Listening to the Past

The Place of Tradition in Theology

Listening to the Past

The Place of Tradition in Theology

Stephen R. Holmes

PATERNOSTER PRESS

Baker Academic

A Division of Baker Book House Co

First published in 2002 by Paternoster Press in the UK
and Baker Academic in the USA

08 07 06 05 04 03 02   7 6 5 4 3 2 1

Paternoster Press is an imprint of Authentic Media,
P.O. Box 300, Carlisle, Cumbria, CA3 0QS, UK
Website: www.paternoster-publishing.com

Baker Academic is a division of Baker Book House Company,
PO Box 6287, Grand Rapids, MI 49516-6287
Website: www.bakeracademic.com

British Library Cataloguing in Publication Data
A catalogue record for this book is available from the British Library

ISBN 1-84227-155-5

Library of Congress Cataloging-in-Publication Data
Holmes, Stephen R.
    Listening to the past : the place of tradition in theology / Stephen R. Holmes
       p. cm.
    Includes bibliographical references and index.
    ISBN 0-8010-2642-3 (pbk.)
    1. Tradition (Theology) I. Title.

BT90 .H67 2002
231′.042—dc21   2002038609

Cover Design by Paula Gibson
Typeset by WestKey Ltd, Falmouth, Cornwall
Printed in Great Britain by Bell & Bain Ltd, Glasgow

For my parents, with true gratitude and much love

Contents

Acknowledgements

Some of the chapters are reworkings of previously published papers, detailed below. In each case I am grateful to the original source both for being willing to publish the work in the first place, and for allowing me to reuse it here.

Chapter 3 is based on a paper entitled 'The Upholding of Beauty: A Reading of Anselm's *Cur Deus Homo*', first published in *The Scottish Journal of Theology* 54.2 (2001), pp. 189–203.

Chapter 4 is based on a paper entitled ' "Something Much Too Plain to Say": Towards a Defence of the Doctrine of Divine Simplicity', first published in the *Neue Zeitschrift für Systematische Theologie und Religionphilosophie* 43 (2001), pp. 137–54.

Chapter 6 is based on a paper entitled 'Edwards on the Will', first published in the *International Journal of Systematic Theology* I.3 (1999), pp. 266–85.

Chapter 7 is based on a chapter entitled 'Baptism: Patristic Resources for Ecumenical Dialogue', in Stanley E. Porter and Anthony R. Cross (eds), *Dimensions of Baptism* (Sheffield: Sheffield Academic Press, 2002).

Introduction

'I have read somewhere or other – in Dionysius of Halicarnassus, I think – that History is Philosophy teaching by examples.' So said Viscount Bolingbroke in his work *On the Study of History*. This book is about theology teaching by examples, and so about historical theology.

As a minister within the Baptist Union of Great Britain (BUGB), much of my experience of church life has been within circles that historically remain identified with Evangelicalism, but have recently been influenced to a greater or lesser extent by charismatic renewal. The Baptist tradition can in turn be traced to similar, if older, 'grass-roots' renewal movements amongst English Separatists and continental Anabaptists. One characteristic position found regularly in all four of these traditions (Evangelicalism, the charismatic movement, Separatism, Anabaptism), and certainly amongst people with whom I have had the privilege of worshipping and ministering today, is an impatience with what tends to get called 'tradition'. God has given us his truth in the Bible; our job is to live it and proclaim it; what other people may or may not have thought about it in the past is of no interest to us; that they were generally wrong is evident from the poor state of the 'traditional' churches.

I remain grateful for all I have learnt and received from this background, and I feel as comfortable within such circles as I ever expect to feel anywhere, this side of the return of Christ. This book, however, is an attempt to combat the sort of view that I have just been outlining: a positive and receptive attitude to the Christian tradition, I will argue, is important, indeed necessary, for us to be faithful to God's calling on our lives.

In this sense, the driving question of the book is one of theological method. It is often said that methodological reflection in theology should follow, rather than precede, the doing of the work. That is, it is best not to think about how to do theology in abstract; rather, one should theologise and then reflect on what one has done.

This book comes after a couple of years of writing papers about Coleridge, Edwards, Calvin and Barth, amongst others, and a conversation with a friend and colleague, Dr Mike Higton, which enabled me both to see that this was an interesting thing to be doing – why should an apprentice theologian trace the arguments of Calvin and Barth more, or at least more explicitly, than he traces those of St Paul and St John? – and to understand something of what it was that I was doing. In a book that is largely about how listening to the masters of old can shape our thinking, it is as well to acknowledge from the outset that theology is an irreducibly communal task (belonging, as it does, to the community of the Church), and to confess that it was talking to a friend that enabled me to understand my own thoughts.

As such, the book is something of a hybrid: most of the chapters came into being with no thought of a relationship to each other, and in some cases their central arguments add little or nothing to the general thesis of the book. They do, I believe, however, belong together: they illustrate and exemplify the contention that is worked out in the three programmatic chapters (1, 2 and 10), and demonstrate how it may be put into practice. Or so, at least, I hope. I do not know to what extent Viscount Bolingbroke's comment is an adequate reflection of current thinking on the nature of historiography; I try to show in this book that theology, at least, by being attentive to its own tradition, can teach by example.

As a result of this genesis, the various chapters do not span out the discipline in the ways that I might have chosen were the book to have come into being in a less haphazard manner. The coverage of topics and periods is wide enough, but patchy: I would have sought to be more systematic in some way if I had conceived the book as a unity from the beginning. The people given significant attention hail from four continents (Augustine and Cyprian from Africa; Basil, John Damascene and John Chrysostom from Asia; Jonathan Edwards from the Americas; and all the others, I think, from Europe), but they all happen to be male. The reasons why most of the significant theologians in the Christian tradition have been male are well enough known, and I do not see any good argument to suggest that a book like this is incomplete without a female voice (the various chapters, after all, serve only as examples from the tradition), but if I had been planning the book from scratch I would certainly have wanted a more balanced presentation.

In editing the papers that lie behind the central chapters, the first task was always the removal of a note of acknowledgement. The monotony with which certain people and fora appeared in those comments only confirmed what I knew already: how much I owe to my teachers and colleagues, to those seminars that have permitted me to give papers, and responded intelligently and generously, and to those friends who continue to take an interest in what I do. Pride of place must go to the various seminars and conferences of the Research Institute in Systematic Theology at King's College, London. There is almost nothing in this book that has not been aired at the Institute at some point, and there is certainly nothing that, having been offered there, has not been greatly improved as a result. The influence of my supervisor and senior colleague Professor Colin Gunton is also everywhere present: Colin's inspiration, example and friendship remain amongst the greatest influences on my life and work as a theologian. Many of the papers underlying particular chapters were also given at the Postgraduate Seminar at Spurgeon's College, and interactions with friends there, particularly Dr John Colwell, have alike been of great benefit to me. Other friends and colleagues have guided my thoughts on various points in the argument: Dr Mike Higton; Dr Murray Rae; Dr Kelly Kapic; Dr Ruth Goldbourne; Prof. John Webster. To all I am grateful.

S. R. H.
King's College, London
The Feast of St Thomas Aquinas, 2002

Chapter 1

Why Can't We Just Read the Bible?
The Place of Tradition in Theology

Many anecdotes have passed into theological folklore about the great Swiss–German Reformed theologian Karl Barth. It is said that on one occasion, for instance, when he was to be visited by a press photographer, he cleared his desk of everything except a Bible, a pad of paper and a pen. The journalist found him apparently writing his *Church Dogmatics* with no other aid or inspiration than the text of Holy Scripture. Professor Barth no doubt intended to make a serious point about the primacy and absolute authority of Scripture in theological work by his jape, but the tale does raise the opposite question in an acute way: why can theology not be done like this? What is it, to phrase the question differently, about the practice of Christian theology that necessitates contact with the theological tradition, the reading of Barth himself and of other theologians of more remote eras? No student of the subject can fail to notice the regular appeals to, and interactions with, earlier writers that occur in almost all dogmatic work. It is not just Barth, although his dialogue with the Christian tradition in the small-print sections of the *Church Dogmatics* is as wide ranging, sustained and insightful as almost any other recent example: most of the great works of Christian theology from this and every previous age are characterised by a sustained listening to, and interaction with, those who have gone before. At the other end of the scale, indeed, few students are introduced to the matter of theology without encountering its history, albeit of course in a very partial way. The greatest statements and the introductory lectures alike demonstrate that theology needs its history.

If this were merely a recent phenomenon, it might be possible to dismiss it sociologically in various ways: a response to the perceived crisis in the academic status of theology that leads to a preference for (unquestionably academic) historical work; or a widespread desire to reinvigorate the discipline by the standard practice of returning *ad fontes*, for example. However, it would appear that there have been interactions with the theological tradition for as long as theology has been done. The process begins as early as the appeals to the 'rule of faith', the codification of early Christian teaching that is claimed as a witness to the apostolic beliefs of the Church, and which is in evidence even in St Irenaeus, whose own teacher, the martyr Polycarp, had been taught by St John the Apostle.[1] In classic patristic theological works of the West and East, this conscious location within a tradition remains significant: in the West, St Augustine locates his meditations on the Trinity within the credally defined faith of the Church and the earlier reflections of the Greek Fathers, and works hard when writing against the Donatists to align his position with the earlier, and apparently rather different, teachings of St Cyprian;[2] in the East the best example might be the *Orthodox Faith* of St John of Damascus, where the interaction with earlier writers is not made obvious, but involves even the reproduction of large chunks of text and their incorporation into his own distinctive reflections. In the medieval period, close to the heart of the 'scholastic method' was the respect paid to earlier theologians, and Peter Lombard's lists of disagreements in the Fathers were often seen not as an invitation to decide between competing authorities so much as a demand that work be done to demonstrate how, read properly, both sides could be correct in what they said. As I argue below,[3] the mainstream Reformation project sought to be responsible to the tradition as it had been passed down, even when disagreeing sharply with certain aspects of it. The pattern changes little through the following centuries.[4]

Even such quick examples should demonstrate the general point: serious Christian theology has almost always involved interaction with the earlier tradition. This fact requires explanation, however: it is not so obvious as to why this should be the case that we may simply notice the fact and pass on. This is particularly true when working from a Reformed or Evangelical tradition,

---

[1] For some detail about the development of the rule of faith see, e.g., J. N. D. Kelly, *Early Christian Creeds* (New York: Longman, 1972). For Irenaeus's invocation of it, see *Adversus Haereses* I.9.5 and *Demonstration of the Preaching of the Apostles* 3; for his account of his relationship to Polycarp, see the letter preserved by Eusebius in *Ecclesiastical History* V.20.6.

[2] *De Trinitate* I.7, V.9–10; *De Baptismo contra Donatistas* II *passim*.

[3] See pp. 13–17.

[4] It is, I think, arguable that there is a fairly widespread loss of tradition in the eighteenth century, for reasons no doubt connected to the dominant ideologies of the Enlightenment project. Even if this is the case, then it provides no more than a brief interruption in the wider pattern, which is clearly resumed in the nineteenth century in the significant theologians (notice, for instance, Schleiermacher's appeals to what has gone before, even whilst seriously reshaping Christian theology), some major church movements (the Oxford movement, most obviously), and the great textual projects: Migne's *Patrologia*; the Ante-Nicene Fathers; the Nicene and Post-Nicene Fathers; the Library of Anglo-Catholic Theology; and so on.

which insists on the *sola scriptura* principle, that authority in matters of faith is found nowhere else but the Bible.[5] It appears that, even in this context, there is none the less something in the nature of the discipline of theology that still demands sustained interaction with earlier writers, with the Christian tradition. Why, instead, can't we just read the Bible? The burden of this book is, by precept and example, to offer an answer to this question.

Answering will inevitably involve offering a defence of the discipline known as historical theology, presently rather out of fashion, as church historians concentrate on social history and systematic theologians concentrate on contemporary issues. The work of tracing the intellectual arguments that shaped earlier ages, arguments that sometimes seem so foreign or irrelevant to our own situation, is a necessary part of the wider theological task of proclaiming the gospel of Christ anew in every new language and situation. I will argue that we cannot merely translate the language of Scripture into our own language, ignoring the intervening ages. Instead, I will suggest, we will only proclaim the gospel faithfully if we make an effort to understand how it has been passed on to us. The middle chapters of the book contain some attempts to demonstrate the utility of this effort by example, but for now I want to argue that it is necessarily the case because of the nature of Christian doctrine.

The question, then, is why Christian theology cannot proceed by listening only to the Bible, but instead must learn from others in history who have been about the same work. Two possible answers to the question can, I think, be disposed of fairly quickly.

First, someone might offer a purely utilitarian justification for listening to the theological tradition: we read St Anselm on the atonement, say, because so doing helps us to grasp what Scripture means – we happen to have found him useful. On this account, the texts of the Christian tradition are no more and no less essential than the lexicons and other linguistic aids we use in reading Scripture: there is no good theological reason to listen to the tradition, it just happens to help. This recognition should not be derided: it is certainly the case that listening to others who have listened to Scripture helps us to see things in that text that we could not have seen on our own, as every preacher who has had recourse to a commentary can testify. It is, however, inadequate: the practice of interacting with earlier writers is so widespread that it demands a better explanation than this, and in any case I believe that I can offer a theological reason that will be much more serious than a merely pragmatic one.

---

[5] This is the tradition from which I come, and so this is the form of the question that interests me most. As I argue below, however, the question framed in a more 'catholic' way, from within a tradition that is prepared to locate authority on matters of faith in other documents – papal, concilliar, or whatever – is not so different.

Second, discussions of the role of 'tradition' in theological methodology usually turn on supporting or opposing accounts of theological tradition that place certain documents – the decrees of the ecumenical councils, or papal encyclicals, for instance – as authoritative alongside Scripture. Such discussions are not my concern in this book. There is, of course, an argument to be had over such issues, but the question I am attempting to address here, of what to do with non-authoritative but orthodox texts within the tradition, will always arise (except in some bizarre limiting case where texts are either regarded as authoritative or heretical, with no middle ground). If, say, the decrees of the First Council of Constantinople are regarded as authoritative, as a part of the canon in some sense, then the question of how to relate to the sermons Gregory of Nazianzus preached immediately before the council remains to be answered. May these be ignored, as non-canonical, or must they be attended to as an important part of the transmission of the canon? I will in what follows assume that the canonical documents are restricted to the Scriptures without further qualification: this is my own tradition, to which I am committed, and it is not obvious to me that the theological arguments are altered in any serious manner by the particular collection of canonical texts to which one subscribes.[6]

In this connection, the most famous account of the place of the doctrinal tradition, John Henry Newman's *On the Development of Christian Doctrine*,[7] must be mentioned. This is still, to my mind, not a sufficiently theological answer, and in any case offers no account of the place of the general tradition, instead only discussing the process of the continuing generation of authoritative (canonical) documents. Newman starts his argument by noting that any set of ideas will necessarily grow and develop and fill out over time. If this is generally true, it will necessarily be true in the particular case of Christian doctrine. It is only at this point that Newman invokes any theological argument, suggesting that God will provide an infallible guide to which developments of doctrine are proper and which are improper (this guide, for Newman, is of course the magisterium of the Roman Catholic Church). As a result, Newman's account reduces to the second of my discarded answers, as his arguments result in an account of tradition that is defined by certain authoritative decisions or documents, and he can offer no interesting theological account of any other writings.[8]

---

[6] By the end of this book I will offer an argument for ascribing a subsidiary authority to certain documents, particularly the ecumenical creeds, as privileged interpretations of Scripture.

[7] John Henry Newman, *On the Development of Christian Doctrine* (London: Longmans, Green, 1890).

[8] I am quite prepared to accept Newman's suggestion that, humanly speaking, the growth and development of Christian theology can be accounted for using only the

I want to sketch two theological arguments that assert the place of listening to the tradition in the practice of theology. Neither of them ascribe authority, as it is commonly understood, to the tradition: that resides in the canonical texts, whether they are restricted to Scripture or expanded to include other ecclesial documents. Rather, my arguments are designed to offer a dogmatic description of theological method, what might be called a theological account of how we should do theology. Just as we would want adequately theological hermeneutics to describe the way we should read the Scriptures, or so I suppose, so I am trying to offer a theological rationale for the theologian's relationship with other, non-canonical, texts in the tradition. One argument, which will occupy the remainder of this chapter, relies on the doctrine of creation to develop a theology of the goodness of historical locatedness. In the next chapter I will develop an ecclesiological argument to suggest that a proper doctrine of the Church requires us to acknowledge both the communal nature of the work of theology, and that that community is not limited to the living, but encompasses those who have gone before as well.

A first way to analyse the Christian tradition might be to notice that the tradition is what both links us to, and separates us from, the prophets and apostles who wrote the Scriptures. The word itself suggests this: the tradition is what has been 'handed on' (Latin *trado*) from the apostles to the churches they founded (1 Cor. 11:23, where the Vulgate reads '*Ego enim accepi a Domino, quod et tradidi vobis*'), and then handed on from generation to generation until finally each of us received it from those who taught us.[9] What is often called 'the tradition' in

---

[8] *(continued)* same factors that account for, say, the development of Greek philosophy or the rules of cricket. Indeed, one of the two major arguments below could be taken to insist that this is the case, inasmuch as it relies only on the doctrine of creation. Newman offers me a theological reason to read the decrees of the councils, but not to read the writings that led up to them and interpreted them. That is to say, on Newman's account (at least in this book) I can do theology without listening to the Fathers. This, it seems to me, is inadequate.

[9] The question of precisely what it is that is handed on is important, of course. I have concentrated on texts, embodying beliefs, concepts and ideas, in this book, but that is only because my interest, as a theologian, is in such things. We also have language, behaviours, ethical intuitions, rites and ceremonies, and so on passed on to us. All of these things should be brought within the general account of the process of tradition as I have sketched it, and all are interrelated in creating and expressing an account of the world, and humanity's place within it, before God. The theology embodied within certain liturgical actions and ethical conformities is certainly a part of what I have in mind in this discussion, although I will not be exploring it explicitly. When I use the term 'tradition', then, this most inclusive sense is in mind, although only *sotto voce* within the text of the book. All that I have received and am still receiving from the

theological work, the collection of texts written by those who came between the apostles and our own day, is in some sense the fossil record of this process of continual handing on: that which enables us to see that what was given to us is no invention, but has been passed down from hand to hand faithfully. As such, it also enables us to trace the changing tradition: those points at which certain ideas were lost from the tradition, or gained particular prominence, or were presented in a new relationship, or were formulated in a new way.

Given this, the way in which theologians gain access to the tradition, in the wider sense of the word, will largely be through these texts.[10] Through them we are able to trace the processes of handing on that have linked us to, and yet separated us from, the apostles. It is this genealogical aspect of the tradition, which may be pieced together from the texts, that is my concern in this chapter. In the next I shall suggest that the texts are not merely artefacts of an earlier age, but lively voices in the Church today: for now, however, the texts are what enable us to tell a story of the handing on of the gospel and all that comes with it, and to locate ourselves within that story.

To attempt to do theology without noticing the tradition, then, is to deny, or at least to attempt to escape from, our historical locatedness. It is worth stressing initially that this locatedness is unavoidable: it cannot be escaped from. If we imagine trying to ignore all who have gone before, and coming to the testimony of the apostles in an unmediated form, we simply cannot do it, as will be clear if we begin to imagine what would be involved in the attempt. We might first claim to listen only to the Bible – but the Bible we have, if it is a translation, is shaped by a tradition of Bible translation, and by its translator(s). Should we attempt to avoid this problem by recourse to the original languages, then we would have to learn those languages from somebody, and so would be inducted into a tradition of translating certain words and grammatical constructions in one way and not another, and we would almost certainly have recourse to the lexicons and other aids, which are themselves deposits of the accumulated knowledge of earlier scholars. Further, the standard editions of the Greek New Testament bear witness on nearly every page to the textual

---

[9] (*continued*) various people who have inducted me into the Christian faith and who continue to lead and teach me is a part of the content of the tradition that has come down to me: hymn books; ecclesial practices; doctrines; forms of language and movement used in prayer; social and ethical attitudes; ways of relating to various people – and whatever else can be thought of.

[10] We might also examine other remains: church (and cathedral) architecture, and so on. The modern practice in cultural studies and similar disciplines of expanding the word 'text' to cover all such artefacts is not one I intend to adopt, but is perhaps helpful to bear in mind at this juncture.

criticism that has come up with this text, and not another, and so we cannot even find a text of Scripture that has not been 'handed on' to us by those who came before. If we push this imagined quest to the last extreme, we might picture a person who has somehow learnt *koine* Greek only by studying original texts, and who has even examined every extant manuscript of the New Testament and developed her own canons for textual criticism: on these bases she might claim to have unmediated access to the Scriptures. Still, however, the claim must be false: apart from the archaeological and bibliographic work that has produced the manuscripts she has used, if she speaks English, German or French, or several other languages, her native tongue even has been decisively affected by earlier theological controversies and biblical translations. There is no escape from the mediation of our faith by the tradition.

That there is no escape is not yet a reason to be happy with this state of affairs. We might ask whether our captivity to tradition is to be celebrated, put up with, or raged against. The driving force of reforming movements throughout church history has, after all, been to set aside tradition and return to the text of Scripture, and we might, similarly, whilst acknowledging our captivity to tradition, none the less seek constantly to free ourselves from as much of it as we can, and so to have as unmediated an access to the apostolic deposit as is possible. This would give us an interesting negative defence of the practice of historical theology: we study the history of theology in order to recognise, as far as is possible, our entanglement in a tradition from which we then seek to free ourselves, again as far as is possible. This would be an entirely defensible account. Indeed, it is not uncommon to suggest that the proper relationship of theology to the philosophic tradition looks very like this, so that a theologian must read Hegel, for instance, in order to escape from captivity to Hegelianism. I want, however, to give a more positive account of the theological tradition, at least, than this.[11]

We cannot have unmediated access to the apostolic witness to Christ (or, indeed, to the *ipsissima verba et acta* of Christ himself).[12] This is a limitation that,

---

[11] The proper relationship of theology to philosophy is too large a topic to introduce here, but the idea I have just sketched, although common, is over simplified, or so it seems to me. There is a proper suspicion, as when a philosopher announces certain truths to be 'self-evident'; in almost every case the proper role of theology will be to deconstruct such claims in order to demonstrate that they are not 'self-evident' at all, but merely attempts to seize power to foreclose on a debate. On the other hand, the philosophical virtues of careful statement, coherent argument and logical consistency must surely be evident in any worthwhile theology.

[12] This may not be something to be bemoaned; the evidence of the gospels does not encourage us to believe that a direct encounter with Christ was guaranteed or even likely to create or strengthen faith!

as human beings, we cannot escape. There is, however, a need with any limitation that we currently experience to discern whether it is a result of being
creaturely (or at least human),[13] and so something good, right and proper, or
instead a result of being fallen and sinful, and so something to be fought against.
Omnipotence, for example, is not proper to human creatures, and so we
should accept that there are things we cannot do – indeed, we should celebrate
it, since that is the way that God was pleased to create us, and he pronounced
our way of being to be good. By contrast, depravity, the inability to do what is
right, is not a part of the way we were created, but rather a result of the
entrance of sin into the world, and so whilst it is the case that, this side of the
resurrection, we cannot live morally upright lives in every particular, this
remains something fundamentally improper.[14] The question is, on which side
of this divide does our historical separatedness from other human beings, and
particularly from the apostles, fall?

A first way to attempt to answer this question might be by seeking a
description of that which separates. Various theological accounts of history
have been proposed, but they generally fall into one of two broad patterns.[15]
On the one hand, we might consider a broadly Origenist account, whereby
history, described as movement and change in time, is a part of fallenness. The
central argument for this contention is intuitively strong: if we posit a state of
human perfection, then any movement or change in that state is, *ex hypothesi*, a
movement away from perfection, and so a fall.[16] A version of this basic position
can be seen worked out in various ways in the writings of St Augustine: his
theological account of time, for instance, pictures it as something that vitiates
our existence, separates us from our past and threatens us. Again, he assumed
there would be a particular age at which we would all be resurrected (thirty

---

[13] As it may be the case that the angels, themselves creatures, are not limited by time in
this way.

[14] This remains the case even within a supralapsarian scheme. Human depravity is
never seen as something proper or good within orthodox Christianity, only sometimes
as something necessary, ordained by God to achieve greater ends than could have been
achieved otherwise.

[15] I am choosing to ignore process theology, and those recent process-influenced
accounts which speak of God's 'becoming' through the creation of the world and its
history, as I do not regard them as Christian in any interesting sense. The doctrine of
creation *ex nihilo* was, I think, the first of a series of patristic theological moves which
served to distinguish the Christian tradition from Neoplatonic philosophy. It also,
with the related assertion of God's aseity, is central to any orthodox account of the
Trinity, in that to deny these points is to deny the key distinction between the
necessary begetting of the Son and the voluntary creation of the world.

[16] See, e.g., Origen, *De Principiis* I.6–8 and II.9, where he says, 'To depart from good is
nothing else than to be made bad' (Anti-Nicene Fathers translation).

years old), because that age was the perfection of human being, and all else was a movement towards, or a degeneration from, that perfection.[17]

On the other hand is a broadly Irenaean account whereby it is a part of God's good ordering of creation for there to be movement towards perfection, and so history. In contrast to Augustine's assumptions about human perfection as represented in his account of the resurrection body, Irenaeus assumes that it is proper for there to be movement and growth.[18] He is perhaps not as radical as he could have been here: it appears that he believes in a final static perfection, but just regards a historical method of reaching that perfection as proper. We could find in the Christian tradition, for instance in Jonathan Edwards, visions of heaven that assume that movement and change will never cease, because they are a part of the proper glory of the created order, just as immutability is a part of the proper glory of God's own life.[19]

It is clear how these divergent positions relate to the question in hand: if Edwards, or even Irenaeus, is right, then historical locatedness is clearly good and proper to human life, and so the mediation of apostolic truth through the tradition is something to be accepted and celebrated; if Origen or Augustine is right, then historical locatedness is improper for human beings, and we should do all we can to escape the process of history. It is possible to offer an account of tradition within such a theology, but it will be an account that denies the link between tradition and history, instead focusing on an a-historical account of the communion of saints to suggest that the Church, and its tradition, exists outside of the change and movement of time, properly understood. Such an account may be found, for instance, in Allchin's *The Dynamic of Tradition*,[20] one of the very few recent book-length treatments of the place of tradition in theology.

Allchin's account is built on a consideration of certain strands of the mystical tradition of Christian theology, and some ideas borrowed from T. S. Eliot about the Incarnation as the 'point of intersection of the timeless and time'. Because of this, Christian prayer is able to transcend time, or to reach the point where all times are gathered up into one, so that historical limitation is overcome, and the communion of saints is realised as we all become contemporaries. 'The moment of incarnation, fully present in

---

[17] For Augustine's theology of time, see *Confessions* XI, on the resurrection body, see *De Civitas Dei* XXII.15.

[18] Irenaeus, *Adversus Haereses* IV.38.

[19] There is a useful collection of many of Edwards's references to heaven as a progressive state, involving constant movement and change, in an appendix in Paul Ramsey (ed.), *The Works of Jonathan Edwards*, vol. 8: *Ethical Writings* (New Haven, Connecticut: Yale University Press, 1989), pp. 706–38.

[20] A. M. Allchin, *The Dynamic of Tradition* (London: Darton, Longman & Todd, 1981).

history, yet opening history to what is beyond it, frees us from the servitudes of history. History is fulfilled ... when it transcends itself into the kingdom of eternity.'[21] Again, we are able to learn from Mother Julian of Norwich, the fourteenth-century mystic, because 'she speaks to us as our contemporary'.[22] This last phrase comes at the end of a long discussion of the radical otherness of Julian's time from ours, of how the attitudes that shaped her life are incomprehensible, irretrievable, today. Yet through her life of contemplation Julian is apparently freed from the particularities of her own time ('one room can contain all the universe, and one life-time can contain all human history') and able to speak to others who can in turn transcend their own particularities.

I mention Allchin's work because I find it interesting, and because it offers what I suspect is the only significant alternative to what I am proposing here. I do not think, however, that it offers an adequate theological account of the process of tradition: after all, on this reading Julian can speak to me precisely because we are both able to transcend the limitations of history, and so there is no need for anything to be 'traditioned', handed on from generation to generation.[23] Historical particularity, on this account, is just not theologically interesting. None the less, it may be the only option available if Augustine and Origen are right, so we are still faced with the two rival theologies of history that I sketched earlier.

The question remains how we are to decide between these two positions. We might try to appeal to biblical texts: there is certainly a suggestion of a proper change in the human situation in the important creation texts, for instance, when the blessing God pronounced over his new human creatures included the gracious command to 'fill the earth and subdue it'. I am not sure, however, that the issue will be settled quite so easily: Origen and Augustine both wrote significant expositions of Genesis, after all, and found little difficulty in maintaining their respective positions in the face of such texts. A supporter of their position might point out that the story of the creation of Adam and Eve seems to describe them as being created as adults, not as having to grow from childhood, which might be an argument against Irenaeus's picture of growth as part of human perfection, and in favour of Augustine's account of the resurrection body, and all the implications of that.

The appropriate way to decide such a question, it seems to me, is by an appeal to christology: in Jesus Christ we see human nature as it was always

---

[21] Ibid., p. 115.

[22] Ibid., p. 10.

[23] In the next chapter I will offer an account of the communion of the saints, which tries to take both the present livingness of the saints and their historical particularity seriously.

meant to be, and indeed as it will be, undamaged by sin.[24] Perhaps the most interesting case to illustrate this point is the event of death: is it a good and proper thing for human beings to die, as many Old Testament texts might suggest,[25] or is this the final mark of the sin-caused disorder of the world, as certain Pauline texts would indicate (e.g. 1 Cor. 15:26)? Christian faith has often been tempted to take the first view, with borrowed Greek conceptions of the need to free the soul from the body so that it may go to a spiritual realm, leading to fairly positive attitudes to death.[26] Even if we do not accept this account, but instead insist (with the creeds) on the resurrection of the body as being the eschatological good awaiting human beings, it would still be possible to construct an account whereby a painless passage through death followed by a restful waiting for the resurrection was proper to human life.[27]

If we try to analyse this using an anthropology based only on the creation texts, we will struggle: references to the 'tree of life', to the punishment of death awaiting Adam and Eve if they eat from the other tree, and even to their fall being followed by the first human death, the murder of Abel by Cain, do not yet establish the point. 'Life', in biblical parlance, after all means much

---

[24] The basic point is, of course, Barth's (see *Church Dogmatics* III.2, pp. 27–54). Two current arguments need to be addressed in passing here, however. First, I believe that my basic point holds whether one asserts that the human nature of Christ was 'fallen' or 'unfallen': for a useful survey of the issues here, and references to the major historical and contemporary works on the subject, see Kelly M. Kapic, 'The Son's Assumption of Human Nature: A Call for Clarity', *International Journal of Systematic Theology* 3/2 (2001), pp. 154–66. Amongst the points of agreement Dr Kapic finds in the debate is '[b]oth positions affirm the Holy Spirit's involvement in allowing Jesus Christ to be "without sin"' (p. 164). Second, I am assuming the orthodox position that insists that the acts of Jesus Christ are genuinely human acts, not divine acts done behind a human mask. For some consideration of the importance of this point, see my *God of Grace and God of Glory: An Account of the Theology of Jonathan Edwards* (Edinburgh: T&T Clark, 2000), pp. 135–8, and works referenced there.

[25] The standard understanding of the Old Testament would seem to be that *premature* death is indeed a tragedy, but to 'rest with one's fathers' when one is 'old and full of years' is an accepted culmination of a life well lived in the grace of God. See, for instance, Walter Eichrodt's comments in vol. 2 of his *Theology of the Old Testament*, J. A. Baker (tr.) (London: SCM Press, 1967), pp. 500ff. As Eichrodt goes on to point out, of course, there are other strands to the Old Testament witness to death.

[26] On this, see Eberhard Jüngel, *Death: The Riddle and the Mystery*, Iain and Ute Nicol (trs) (Edinburgh: St Andrew Press, 1975), pp. 41–55, where the example of Socrates asking Asclepius to offer up a cockerel to celebrate his recovery from the sickness that is mortality is to the fore.

[27] This would seem to be the view of Robert Jenson: see his *Systematic Theology*, vol. 2: *The Creatures* (Oxford: Oxford University Press, 1999), pp. 329–31.

more than continued biological existence,[28] and the threat of death and the
coming of murder could be read as references to untimely death, although this
is perhaps not the most natural reading. If, however, we ask whether death is
natural to human nature as revealed in Christ, the case becomes clearer:
although Christ died, this is always pictured as his giving up his life for the
sake of others, not as something necessary because he was human; indeed, St
Anselm's reading of the texts suggests that the whole point of Christ's death
was that it was unnecessary, and so able to be atoning.[29] When Jonathan
Edwards was confronted with an opponent, John Taylor of Norwich, suggesting that death might be a good thing, his angry response was to insist that
Christ meets death as an enemy, not as something good and to be welcomed.[30]

The final answer might be found by performing the thought experiment
proposed variously by St Irenaeus and John Duns Scotus, amongst others: if sin
had not entered the world, would Christ still have become incarnate? The
standard answer given is that he would have, but that his Incarnation would
have been glorious and not humble, and a time of joy and not suffering.
Emphatically, it would not have ended in death, since his death is only
atoning. For all these reasons, then, we may say that death is a result of the fall
and sin, and not something proper to human nature.

What, however, of historical limitations? Can we find a Christological argument one way or the other here? Several lines present themselves: we might
notice, first of all, that the human body of Jesus was not created all at once at age
thirty, or at any other particular age, but instead that he was born as a baby,
and 'grew in wisdom, and physically, and in the esteem of God and other
people' (Lk. 2:49).[31] This suggests that, contra the implication of the Genesis
texts, growth, development and change are indeed proper to human life, just as
Irenaeus suggested.

We might secondly note that Christ was undeniably historically located,
and that there is no suggestion in the gospels of this being something
from which he was insulated, or which he strove to overcome. The various
examples that are often quoted of Jesus sharing first-century Jewish beliefs and
attitudes will attest sufficiently to that point.[32] A series of modern questions
about the particularity of the humanity assumed by God the Son are of

---

[28] On which, see again Eichrodt, *Theology of the Old Testament*, vol. 2, pp. 497–500.
[29] On which, see Chapter 3.
[30] On which, see again my *God of Grace*, pp. 225–6, and the references there.
[31] All biblical quotations are my own translations.
[32] A volume of N. T. Wright's massive and magisterial contribution to the renewed
'Quest for the historical Jesus' demonstrates this point very fully: *Jesus and the Victory of
God* (London: SPCK, 1996).

relevance here. On the one hand, in dialogue with various feminist theologians, it is now usually assumed or asserted that the maleness of that humanity was not constitutive for the mission, or was only contingently constitutive – as when it is argued that in the particular historical location Jesus was, it was necessary for him to be male to do what he did. On the other hand, it is increasingly recognised in modern theology that the Jewishness of Jesus was necessary to his mission, that the Incarnation makes no sense without this organic link to God's election of Israel. In all of this there is an attempt to notice which factors concerning Christ's particular humanity are theologically interesting and which are merely contingent. The fact that some *are* merely contingent suggests that for Christ to exist in a particular historical location, with all that that implies, is not something problematic, but is a necessary, and so good, implication of his being human.

Finally, the thought experiment described above will also help us here, resulting as it does in the suggestion that if there had been no need for redemption, still the Son would have become incarnate. There is thus a necessary change in the human situation, and one of decisive importance, so history, defined as movement or change in human life, is not improper, but something God had always intended. This is a part of the good ordering of creation in which God was pleased to place us. Just so, it is proper to human reception of the apostolic witness that it is mediated through a process of tradition, of handing on. We should not attempt to escape from our embeddedness in the Christian tradition, but should rather celebrate it. To attempt to engage with the scriptural witness in any other way than as that which has been handed on is simply theologically improper, a refusal to accept the way in which God has created us.

Let me emphasise that this is not to ascribe any authority to any particular tradition, or to insist that historical developments are necessarily good: it is, after all, a proper way to relate to a tradition to stand against particular developments and suggest that they are improper and should be done away with. What is improper is to attempt to pretend that the tradition is absent or irrelevant. Theology needs always to be in dialogue – conversation – with its tradition, but that dialogue may well be sharply critical.

Perhaps the best examples of the distinctions that I am trying to make here are found in the various controversies during the Reformation. On the one hand, and relatively simply, there was an insistence by the Roman Catholic Church on the authority of (a particular reading of) the tradition. This is perhaps best represented by the Council of Trent,[33] where we read precisely of a process of

---

[33] Translations are from Mark A. Noll (ed.), *Confessions and Catechisms of the Reformation* (Leicester: Apollos, 1991), pp. 169–210.

'tradition', of the passing 'from hand to hand' (*per manus tradite*) from Christ and the apostles of 'these truths and rules [which] are contained in the written books [i.e., Scripture] and the unwritten traditions ...' Hence, 'the traditions [*traditiones*], whether they relate to faith or morals' are to be 'received and venerated' in just the same way as the Scriptures are, because, like the Scriptures, they have 'been dictated orally by Christ or by the Holy Ghost, and preserved in the Catholic Church in unbroken succession'.[34] The Profession of the Tridentine Faith, the creed which the council promulgated, demands assent to similar points: 'I most steadfastly admit and embrace apostolic and ecclesiastical traditions, and all other observances and constitutions of the [Holy Roman] church.' The response of all the Reformers was simply to deny that authority should be thus ascribed.[35]

More interesting and less well known, however, is a debate internal to Reform. Alongside the 'mainstream' or 'magisterial'[36] Reformers, such as Luther, Zwingli, Bucer or Calvin, there was a 'left wing', or 'Radical Reformation', composed of various groups of Anabaptists, Spiritualists, Evangelical Rationalists and so on.[37] Both sides of this debate thought that the tradition that had been handed to their generation was in serious need of critique and reformation, but they disagreed over how to relate to it. The arguments took various forms, for instance, over certain issues in reading Scripture (variously, the relationship between the Old Testament and the New, or a strict [nothing not commanded in the Bible may be done] or liberal [anything not prohibited in the Bible may be done] interpretation).[38] The interesting discussion for our purposes is, however, the working out of the *sola scriptura* principle, with the opposing sides perhaps best represented by Calvin and his Anabaptist opponents.

Calvin,[39] although committed to the principle of *sola scriptura*, none the less thought it important to stand within the tradition of the Church. It is not just

---

[34] 'Decree concerning the Canonical Scriptures'.

[35] As I have indicated above, nothing in my argument depends on which documents are regarded as canonical, and so, whilst I think the Reformers were simply right at this point, I make no attempt to prove it here.

[36] 'Magisterial' because they submitted to and used the authority of the magistrate to promote Reform.

[37] George H. Williams, *The Radical Reformation* (Philadelphia, Pennsylvania: Westminster, 1962), might be considered as the beginning of modern scholarship on this subject, and is still a significant source.

[38] See, for instance, Scott A. Gillies, 'Zwingli and the Origins of the Reformed Covenant 1524–7', *Scottish Journal of Theology* 54/1 (2001), pp. 21–50, for some discussion of how such issues worked out in Zurich.

[39] English quotations from the *Institutes* are from the Battles translation: *The Institutes of the Christian Religion*, 2 vols (Library of Christian Classics, vols XX & XXI), Ford Lewis

that Calvin owes much (indeed, more than is often recognised) to the immediately preceding theological tradition, although he does;[40] the relevant point is that both in the *Institutes* and in other places he devotes considerable energy to demonstrating that the positions the Reformers are urging against the Roman Catholic Church are in fact more faithful to the Christian tradition than the Roman alternatives,[41] and, even where he disagrees with the recent tradition, he is mindful of the need to specify those disagreements with some exactness, and to defend precisely those points with particular energy. This is no doubt in part due to the polemical nature of his work, but a comparison of that work with his Anabaptist opponents reveals a radically different temper: whereas they were prepared to merely insist on what they believed to be right from Scripture, Calvin felt the need to be in dialogue with earlier theologians. Whilst some, at least, of the Anabaptists explicitly denied having any respect for the teaching of any human authority,[42] it mattered to Calvin that his thought was in continuity with the Christian tradition; he respected the tradition of the Church as something to be taken seriously, even when violently disagreeing with it.

This works out in various ways. The difference between Calvin and the Anabaptists is not to do with their estimation of the authority of Scripture, although there are no doubt various technical hermeneutical differences. Rather, it is to do with their estimation of earlier writers, and so, put theologically, to do with their ecclesiology.[43] For Calvin, the Church explicitly includes 'all God's elect, in whose number are also included the

---

[39] *(continued)* Battles (tr.) John T. McNeill (ed.) (London: SCM Press, 1960). Latin quotations are from the Barth and Niesel edition: *Joannis Calvini: Opera Selecta*, 5 vols, Petrus Barth and Guilelmus Niesel (eds) (Christian Kaiser, tertio ed. 1967–74).

[40] On which see Richard A. Muller, *The Unaccommodated Calvin* (Oxford Studies in Historical Theology) (Oxford: Oxford University Press, 1999); David C. Steinmetz, *Calvin in Context* (Oxford: Oxford University Press, 1995) (particularly good on Calvin's practices of biblical interpretation); and Chapter 5.

[41] On which see especially Anthony N. S. Lane, *John Calvin: Student of the Church Fathers* (Edinburgh: T&T Clark, 1999), *passim*, but note for instance p. 54 ('Calvin's use of the fathers was a masterly sixteenth-century attempt to relate Protestantism to historic Christianity: to trace many of its doctrines to the Early Church and to show how Roman error had arisen').

[42] On which see Walter Klaassen (ed.), *Anabaptism in Outline: Selected Primary Sources* (Scottdale, Pennsylvania: Herald Press, 1981).

[43] Calvin has a 'high' ecclesiology and takes seriously God's decision to use the Church, calling it the '*piorum omnium mater*' (*Institutes* IV.1, title, see also IV.1.4). On this, see for instance K. McDonnell, *John Calvin, the Church and the Eucharist* (Princeton, New Jersey: Princeton University Press, 1967), or B. Milner, *Calvin's Doctrine of the Church* (Leiden, Netherlands: Brill, 1970).

dead'.[44] Given this, Calvin relates to Augustine (say) as he would any other member of the Church, with charity and respect.[45] Whilst Scripture was of course the sole source of authority in matters of faith for Calvin, he also has great respect for the teachings of the Fathers: in the 'Prefatory Address' to the *Institutes* he refers to them as 'the ancient writers of a better age of the church',[46] and states that they have written 'many wise and excellent things'. The excellence of the patristic Church was that it had maintained the apostolic doctrine, handed it down and carefully guarded it against erroneous interpretations.[47] The teachers of the ancient Church are thus not to be despised or ignored, but respected, as those who have laboured to pass on the faith unblemished.

For the Anabaptists, the history of the Church was a narrative solely of decline;[48] the New Testament was God's gift to his people, but all that had come afterwards was a losing and falling away from this point. The process of tradition, the handing on of the faith, was a wholly negative process from which true Christians would only seek to escape.[49] Calvin, by contrast, not only saw the patristic period as a largely successful attempt to hold on to and to explore 'the faith once for all delivered' (the ecumenical creeds, for example, were useful summaries of the heart of biblical faith, and so to be welcomed

---

[44] '*omnes quoque electos Dei, in quorum numero comprehenduntur etiam qui morte defuncti sunt*': *Institutes* IV.1.2.

[45] It has often been noticed that Calvin will cite Augustine (particularly) when he agrees with him, but will merely say 'someone has said …' when disagreeing with a point he surely knows was made by the Bishop of Hippo. I have no doubt that the usual reason offered for this, that it is good polemics, has much truth in it, but I wonder also if there is not also a subsidiary ethical reason, leading Calvin to be properly reticent of criticising a fellow-member of the Church.

[46] '*antiquos et melioris adhuc seculi scriptores*'.

[47] *Institutes* IV.2.3, where this maintenance of doctrine is contrasted with episcopal succession. See also IV.4.1.

[48] To take only one example, see the 'Dedicatory Epistle' to Balthasar Hubmaier's *Christian Catechism*. See Denis Janz, *Three Reformation Catechisms: Catholic, Anabaptist, Lutheran* (Lewiston, New York: Edwin Mellen Press, 1982), pp. 133–40, where it is asserted that 'the mud holes and cesspools of human dogmas' impede the progress of the divine word, and the works of 'Thomas, Scotus, Gabriel [Biel], Occam' and 'decrees, decretals … and the other high-thinkers [scholastics]' are described as 'hellish scriptures'. It has been said of Hubmaier that '[m]ore than anyone else, he defined the theological core of Anabaptism' (Tim Foley, 'The Anabaptism of Balthasar Hubmaier', *Anabaptism Today* 22 [1999], pp. 14–22, 21).

[49] Later Anabaptist writings would recognise the importance of the process of tradition, and so an alternative tradition, traced through various marginalised and heretical groups, and culminating in the Anabaptist movements, was regularly sketched.

and affirmed),[50] but also saw even the recent failures of tradition as important, as part of the context in which the work of recovery had to be done. To make the point with a slogan, the Anabaptists sought to refound the Church, whereas Calvin sought to reform it.

It is this account, of a historically located theology that is none the less *reformata et semper reformanda*,[51] which I am trying to recapture, in contradistinction to both the Tridentine account, which ascribe too much to tradition, and Anabaptist accounts which ascribe too little. I have thus far sought to argue that, because of the doctrine of creation, historical locatedness is something good. The tradition we inherit is a part of our location in history, and so in doing theology it is necessary to relate to the tradition. In the next chapter I will explore how we should relate to it.

---

[50] So, for instance, in the very earliest edition of the *Institutes* (1536), Calvin asserts that 'we may readily learn [what the nature of … faith ought to be] from the Creed (which is called "Apostolic"), a brief compend and, as it were, epitome, of the faith agreed upon by the catholic church' (translation from Ford Lewis Battles, *Institutes of the Christian Religion*, 1536 Edition (Grand Rapids, Michigan: Eerdmans, 1986), p. 42).

[51] 'Reformed and always being reformed', a slogan that indicates the constant desire of the Reformed Churches to seek further reformation from God.

Chapter 2

On the Communion of Saints

Thus far it may appear that I am arguing for a genealogical method, for an account of theology whereby a doctrine is not understood unless the arguments that led to it and shaped it are understood. Such an account, I think, leads to the complaints of various of those who are engaged in studying the history of doctrine that systematic theologians tend to play rather fast and loose with the texts with which they interact. In some cases, of course, this charge is justified, and I certainly want to insist on a properly scholarly engagement with the tradition; I think that such an engagement can take place without the need to construct full genealogies, however, and the alternative model I want to propose is based on an account of the communion of saints.

The account in the previous chapter, whilst it was a specifically theological argument, could apply not just to theology, but to any academic discipline, or at least any discipline that sees the explication of historical texts or artifacts as a part of its work.[1] It is a part of the human condition to be separated from previous generations by the passage of time, and what I have called 'tradition' is merely an account of the way in which we endeavour to prevent things being lost through that separation. Inasmuch as the basic theological move in the last chapter relied on the doctrine of creation, it is no surprise that the arguments are widely applicable, of course: the doctrine of creation out of nothing asserts that there is no reality that is not a part of God's creative order, and so any adequate talk about creation must be true of all human realities.

The burden of this chapter is to ask if there is anything specific to the discipline of theology that adds to this picture. Theology often seems more concerned about its relationship to its tradition than other academic disciplines (philosophers, for example, whilst employing intellectual skills that are very similar to those used by theologians, do not seem to have anything like the same interest in how it is that a particular medieval text should be used in current arguments). I want to suggest that theology, as a discipline, belongs to the Church, and so to argue that the particular way in which God has

---

[1] Hence it would not apply to an experimental science, for instance.

constituted the Church affects the relationship of theologians separated by their historical locatedness. Because theology is the only academic discipline that is intrinsically related to the life of the Church,[2] the arguments in this chapter will be specific to the practice of theology.

The claim that theology belongs to, or is intrinsically related to,[3] the Church is a contentious one.[4] It seems to me, however, that almost any account of the nature of academic theological work that sees it as more than merely a subset in the history of ideas field will be committed to this claim, or something like it. Historically theology has generally been assumed to depend on revelation, on the gracious self-giving of God as he lets himself be known. This account is common in the Fathers,[5] and may be found in a text like Anselm's *Proslogion*.[6] It may also be found, however, in texts that are regarded as classical statements of natural theology, such as right at the beginning of Aquinas's *Summa Theologica*.[7] Again, it is the vision of the nature of theology that has inspired Reformed theologians from Calvin,[8] through Puritans such as Edwards,[9] to Karl Barth in the twentieth century.[10] Under this account, any knowledge of God depends on a gracious work of the Spirit that enables us to know and understand. Without this work, theological truth will remain simply opaque to us.

At the heart of a vision like this might be a sense that the ultimate aim of theology is not so much to understand a system of logic, as to give an account of the being and act of God, who is personal. When we consider the ways in which we come to know human persons, to do so without their cooperation is difficult – the limitations of the unauthorised biography are notorious. To attempt to get to know a person who is actively seeking to prevent our success,

---

[2] Understanding 'theology' here in the wide sense, to include all theological disciplines (church history, biblical studies, etc.).

[3] I recognise that these two ways of phrasing the relationship imply different claims; both seem to me to have strengths and weaknesses. There is, I think, no particular need to decide between them for the argument presented here to work.

[4] For a fascinating display of some of what is at stake, see the exchange of letters between von Harnack and Barth in James M. Robinson (ed.), *The Beginnings of Dialectical Theology: Volume I* (Richmond, Virginia: John Knox Press, 1968), pp. 165–87.

[5] See, for instance, St Augustine, *De Trinitate* I.1–3, or St Gregory of Nazianzus, *Orations* 28:3–6.

[6] See particularly chapter one.

[7] *Summa Theologica* Ia q.1 art.1.

[8] *Institutes* I.1–6.

[9] See particularly the sermon 'A Divine and Supernatural Light …', *The Works of Jonathan Edwards*, 2 vols, S. E. Dwight and E. Hickman (eds), (Edinburgh: Banner of Truth, 1974), vol. II, pp. 12–17.

[10] *Church Dogmatics* I/1, pp.17–24.

particularly when that person wields great power, might be considered to be an almost impossible task. If that person is God, in whom we 'live and move and have our being', and who is omnipotent, the impossibility is assured, or so it has seemed to many.

Is it, however, the case that God ever actively seeks to prevent his being known? According to this sort of argument, it is not so much that, as that God desires to be known through the Church, however that is understood.[11] One attempting to know God – to do theology – is hence far more likely to succeed within the fellowship of the Church, and so theology as a discipline may be considered to stand in a particular relationship of dependence to the Church.

There are of course other visions of the work of theology that may be advanced. One that has been particularly influential over the past two centuries finds its foundational and classic statement in Freidrich Schleiermacher's *The Christian Faith*.[12] According to Schleiermacher, and the 'liberal' theology that has followed him, the beginnings of Christian experience are not in God's giving of a special revelation to particular people, but in a universal human experience,[13] which when analysed can only be made sense of if the truth of one or another religious scheme is assumed.[14] Schleiermacher believed that Protestant Christianity was the most profound analysis, and so the best religious system.

---

[11] This argument can be used without modification whether the Church is identified by a historical continuity of episcopal succession stretching back to the apostles, or as the place where the Word is read and preached rightly, and the (two) sacraments are administered in accordance with Scriptural warrant – or, indeed, on any other account of which I am aware.

[12] Quotations are taken from the English translation of the second edition, F. D. E. Schleiermacher, *The Christian Faith*, H. R. Mackintosh and J. S. Stewart (eds) (Edinburgh: T&T Clark, 1999).

[13] Schleiermacher's account, particularly of the nature of this experience, is considerably more subtle than this summary suggests, but this brief account should nonetheless display those features of the position that are both commonly held and necessary to my argument. For Schleiermacher's mature version, see *The Christian Faith*, §3–7.

[14] It seems to me that Ludwig Feuerbach's criticism of this position is devastating, so much so that I confess that I struggle to understand its continuing popularity. In essence, Feuerbach pointed out that there is no particular reason (if the existence of a good God is not regarded as axiomatic) to assume that our experience of the world makes any sense, so to argue that there must be a basic truth to religion because without it our shared human experiences would be ultimately meaningless, is not logic, but wishful thinking. (For this, see his *The Essence of Christianity*, George Eliot [tr.] [Amherst, New York: Prometheus, 1989], pp. 283–7). I mention the position Feuerbach critiqued here because it has remained popular, and to demonstrate that even if it is correct my arguments hold.

Under such an account, a person seeking to do theology must first be religious, in the sense that she must know the core religious experience in her own life. To not know it, and still to seek to do theology, would be akin to a tone-deaf person seeking to become expert in musical analysis: the initial disadvantages to be overcome are so great that failure is inevitable. Secondly, this account, in Schleiermacher's version at least, assumes that religious experience is undeveloped unless related to a particular religious tradition,[15] and so will assert that any serious theology will always be linked to one or another of the religious traditions of humankind. Thus, Schleiermacher was prepared to argue that Christian theology is necessarily linked to Church life, and, indeed, that the same knowledge should not be called theological if it is not so linked.[16]

There are of course other ways of conceiving of the nature of theology, but these two are the ones that have generally been found convincing in academic theology (and in much Church life) over the past two centuries. In either case, theology is intrinsically linked to the Church, in the sense that it is not possible to practise theology without being somehow involved in the life of the Church.[17] In giving an account of how a theologian should relate to theologians of previous generations, then, it is not just the differing historical locations that are important, but the shared ecclesial location too. If, that is, it is the case that there is good reason to suppose that membership of the Church establishes some form of connectedness between people that is not undermined by historical separation, that must be considered alongside the arguments of the previous chapter.

Can there be such a form of connectedness? People can be connected to one another in a number of different ways, many of which clearly are affected by historical separation. Family relationship, for instance, as commonly understood in the Western world today, is a way of being connected to other people that is unquestionably weakened by historical distance. On the one hand, the further I am from an ancestor or descendant in generational terms, the more distant I consider my relationship: children are closer to their parents than to their grandparents, and closer to their grandparents than their great-grandparents, and so on. On the other hand, the historical distance that prevents me from physically meeting a descendant or ancestor is an interesting case: psychologically, this also increases separation, in that I feel myself closer

---

[15] Schleiermacher, *The Christian Faith*, §6–7.

[16] See *A Brief Outline of the Study of Theology*, T. N. Tice (tr.) (Richmond, Virginia: John Knox Press, 1966), pp. 19–27.

[17] In the normal run of things, of course. The account based on revelation leaves open the space where God may choose graciously to make himself known to someone who is utterly unconnected to the Church, but, inasmuch as it is claimed that God's normal way of working is through the Church, the general point holds.

to those grandparents I have been able to form adult relationships with than to those I never knew; legally and linguistically, however, there is no distinction in relationship to be made – both are my grandparents. Again, other factors (living in the same house, or pursuing the same profession, as an ancestor did, perhaps) may increase or decrease my psychological sense of connectedness or separation, but these will not change the fundamental relationships.

This sort of distinction will also apply to any ecclesial connectedness that may be found: for a variety of reasons – social, temperamental, geographical, theological, denominational – I may feel psychologically closer to some members of the Church than others, but I am not aware that any of these factors has ever been claimed to have theological significance.[18] That is, whatever theological language I may use about my relationship with fellow Christians (most obviously, perhaps, the familial language derived from the Scriptures, 'brothers and sisters') applies as strongly to a believer I have never met, and with whom I do not share a common language, as it does to my closest friend in my own local fellowship.[19]

To establish the sort of connectedness that I have argued should make a difference to the way theology is done, two further questions must be answered: one is simply the question of whether the language of 'brothers and sisters', or other ecclesial and/or theological language describing relationships within the Church, implies any actual connection: has God in fact established a real bond of some sort between Christian believers? The second question is whether 'historical' may be added to the list of factors in the previous paragraph: do five hundred years make as little difference to Christian fellowship as five hundred miles?

Consideration of the first question might begin with an examination of St Paul's central metaphor for Christian existence: being 'in Christ'. This phrase, or something equivalent ('in him', for example), occurs over two hundred times in Paul's letters.[20] Most recent interpreters of Paul seem to regard it as

---

[18] Some recent theology gives a sort of significance to denominational differences, by claiming that some denominations are somehow 'defective' (see, for example, the Dogmatic Constitution on the Church from Vatican II, *Lumen Gentium* 15). I do not, however, see how this could apply to the Christian existence of individual members of those denominations: it may be more difficult to be a 'good' Christian, however that may be defined, but there is little theological room for someone to be considered a 'half-Christian'. A person is either in Christ or in Adam, dead in trespasses and sins or alive in Christ, and so on. There is no middle ground (Mt. 12:30).

[19] This assertion ignores any covenant members of a particular fellowship may have made to one another. To the extent that such a covenant is theologically valid, it clearly establishes a particular relationship between those covenanting.

[20] So A. M. Hunter, *Introducing New Testament Theology* (London: SCM Press, 1957), p. 96.

fundamental in his theology.[21] It clearly has a variety of meanings.[22] Sometimes a particular person is described as 'in Christ', indicating little more than that they are a Christian (Philem. 16). Sometimes it indicates the relationship of the particular believer to the Lord (Phil. 4:13). The heart of the image, however, would seem to be corporate: to be 'in Christ' is to exist in a new reality, together with all others who are 'in Christ'. The precise details of this reality are disputed by interpreters,[23] but only one question is relevant to the issue here: is this reality irreducibly, or merely incidentally, corporate?

The difference between these two positions might be illustrated by considering the different relationships in which a football supporter and a football player stand to their comrades. A supporter could follow his team happily without any corporate involvement in supporters' events. He might, in an extreme case, book a box at the ground so that he could enjoy the games in total isolation, without any human interaction with others who felt similarly about the team. Although the picture is somewhat ridiculous, it makes the point that football supporting, whilst normally highly corporate, is only incidentally so: there is nothing in the nature of the activity that demands entrance into a particular set of relationships. A player on the team is in a very different situation, however: it is necessary for him to relate in a series of ways to the other players if he is to do his job properly. Playing on the team is irreducibly corporate, and to attempt to do it without relating to the other team members would not be an idiosyncrasy, but a serious failure to be what he is supposed to be.

At the heart of any theological account of conversion, of the movement from being 'in Adam' to being 'in Christ', to continue to use that language, is a changed relationship with God. That much is not in doubt. Reconciliation, justification, adoption – all the richly resonant soteriological terms point to that change of relationship. This is, of course, a change of actual, theological, relationship, which may, but need not, involve a change of experienced, or

---

[21] Taking examples almost at random: C. K. Barrett describes this phrase as 'primary' and 'fundamental' (*Paul* [Outstanding Christian Thinkers series] [London: Geoffrey Chapman, 1994], pp. 131, 105); Herman Ridderbos includes it amongst the 'fundamental structures' of Paul's thought (*Paul: An Outline of His Theology*, J. R. de Witt [tr.] [London: SPCK, 1977], pp. 57–64); G. E. Ladd merely describes it as 'one of Paul's most characteristic formulations' (*A Theology of the New Testament* [rev. ed.] [Grand Rapids, Michigan: Eerdmans, 1993], p. 523); Günther Bornkamm claims it 'has a significant place ... among the descriptions of the believers' new existence' (*Paul*, D. M. G. Stalker [tr.] [London: Hodder & Stoughton, 1975], p. 154).

[22] Hunter and Bornkamm both offer some indication of this range, with examples, from which I have borrowed in what follows.

[23] Ladd offers some history of the disputed interpretations of the phrase, together with bibliographic notes indicating where more can be found.

psychological, relationship. The new believer may not feel that they have been adopted as a child of God, may not even know this on an intellectual level, but it remains a reality. The question is whether that movement also necessarily implies a similar change in actual, theological relationship with other believers. That there need not be any experienced change in social relationships is clear: when, after Philip's explanation of Isaiah, the Ethiopian eunuch believed and was baptised in the desert, he joined no fellowship, but returned to the service of his queen.[24] Had he met Peter or Dorcas, however, he would have been called 'brother'; would this term have reflected an already existing relationship, instituted by God?

The classic image of existence 'in Christ' is the picture of the body of Christ, used in four letters in the Pauline corpus.[25] The roots of this image are obscure,[26] and it is quite important to note the slightly different nuances it is given in the various uses,[27] but the basic point, at least in Romans 12, 1 Corinthians 12 and Ephesians 4, is clear: individual Christians can no more exist apart from one another than individual organs or limbs of a human body. Their very survival depends on their interrelationships with each other, and the vivification of the whole by Christ, through the Spirit. It is not that the relationships of Christians to each other are fulfilling, but incidental, like membership of a club; even the common preacher's image of lumps of coal, that together can blaze but apart grow cold, is inadequate; a Christian apart from the Church would be like an eye apart from its body: grotesque, dead and doomed only to decay. Like the bones in Ezekiel's vision, the parts of the body must come together before there can be any God-given life.

It may be argued that this image in Paul applies only to the local fellowship, and so attempting to discover any more general account of Christian being, one that asserts the interdependence of Christians who have never met one another, is forcing the text to say more than it in fact does. I believe this argument may be countered, however, on three grounds. First, the Church is in fact one Church, and whilst the relationship of that universal Church to each particular local fellowship needs careful statement, it is surely the case

---

[24] Tradition has him converting his countrymen. As far as I am aware, there is no historical evidence to support this tradition (the Ethiopic church that survives today can be traced to a later time), but none to discredit it either.

[25] Romans 12:4–5; 1 Corinthians 10:17, 11:29, 12:12–27; Ephesians 1:22–3, 2:14–16 (possibly), 4:12–16, 5:21–32; Colossians 1:24, 2:17–19, 3:15. For an exhaustive discussion of these passages, see Ernest Best, *One Body in Christ: A Study of the Relationship of the Church to Christ in the Epistles of the Apostle Paul* (London: SPCK, 1955).

[26] Best, *One Body in Christ*, offers a discussion, pp. 83–95; see also J. A. T. Robinson, *The Body: A Study in Pauline Theology* (London: SCM Press, 1952), pp. 55–8.

[27] On which again see Best, *One Body in Christ*.

that, if Paul's image does indeed convey theological insights, these insights apply universally, as there is nothing in the image to suggest local limitation or reduplication. Indeed, second, the image surely cannot be applied to a multiplicity of local congregations, since Christ has one body, and there is one eucharistic bread that is shared (cf. 1 Cor. 10:17). It would be possible to insist that the metaphor has nothing at all to say about relationships beyond the local fellowship, but, to the extent that it does, it would seem to imply that these relationships are as necessary and fundamental to proper Christian existence as those within the local church.

Third, what is presumably the latest use of the image in the Scriptures does actually imply its application more widely than the local fellowship, albeit *sotto voce*. Ephesians 4:7–16 presents a picture of the exalted Christ, 'who ascended … so that he might fill the universe' (v. 10), giving leaders ('apostles, prophets, evangelists, pastors and teachers', v. 11) to edify his body, the Church. At least two, and possibly three, of the ministries mentioned were translocal, not confined to a particular fellowship, which makes the logic of the passage difficult if the body metaphor is to be restricted to such. Further, the great Ephesian vision of Christ filling the universe that forms the immediate context of the passage suggests strongly that the universal Church is in view. Finally, the wider context includes the ringing affirmations of unity of vv. 4–6 'there is one body and one Spirit … one hope … one Lord, one faith, one baptism, one God and Father of all …': in the light of such a text, linking the oneness of the body with the oneness of the Father, could the image really be restricted to particular and plural local fellowships just a few verses later? In chapter 5, the image is recalled again when moral standards concerning behaviour within marriage are justified by an appeal to Christ's relationship to the Church (vv. 21–33; the body image is used in v. 23 and vv. 28–30). Once again, the imagery used simply demands that Christ's body be understood as the one Church, and not restricted to each particular local fellowship.

So, I suggest that not only does the internal imagery of the body metaphor resist its limiting to particular local fellowships, but that also there are both theological and exegetical reasons why this limitation should be refused. The image must be applied universally, as well as locally; in God's good ordering of things, the faith of the Ethiopian eunuch did indeed depend on a real connectedness with Peter, Dorcas and every other Christian believer.

This result might seem difficult, as the form of this connectedness might be hard to imagine. There are resonances with other theological themes, however, which may illuminate it. Accounts of Christ's saving work, for instance, have often stressed the unity of the Church in salvation: Christ acts to win the Church, and particular people are won inasmuch as they are a part of that Church. This theme can be found in Scripture, where it is linked to the body metaphor, and to the picture of the Church as the bride of Christ:

'Christ is the head of his body the Church, of which he is the Saviour ... Christ loved the Church, and offered himself up for her, to make her holy, cleansing her by the washing of water through the word, and to present her to himself as a radiant Church ... holy, and without blame' (Eph. 5:23–7).

In later dogmatics, this theme is developed in various ways. More catholic discussions tend to stress the Church as the locus of God's grace, particularly in the sacramental ministry. The sacraments, particularly baptism, are held to be necessary to salvation, and so outside of the Church none can be saved. Reformed discussions often link this sort of theme with the doctrine of election, stressing that the election of believers is consequent upon, and included in, the election of the Church, and that in turn that is consequent upon, and included in, the election of Christ.[28] In whatever way the theme is worked out, however, it demonstrates that the Church as a whole is theologically important, and so that those relationships that are established between its members are not incidental but vital.

The second question raised above concerned the extension of this fellowship across time as well as space. To what extent can the relationships established by God within the Church continue to be regarded as real when death, in particular, separates two Christians? The obvious place to look for an answer is in theological reflection on the credal confession 'I believe in ... the communion of saints.' This phrase has usually been taken to imply the unity of the church militant (i.e., on earth) and the church triumphant (i.e., in heaven), and lies behind that hymnody which speaks in such terms as 'mystic sweet communion with those whose rest is won'.[29]

The doctrine of the communion of saints, then, would teach us that those who have died in the faith of the Church are not lost to its membership. At its most basic, it is the confession we make in our eucharistic liturgies, that it is only 'together with all [God's] saints' that we can stand in the Spirit before the Father's throne as the Church of Christ. In order to determine whether there is a real and irreducible connectedness that is not destroyed by historical distance, it is necessary to describe the character of this communion with some exactness. Three disputed issues in particular stand out, two bequeathed as problematic by the tradition, the last rendered so by modern discussions. They are: the question of the status of those designated 'Saints' by certain ecclesial communions or authorities which claim for themselves the right to so denominate;[30] the

---

[28] See Chapter 8 below for a discussion of these themes in various Reformed writers.

[29] From 'The Church's One Foundation ...'

[30] I will adopt the practice of using 'Saints' (capitalised) to refer to those so designated, and 'saints' (uncapitalised) to refer to all Christian believers, after the manner of the Reformation.

Reformation question of the practice of addressing those so designated; and the modern attempt to render orthodox the ancient Arabian heresy of 'soul sleep'.

With regard to the first, there is, it seems to me, theological value in identifying certain people as exemplary practitioners of the Christian life.[31] I have already asserted (in the previous chapter) that the proper way to understand what it is to be human is by looking to Jesus Christ. The ethical converse of this dogmatic statement is the ancient practice of the imitation of Christ. However, if we take seriously the historical locatedness of human existence, as I have argued that we should, then we have to acknowledge that even Christ's life is historically particular in all sorts of ways, and so take seriously the possibility that 'imitation', in this sense, may involve a very different way of life, which seeks to respond to the particularities of a different historical location in a manner that is authentically Christlike.[32] This raises a problem of discernment, or hermeneutics: how are we to decide what is an authentic and successful attempt at imitation, given that an apparent likeness, and still more its lack, has the potential to be seriously misleading?

A position commonly advanced by feminist theologians offers a lead here: if, as it is often argued, the embracing of humility and self-denial are virtues which respond to peculiarly male patterns of sinfulness, then how are we to know what is Christlike living for a woman?[33] Proper imitation, that is, might be unlike the original because of the constraints and possibilities offered by each particular historical location. To pretend that conforming ourselves to Christ will involve wearing what he did, eating what he did, living as he did, is foolish: these things are part of the particularity of his historical location, and in a different location we will find different particularities. I read the denomination of certain Christians as 'Saints' as a way of answering this problem.

The Saints, that is to say, are those whom the Church commends to us as people who have successfully 'imitated' Christ in their particular situations, thus giving us an expanded and enriched view of what it might mean to be Christlike. It would take great wisdom and greater discernment to be able to imagine all the ways of living that might be authentically Christian in even one location (as even the very different lives of the apostles might teach us); given the deceitfulness of the human heart, it would take great courage too. Hagiography invites us to enlarge our perceptions, and to see more examples, in order to gain wisdom in this area, and perhaps even discover examples

---

[31] The argument that follows is my own development of a line first suggested to me by Dr Mike Higton.

[32] The most famous treatise *de Imitatione Christi*, that of Thomas à Kempis, would seem to be well aware of this dynamic.

[33] I should say that I find this position rather unconvincing, but it is a useful and currently common illustration of the basic point.

whose locatedness is close enough to our own that we might learn directly from them.

Telling the stories of the Saints, then, is an activity that invites us to enlarge our perceptions of what faithfulness to Christ might mean. It is an attempt to see ways of living and acting that are genuinely Christlike, but are muted to the point of inaudibility in the gospel stories because of the necessary particularity of Christ's own life. Proper hagiography amplifies the life of Christ without adding to it, enabling us to hear notes and melodies which are a part of the infinitely rich beauty of that life, but which we might never hear without this aid. For this to be achieved, the stories told of Saints must be true, and must model genuinely Christlike behaviour.[34]

If this is a correct reading, then it does not greatly matter who identifies those whose stories will serve as our examples, provided the identification is credible. It seems to me clear that, formally or informally, every Christian tradition has generated a hagiography, a selection of stories that are intended to fulfil this function, of displaying the varieties of the Christian life. In those Reformation communions that have chosen to discontinue the practice of denominating certain individuals as 'Saints', instead reserving the word for all Christian believers, a series of denominationally particular exemplars of the Christian life has been effectively created by no more discerning a process than popular acclaim. One need only think of the martyrologies of the early days of Reform (whether it be the *Martyr's Mirror* of Anabaptist tradition or the Anglophone work of Foxe) or later examples such as Jonathan Edwards's *Life of* [David] *Brainerd*. Once this is noticed, however, the question of how the title 'Saint' is conferred is not especially relevant to my purposes; I have argued that the practice of so denominating some people is useful; that is all that matters.

What is the relevance of this to theological work? It has often been noticed that some theologians interact with history by identifying certain 'heroes' who are listened to and conversed with extensively, often without any particular regard for their context or original conversation partners. This has sometimes been derided as a failure of historiography: such theologians, it is claimed, are stuck within a model of history borrowed from a pre-critical age, whereby it is thought to be exclusively the story of the doings – or in this case thinkings – of great men. Genealogically, this may be an accurate account, but I suspect it is inadequate. Certain theologians – let us call them the doctors of the Church, again without worrying unduly about how such a title might be conferred in any particular case – certain theologians are recognised as outstanding

---

[34] I am certainly not suggesting here that these conditions are both fulfilled for every piece of hagiography that is currently accepted by one church or another – although I wonder sometimes whether we are too quick to dismiss as bizarre or unbalanced behaviour which might indeed teach us something of Christ.

examples of how to think through the way in which God's all-sufficient gift of his Son is sufficient to meet the needs of a particular age or circumstance. They thus become examples to be lived with and studied, whose writings amplify without adding to the teachings of Scripture in just the same way as the lives of the Saints amplify without adding to the example of Christ. That is, there is a proper intellectual hagiography within the Church, just as there is a proper intellectual apostolate; it is appropriate to dwell long and lovingly on the writings of certain heroes, and it is by so doing that one becomes a theologian.[35]

This is not yet enough, however, to establish the point under consideration: there is no irreducible connectedness established yet. There is, though, a suggestion in the tradition that we can go further, as there is substantial, albeit disputed, witness to the practice of speaking to (and even, occasionally, hearing from) the Saints. This practice, if it is theologically legitimate, would certainly establish the sort of connectedness that is under discussion: if the aid of the saints as intercessors may be sought, then clearly our shared ecclesial context makes a difference. Even if this practice is not theologically legitimate, the sorts of theologumena that are invoked in the discussions may point to ways forwards.

The first of these is a modern question that is logically prior to the question of praying to the Saints, and must be addressed. Both sides in that Reformation debate, after all, were united in denying what Augustine had called the 'Arabian' heresy, the idea of 'soul sleep'.[36] Indeed, Calvin's first published writing was a defence of this orthodoxy.[37] The idea in question concerns the state of a person between physical death and the general resurrection: Christian teaching had always maintained that our souls survive in a conscious state, and experienced a foretaste of the rewards or punishments that were to be our lot come the resurrection;[38] at various points this had been denied, and the suggestion had been made that the soul 'slept', or that somehow the person is

---

[35] These arguments might be developed to offer a theoretical reason as to why church history can be regarded as a theological discipline, and not merely a historical one. The study of the Saints and doctors of earlier ages, in their social contexts and so on, is a study that can be directed towards a clearer vision of the face of Christ, the proper final aim of all theological endeavour.

[36] *De Haeresibus* cap. 83.

[37] *Psychopannychia,* published in 1534.

[38] Dante's pictures of hell, purgatory and heaven are explicitly of this intermediate state, and he questions Virgil at one point as to whether the torments of the damned will be lessened or increased by the resurrection, citing the orthodox belief (that was never really lost sight of, contrary to modern polemic) that a soul desired to be embodied, but unable to believe that the coming judgement will in any way lessen the torments of the damned.

insensible whilst awaiting resurrection and judgement. In the last century, under the influence of a historiography that sees Christian theology as thoroughly infected by Greek philosophical metaphysics, this orthodoxy has often been considered to derive from a Greek suspicion of the body[39] and so denied.

Without entering fully into the argument,[40] it seems to me that the biblical evidence is compelling. The repeated Old Testament references to *sheol*, for instance, apparently indicate a genuine post-mortem existence which, although shadowy, is in some sense conscious.[41] Again, St Paul's discussion of being 'absent from the body' but 'present with the Lord' after death[42] is difficult to make sense of without postulating some form of conscious post-mortem, but pre-resurrection, existence. Other strands of evidence are more minor or contentious, but add to the overall impression: the raising of Samuel's 'ghost' by the witch of Endor; the traditional interpretation of Christ's preaching to the imprisoned spirits; the martyrs under the altar who cry out to God for justice as they await their resurrection.[43] In the face of all this evidence, and in the absence of any adequate alternative exegesis of the various passages, it seems difficult to deny the traditional view. The Saints (and saints) and doctors who have gone before are alive in Christ, fully conscious, enjoying the beatific vision, and awaiting the resurrection.[44]

If in Christ they are alive and remain members of his body, then the Church's dogmatics, to which all theological work should aspire to be a contribution, cannot proceed by pretending otherwise. The doctors are not dead and gone, but living and active, and members together of the same body of Christ to which we belong. God has established a real and irreducible connectedness between us and them. Thus, to deal with the theological

---

[39] For a recent example of this tendency, see E. Jüngel, *Death: The Riddle and the Mystery* (Edinburgh: St Andrew, 1975), pp. 41–3, 53–5. Jüngel ignores the constant insistence within the Christian theological tradition that to be embodied was the proper mode of being of a soul, which insistence decisively differentiates Christian accounts of the immortality of the soul from Platonism, however superficially similar some of the language may be.

[40] Some pointers towards a way through can be found in Mike Higton and Stephen R. Holmes, 'Meeting Scotus: On Scholasticism and Its Ghosts', *International Journal of Systematic Theology* IV.1 (2002), pp. 67–81. I have also been helped on this point by a forthcoming paper on soul–body dualism by Randal Rauser.

[41] See, for instance, Eichrodt, *Theology of the Old Testament*, vol. 2, pp. 210–23.

[42] 2 Corinthians 5.

[43] 1 Samuel 28:15; 1 Peter 3:19; Revelation 6:9–11.

[44] I am fully aware of the problems of this position, many of which are considered in some detail in Higton and Holmes, 'Meeting Scotus', but I believe it is easier to answer those problems than to find an alternative view that does justice to the biblical evidence.

tradition only by doing straightforward genealogy is improper, as it denies this central ecclesiological dogma; instead we must find a way of relating to the doctors of earlier ages that recognises the asymmetry of the relationship in which we stand to them – we can read their works but they cannot respond to ours; conversely they now gaze upon the face of the living God, whilst we still see as through a glass darkly – but does not ignore a proper ecclesiology and so collapse this relationship into one that is merely historical.

The first stage of this argument is to recognise the context we share with the doctors of the Church. Much of my argument thus far has stressed the difference that our created particularities create between us; it is now time to point to a key similarity. The Saints and doctors who have gone before certainly have their own national, social and historical locations, and nothing can remove that fact, but they – and we – are also located ecclesially, as members of the body of Christ, and so are bound together as well as separated by our particular locations. We share a context with them, and so we can hear their voices as fellow voices, as less strange than mere genealogy might suggest they should be. Within the Church we are sisters and brothers, members of the same body, sharers in the one Spirit, seeking and claiming to possess the mind of Christ. To make the point with a slogan, the thoughts of Martin Luther cannot be utterly foreign to anyone who can say *baptismus sum*.

There is, thus, an important truth behind Allchin's suggestion that we are able, in the communion of saints, to transcend the particularities of our own times – but this transcendence has a complementary immanence. We remain the particular, located creatures that God has been pleased to make us, even whilst, in the Spirit, we are able to learn from those who have gone before. History is not done away with by the Spirit, but its vicious aspects are transformed so that they are no longer barriers but gifts, so that the glorious diversity of God's human creation does not separate us from other Christians but rather enriches our communion. The babble of voices at Babel that is overcome at Pentecost will finally resolve, not into a monotonous unity, but into a glorious harmony as 'every tongue, tribe and nation' is engaged in praising God in heaven. Just so, the various historical particulars which make up the Church are not destroyed by the Spirit, but transformed, so that they, too, may add to the richness of the praises of God that are sung by the redeemed.

Living before the final eschatological inauguration of the Kingdom, we do not experience the fullness of this truth, of course. History remains a barrier, and one that requires hard intellectual work, and great humility (and, no doubt, other virtues), to overcome. As with the gift of sanctification, or the progress of the gospel, however, we may be certain both that the barrier will, one day, be overcome, and that in various ways it is at present being overcome. In the Spirit, in all our glorious particularity, there is a way in which we can hope and expect to experience the relationship God has put us in with the doctors of the Church.

A part of the experience of this relationship will be the occasional recognition that, despite all their historical particularity and strangeness, we none the less share certain thoughts and questions with the doctors, because we also share a context with them. As well as thinking in many ways that are unlike the ways we think, they also think in some ways that are similar. We ask similar questions, perhaps, or try to apply the same texts, stories and insights to our own situations. There should, then, be something familiar in the writings of fellow theologians: compared to other writings of the same period, we ought to find more that is more easily accessible to us in avowedly theological writing.

Can we say more than this? If the Saints and doctors are living and active still, and still too a part of the one Church of Christ, can we relate to them more directly? This is the Reformation question of whether the Saints – and, we may add, the doctors – may be addressed, and it remains relevant. In their present existence they are conscious and enjoying the beatific vision of the glory of God in the face of Christ whilst they await the final consummation of the resurrection. It is, thus, not inconceivable that they might be addressed by believers, or indeed by others, who remain on earth. God may have established a mode of communication that makes this possible. May, then, we properly seek the aid of the Saints as intercessors, or the doctors as teachers?

Again, I do not want to attempt a summary of a complex and long-standing debate, but, with Calvin, I see little reason to be confident that the Saints can hear our addresses,[45] and so little reason to seek their aid as intercessors. In Scripture, we are promised the presence and intercession of Christ but not of our fellow Christians. Even if, however, there is no good reason for us to believe that we can speak directly to those who have gone before, the Scriptures do give us a tantalising glimpse that suggests ways in which we might perhaps gain from their presence with Christ. We are told of a time when Jesus ascended a mountain, taking with him three living disciples, and there in his glory he met and spoke with Moses and Elijah.[46] At least once in the history of the Church, according to this text, living disciples have witnessed the familiar converse of the saints with their Lord.[47]

It may be that we should read nothing into this text, but if we are to give an account of a continuing ministry to the church militant of those who have gone before, then it is surely the most fruitful place to start. It might, first,

---

[45] *Institutes* III.20.24.

[46] I am grateful to John Colwell for suggesting to me the utility of this text, although the development that follows is entirely my own responsibility.

[47] I take it, not least from Jesus' parable of the rich man and Lazarus, that the patriarchs were not forced to wait till after the resurrection of Christ before they could enter heaven.

suggest that the speech of the doctors is now directed only to Christ: we should not expect to hear from them. Their ministry, still, is to witness to Christ, to assure us that he is who he claims to be, that although we sometimes question and doubt the faith on earth, troubled and confused (as Peter, James and John were) by the humiliation of our Lord, beyond the grave it will be luminously clear, and the Lord whose presence is now so often hidden will then speak to us as friends. There is no suggestion in the text that we can know or overhear the secrets which Christ shares with them: that he lives, and reigns, and holds familiar converse with our brothers and sisters, is all we can hope to know. Like Peter, we may expect to be utterly undone by the realisation of such knowledge, but such experience is perhaps valuable for those of us who presume to speak often about God. If the doctors still have a teaching ministry, then, it is always and only to point to Jesus the Lord, not to answer curious questions, but to affirm that all truth may be found in him. This, I think, is as much as we can say concerning any such ministry.

To return, then, to the main argument, asserting that theological writings should be more familiar to us than other writings might raise the question of who counts as a theologian, or what counts as theology. I am not sure that the issue is quite so clear-cut as this question suggests, however: I am claiming that we will find a surprising commonality which can be theologically explained by a shared ecclesial context, and which is based on the fact that, although living in very different locations, we and they are trying to submit our thinking to the truths of the gospel of Jesus Christ as found in Scripture. On the one hand, I have suggested that those who might be termed the doctors of the Church are so denominated precisely because they have been judged to be particularly successful in doing this, and so their writings will form the major resources for this form of theological study. On the other hand, with any writing, the extent to which successive theologians find this familiarity will be some sort of measure of the extent to which the writing or writer is indeed shaped by the gospel.

This argument may also be reversed, in a sense, and used as a test of our theology rather than that of our brothers and sisters who have gone before. If a text is acknowledged widely to be a theological classic, then the extent to which we find a familiarity in its thoughts and arguments might reveal how much our thoughts have been shaped by the gospel. To this extent, I think, it is theologically proper to ascribe a relative and dependent authority to the tradition in theological work: if many other Christian believers, seeking to submit their minds to the authority of the gospel, and living in a variety of different intellectual climates and historical circumstances, agree on a particular point, then that fact establishes a presumption in its favour, unless and until it can be demonstrated to be inconsistent with other, more central points of the gospel. I will return to this discussion in the concluding chapter, which will offer an account of the proper authority of the tradition.

In the previous chapter I argued that it was in fact necessary to theological work to approach the Scriptures by way of the tradition, and that, as the necessity was a result of the way God has been pleased to create us, that fact was something to be celebrated rather than resisted. The argument of this chapter allows that point to be extended: to respect, learn from, and listen to those who have struggled with the Scriptures before us is a part of taking seriously our life as God's people together in the Church. To refuse to learn from the tradition in doing theology is to succumb to the pride that says 'because you are not a hand, I don't need you', and to spurn the most excellent way of love, without which all insight and all knowledge is only and precisely nothing.

What, finally, of the disputed tradition of the Church? In what sense can these arguments apply when so many of the writings of the great theologians of earlier ages are controversial, directed towards demonstrating the failure of other writers to conform to the gospel? The first point to make is that the controversies, however much they were marked by the *odium theologicum*, did not always, and perhaps not often, involve the suggestion that the opponents had left the Church behind. This is clearly true in most conflicts that were internal to a particular communion, and can be shown to be true of many others.[48] Disagreement, even when sustained,[49] need not result in division, and so in a split tradition. Further, whatever one may think of the structures and ideas that have been created by the ecumenical movement over the last century or so, the realisation of just how much is shared by all Christian communions (in matters of belief, but also in traditions of worship, ethical principles and so on) has become very common, and helps us to recognise that, even when disagreement has grown so serious as to result in a breach of communion, still such disagreements are internal to a tradition of discourse.

The concept of heresy may be helpful here, as a limiting case. A heresy is a system of belief that grows up within Christian life and thought, but which is

---

[48] To take merely one example, François Turretin, in a work devoted to controversy, which exposes again and again (what he regards as) the errors of the Lutherans, nonetheless asserts, 'we do not cease to honour them with brotherly affection'. *Institutes of Elenctic Theology*, 3 vols, G. M. Giger (tr.) J. T. Dennison (ed.) (Phillipsburg, New Jersey: Presbyterian and Reformed, 1992–7), XVIII.15.11.

[49] Controversies over the proper mode and subjects of baptism (between Independents and Baptists in England and Wales), over the presence of Christ in the Eucharist (within Anglican churches) and over the authority of Scripture (within many communions) are all examples of disagreements that have lasted centuries without causing a breach in communion.

judged (properly by an ecumenical council) to be in fact inimical to Christian belief and practice. In this, it contrasts to a religious or philosophical tradition that is simply foreign to the Christian faith (ancient Greek philosophies, or Hinduism, perhaps). Heresy, however dangerous and wrong it may be judged, and however much it should result in a breach of communion, is still clearly a part of the Christian tradition, albeit a part that has been judged inadequate and wrong, and not something foreign.

Just so, there is family resemblance in our errors and failures, however severe. Arianism, Pelagianism and Sabellianism are constant dangers because they each seem superficially to be congruent with Christianity. It may be that heretics, particularly those whose errors are the result of pride and hatred, cannot be considered to be a part of the Church, the body of Christ, but those who remain in the Church still share something of a context with them. The same arguments will apply, but much more strongly, for others who we consider to hold to errors which none the less do not remove them from the Church. Thus the first two arguments that I have advanced above, concerning the handing on of the faith and the shared intellectual context, still apply even to those who are in error.

Finally, most of us are ready to accept that there are disputes that do not damage the unity of the Church. We may disagree about the proper form of Church government, or the interpretation of certain scriptural passages relating to the eschaton, or various other things, but we do not suppose that such disagreement damages our fellowship in Christ in any fundamental way. Unity in the body is a result of being in Christ, and of the Spirit's being in us, not of agreement in all matters of doctrine. Thus for most disputes, all the arguments I have advanced in this chapter will continue to apply.

$$\star \qquad \star \qquad \star$$

Thus far I have argued that it is both necessary and useful to pay attention to the Christian tradition when doing theology. I have hinted at ways in which this should be done, but not explored the practice in any detail. The next two sections of the book will add further support to these claims by offering a variety of examples of how theology might be enriched by attention to the tradition. They will also seek to explore and exemplify the practice of interacting with the tradition by demonstrating the various techniques and virtues that are necessary for successful interaction. These chapters will range widely across the theological tradition, looking at writers from different ages and different communions. Given the way this book came into being, this is largely an accident, of course, reflecting no more than the range of topics that I found occasion to write about, whether through personal interest or request. It is, I think, a happy accident, however: to trace the history of one particular strand of the tradition over a narrow time period would be more coherent, certainly, but would perhaps be less illuminating as to how the principles I have outlined can be applied.

Chapter 3

The Upholding of Beauty:
A Reading of Anselm's *Cur Deus Homo*

The first skill that is necessary to learning from the tradition is that of listening. There is a need to allow historical voices their own particularity and strangeness, to recognise that they are, as I have argued, located within an intellectual and cultural context that is other than ours. The three chapters in this section are all attempts to explore that art, to recognise how our own intellectual assumptions and contexts cause us to mishear what our predecessors have said, and to seek to demonstrate that careful listening can none the less enable us to hear the voices of the doctors in all their particularity. Any reappropriation, any attempt to use a text to illuminate or critique theological work today, must come second to this fundamental work of listening.

St Anselm of Canterbury's *Cur Deus Homo* provides an interesting example of the necessity for this art of listening, simply because the accounts of its argument that are regularly offered in introductory works so clearly demonstrate a failure to listen. In this chapter I offer a straightforward reading of the text, an attempt to pay sustained attention to it on its own terms, and so to hear what it has to say. Anselm remains famous today for two things: he is the originator of the ontological argument for the existence of God; and he is the source of the satisfaction theory of the atonement. These positions do not exhaust his theological contribution: he also wrote works defending and defining Western Trinitarian doctrine, against Sabellianism and tritheism, and arguing for the *filioque*; he wrote on the Incarnation; and was influential in modifying Augustine's account of the transmission of original sin. There is also a collection of meditations and prayers, traditionally attributed to St Anselm, which at their best rank alongside almost any devotional literature of the medieval period.[1] His memory, however, is firmly attached today to just the

---

[1] For a reasonably up-to-date list of critical editions and translations of Anselm's writings, see G. R. Evans, *Anselm* (Outstanding Christian Thinkers series) (London: Geoffrey Chapman, 1989), p. xi.

two points with which I began. It would not be an exaggeration to claim that on both he has been fundamentally misrepresented by the popular accounts of his thought given in theological and philosophical introductions and histories. What he has to say is recognised as important, but too often the effort of simply listening to it is not made.

The problem seems to be that, whilst it might be clear that Anselm did not think that he could prove the existence of God from a particular definition of God, and nor did he derive a theory of the atonement from the penitential system, quite what he did say and do is the subject of major disagreement, and so it is easier to perpetuate the caricature than to attempt a more accurate reading. Nearly fifty years ago, a survey of what the famous slogan *credo ut intelligam* had been taken to mean could find interpreters who classed Anselm as anything from a rationalist philosopher who would not be out of place amongst eighteenth-century Enlightenment deists to a parody of a Barthian who would argue from nothing that was not a direct quotation from either Scripture or the Creed.[2] On the atonement, there has recently been criticism of Vladimir Lossky's depiction of Anselm as the epitome of legalism, rationalism, crucicentrism and everything else that the Eastern tradition has found objectionable about Western theology by another Orthodox interpreter who finds Anselm offering fundamentally the same narrative-based theology as St Athanasius had done in his *De Incarnatione Verbi Dei*.[3]

This variety of interpretation offers, I think, an interesting example of the problem of historical particularity. St Anselm occupies a curious place in history just close enough to our own for us to feel kinship, and just far enough away for that feeling to be misguided. When we read his more philosophical works, we feel that he is speaking the same language as St Thomas or Descartes or Kant; the same words are there, and many similar ways of arguing, and this is enough to blind us to the fact that the words and the syllogisms are being used very differently, not least because he lived before the Aristotelian renaissance of the thirteenth century. Again, and more to my purpose here, *Cur Deus Homo* will talk about satisfaction, and so remind us of the Reformation accounts of the atonement that did owe something to the penitential system; or it will speak of debt, so that the whole spectre of what Edward Irving dismissed as 'Stock Exchange Divinity' comes to our minds. When language of necessity and proof is used, we think immediately of the sort of systematisation that was first attempted in Germany in the nineteenth century. The

---

[2] John McIntyre, *St Anselm and His Critics: A Re-Interpretation of the* Cur Deus Homo (Edinburgh: Oliver and Boyd, 1954), pp. 15–38.

[3] D. B. Hart, 'A Gift Exceeding Every Debt: An Eastern Orthodox Appreciation of Anselm's *Cur Deus Homo*', *Pro Ecclesia* VII/3 (1998), pp. 333–49. On Lossky see particularly p. 340.

Ritschilian misreading that is still too regularly reproduced by people who should know better has its origin, I think, in such failures to be properly attentive to the particular and strange historical context of Anselm's work.

In attempting to listen to what Anselm actually does have to say, then, the first question needing attention is methodological. In the *Cur Deus Homo* Anselm famously claims to be arguing, *remoto Christo*, for the rational necessity of the Incarnation and passion of the divine Word. Stated baldly like that, the temptation of the modern reader is to assume that what is going on is a thoroughgoing natural theology, claiming that the human mind unaided by revelation can discern the truth of the gospel. A knowledge of Barth's admiration for Anselm's theological method should be enough to convince us that this is a misreading, but the question still remains as to what this odd procedural announcement might mean. Anselm does, after all, appear to assume a variety of theological positions at various points in the text, including a robust doctrine of God (his attributes and, in particular, his Trinitarian existence) which are hardly uncontested dictates of natural reason, either now or then. An understanding of the method of argument he adopts will be crucial to any attempt to read the text properly.

John McIntyre, in a careful study of the various interpretations of Anselm's method,[4] suggests that in each of his works Anselm has a particular audience in mind, and he starts from what he regards as common premises in order to demonstrate the disputed conclusion for which he is arguing. In *De Processione Spiritus Sancti*, for example, the opponents are Eastern Orthodox theologians who deny the *filioque*. So Anselm is able to assume the doctrine of the Trinity and the procession of the Spirit from the Father, and argues from these common starting points for the double procession. Again, in the *Monologium* a broadly Platonic doctrine of the forms is assumed;[5] living prior to the rediscovery of Aristotle by the West, this can be taken as a common starting point to be reasoned about and applied in a Christian way. Anselm's methodology, that is, is intimately bound up with his historical locatedness.

In the *Cur Deus Homo*, the aim is to confound infidels who 'despise the Christian faith because they deem it contrary to reason' (Preface)[6]. In particular, as the first chapter suggests, the question is why God should do what he did in Christ; granted the premise that humanity needs salvation, the Incarnation and passion of Christ is surely an absurd and unreasonable way for

---

[4] McIntyre, *St Anselm and his Critics*, pp. 47–8.

[5] Ibid.; see *Monologium* VII.

[6] References to Anselm's works will be by chapter division. English quotations will be taken from *St Anselm: Basic Writings*, S. N. Deane (tr.) (Chicago, Illinois: Open Court, 1962²); Latin from the corrected Nutt edition of the *Cur Deus Homo* of 1895.

God to bring about that salvation. The question thus concerns the internal coherence of Christian theology; we might compare it with the theodicy question that is so often raised today, as they share the same form: in both cases, the challenge is, 'if what you say about God is true, then surely this doesn't make any sense?' Anselm is thus able to assume many Christian theological positions, as they are granted, as hypotheticals at least, in the particular question he is addressing in *Cur Deus Homo*. The challenge is to show that, with these positions granted, the gospel story is rational and necessary. He is seeking to show, that is, not just that God could have done this thing (the Incarnation and passion), but, because he accepts the premise that this actually seems a rather bizarre thing for God to have done, he needs also to show that there was no other way.

There are two categories that appear to be central to the construction of the argument: one is reason, the other is fittingness. Many points are established by an appeal to one or the other of these. What Anselm means by these two concepts and the relationship between them is the central question in under-standing the method he adopts. Both must be understood in terms of the particular historical location in which the work was written; otherwise they will be just misunderstood. Because of this, the second category, fittingness, is in some ways the easier to understand, as it is obviously a strange category to the present-day reader, and so less likely to be misunderstood.

A passage from the book that has usually been regarded as peripheral, mistaken, or both will serve to illustrate the concept of fittingness. Anselm at one point (I.16–18) discusses the relative numbers of the angels and the redeemed. In essence, his argument begins with an assertion that God always intended a certain number of intelligent beings as the inhabitants of heaven. There must, thinks Anselm, be a perfect number of such beings, and God being God must know that number and have planned towards it. The first premise here seems highly dubious but, as our interest is currently in method not doctrine, let it be accepted as a hypothetical for the moment. Now, God would not have made angels merely to waste them, as that would be unworthy, so the total number of created angels must be equal to or less than this number. Even in the limiting case of it being equal, some angels fell and so the perfection of heaven would be incomplete without the number being made up from somewhere. The only possible source is human beings. Now, the number of blessed beings may not exceed the perfect number, since that too would be imperfect, and so God would not do it, and God would not have created humanity without intending to admit them to his presence, so we must assume that the total number of created angels was less than this hypo-thetical perfect number, with room for human beings. Again, if humanity was only to gain happiness as a result of the fallen angels' misery, God would have so ordered things that blessed humans would rejoice in the fault of the fallen angels, as providing the opportunity for their own happiness. But God would not so order the world as to encourage rejoicing in another's sin, so there must have been space.

As I have said, I find the initial premise of this argument unconvincing, but it does display well what is meant throughout the book by 'fittingness'. God being who he is, perfect in every way, all wise and all good, and also omnipotent, it is a sufficient argument against a particular thing that the all-wise and all-good God could not have wanted it so. The image of the feudal overlord has often been used in interpreting Anselm, but it must be understood the way Anselm would have understood it, as far as that is possible. On this particular point, a part of that image which is often forgotten today is crucial: the lord–vassal relation was not just about the obedience owed by the vassal, but about the lord's responsibility to maintain order and uphold justice.[7] There is, for Anselm, an order and a beauty in the creation that God has put there and, being good and just, will necessarily maintain. If something threatens to mar that beauty (the fall of some angels, for example), God will act in such a way as to preserve or restore it (the election of more human beings).

'Reason' must be understood in a strict sense, as simply logic. When Anselm asserts that a position is 'reasonable', he is claiming nothing more than that he has shown how it may be derived from previously argued positions and agreed premises. There is no sense of an appeal to natural theology or to universal a priori positions – or rather, where there is, these are in the category of agreed starting points, and not what is 'reasonable'. What then is the relationship between that which is fitting and that which is reasonable? Simply this: the most regular argument used by St Anselm in this text takes the form that it is unreasonable to believe God would do something unfitting. Almost the whole discussion proceeds by establishing disjunctions that either x or y must be the case, then showing that it would be unfitting for God, *this* God, to do x, and so asserting that y has been rationally demonstrated. Recently, a claim has been made that Anselm only ever uses this negative form of the argument, that is, that he refuses to argue from 'z is fitting' to 'z is necessarily the case';[8] I am not sure that this is the case, as there are, I think, one or two counter-examples,[9] but certainly the negative form predominates.

The important point about the relation between these two, however, is that they are not merely synonymous; to move from 'z is fitting' to 'the existence

---

[7] I owe this point to Colin Gunton, *The Actuality of Atonement: A Study in Metaphor, Rationality and the Christian Tradition* (Edinburgh: T&T Clark, 1988), p. 89.

[8] See Michael Root, 'Necessity and Unfittingness in Anselm's *Cur Deus Homo*', *Scottish Journal of Theology* 40 (1987), pp. 211–30, and particularly p. 215.

[9] The two initial arguments of I.19, for instance, one made by Anselm and one by Boso, seem to contradict this assertion.

of z is rational' requires an argument, not merely a restatement. Because of this, I have used the slightly anachronistic word 'beauty' to describe what is 'fitting' alongside 'order', which is closer to Anselm's Latin. The order of the creation is not only a matter of rationality – although it is that as well, in that God is perfect in reason as well as justice, mercy and love. Anselm is not attempting to build a system after the pattern of the magnificent, but fatally flawed, Hegelian examples; the universe is not merely rationally necessary in each particular and in general. Indeed, Anselm's reticence, if not refusal, to argue from 'z is fitting' to 'z' could be read as an insistence that there is a plurality of possible worlds, and so that a thing could rationally be is no reason to suppose that it is. The world makes sense as the creation of this particular God; that allows much to be rejected, but more than that Anselm will not claim.

All of which is to say that what may be regarded as proper, or fitting, for God to do is absolutely central to the argument, and so the underlying doctrine of God is of great importance. At no point does Anselm spell out the things that he feels at liberty to assume about God; if his method is as I have described, seeking to demonstrate the internal rationality of the Christian faith, he may and does assume anything that is a part of the faith that does not violate the condition he has set of thinking *remoto Christo*. Now, a statement like that should produce howls of protest: we know *nothing* of God apart from Christ. Quite so, but that is to miss Anselm's point: he is not attempting to derive a doctrine of God apart from Christ; rather, he is attempting to respond to a charge that the Christian doctrine of God is not compatible with the Incarnation. To fulfil this apologetic purpose, he must in a sense reverse the order of the theological logic that argues from the gospel narrative to a doctrine of God, and instead begin with the received doctrine of God and show how the gospel narrative may be coherent with this. Given this, some comments regarding Anselm's assumed doctrine of God seem in order.

Having been required to leave out the Incarnation, Anselm is unable to give much content to Trinitarian doctrine, although he does assume the truth and basic contours of an Augustinian Trinitarianism. Instead, he concentrates on the classical attributional language about God, focusing on his justice, his mercy, his omnipotence and particularly his aseity. Two particular comments need to be made, one concerning what is meant by justice, and how this relates to mercy, the other concerning the assumption of God's aseity.[10]

First, concerning justice, mercy and God's forgiveness. Much of the first book is taken up with establishing that God could not simply forgive sinful human

---

[10] 'Aseity' is the idea – common in patristic, medieval and early modern theology – that God is *a se*, self-caused, so that he cannot be affected by anything beyond his own life.

beings without the need for either punishment or satisfaction. Boso's repeated question[11] is why could God not simply forgive, or why praying for forgiveness (as we do in the Lord's prayer) is not enough, or why penance is not enough (I.12, 19–21). It is in this last context that Anselm famously asserts 'you have not yet considered how serious a thing sin is' (I.21, although phrased differently in the English translation referenced). Boso at one point urges God's omnipotence and liberty to do as he wills and his ultimate mercy, as reasons why God could just forgive without any need for satisfaction. Anselm's response is important: he insists that God's liberty and compassion must not be interpreted in such a way as to interfere with his honour (*dignitatus*). That is, just as God's freedom cannot be interpreted in such a way that he is free to lie, so neither his freedom nor his compassion may be interpreted in such a way that he is seen to be unjust (I.12).

The text offers three reasons why the free forgiveness of sins may be considered to be unjust, which between them offer an important insight into what it means for God to be just, according to St Anselm (I.12). First, it is right order for sin to be either satisfied or punished (I.12),[12] and so if it is simply forgiven the universe will be disordered (*inordinatum*). Second, to simply forgive sin is to treat the guilty and the non-guilty just the same, and this is unfitting for God (*quod Deo non convenit*). Third, God has established a law for humanity, which lays down a penalty for sin. If God just forgives sin, then sin is freer than righteousness, being subject to no law, and this is clearly inappropriate. In each case, the argument turns on a particular result of God's forgiveness of sin that is regarded as unjust, in that it fails to fulfil the condition of God's perfect upholding of the beautiful order of creation, whether in the law that he has established or the winking at the introduction of disorder.

This, for St Anselm, is the final demonstration of how serious a thing sin is: not the infinite guilt of the sinner, but the disordering of the beauty of God's creation. God, being just, cannot allow his creation to be, and to remain, disordered. It is the need of the creature that means that sin requires a response (as we shall see in a moment, sin does not damage God), but God, as the creator and governor of the world, would be less than perfect if he did not make that response. God's response is to bring good out of evil, to find a new way of ordering the world that responds to the disruption of sin in such a way that the world is restored to a beautiful order. St Anselm suggests this can be done either by punishment or by satisfaction. His arguments concerning punishment (I.14) are not as cogent as others in the work, but that is perhaps because they are made only in passing; it is as inconceivable that God should punish human sin as it is that he should wink at it. Anselm's real interest is in

---

[11] The book is cast in the form of a discussion between Anselm and Boso.

[12] '… *quoniam recte ordinare peccatum sine satisfactione non est nisi punire*'.

showing how God is both perfectly just and perfectly merciful in providing a way for satisfaction to be made for human sin.

The second point concerns God's aseity. Anselm is very clear in insisting that sin does not harm God, because God cannot be harmed by any creature in any way. Sin does not lessen God's honour, it lessens the honour done to him by creation (I.15). This is an important distinction, which makes Anselm's concept of the harm done by sin much clearer. God, insists Anselm, has no need to act to preserve his honour; it is the height of arrogance and absurdity to presume that we could ever place God's honour in jeopardy. Rather, what is put in danger is, as I have indicated, the perfect ordering of creation. The world and every creature in it exist to honour God; this is so much their purpose that, as Anselm and Boso discuss (I.21), it would be better that the universe cease to be than for one glance to be cast contrary to God's will. Sin dishonours God, not in the sense of detracting from his actual dignity in himself, but in the sense of preventing or perverting the honouring of God that is the centre and height of the order of creation.

This issue of aseity introduces a reason why Anselm insists that sin must be satisfied rather than punished: were God to punish the human race, his purposes for humanity would be frustrated. That, however, requires us to assume that a human action (sin) can frustrate God's purpose, which contradicts God's aseity (I.25). So God will not punish sin, but fulfil his purposes through its satisfaction. I have said it already, but it is perhaps worth making absolutely explicit, given the caricatures of Anselm's position that still occur, that it is as inconceivable here that sin be punished as it is that sin be undealt with, in that one would suggest that God has failed to be perfectly just, whilst the other would suggest that God has failed to be perfectly merciful. Neither may be supposed, and so the famous dilemma, *aut poena aut satisfactio* (sin must either be punished or have satisfaction made for it) cannot, according to Anselm, be settled on the side of punishment. The question remaining, then, is how satisfaction may be made.

Much has been written about the origins of St Anselm's theory of satisfaction. The initial statement of the theme is in I.11, where Anselm simply asserts that a willful injury should be dealt with by recompense and an additional penalty to satisfy the outrage of having injured the other in the first place. This is not argued for by Anselm, or against by Boso, so we must regard it as one of the things Anselm feels able to assume in constructing his argument. No doubt various backgrounds in Roman law, in Teutonic *Wergild* and in the Church's penitential system contributed to this being a commonly accepted concept, but that should not lead us to suppose that an analysis of one or all of these will enable us to understand Anselm's meaning. Just as he takes a general concept of sin and, by arguing from the nature of God, fills it out in surprising ways, so the particular contours of his idea of satisfaction will be defined by the way he uses it, not by any prior history of the concept. This is a place where, I think, the ecclesial context which present-day theologians share with Anselm is important: satisfaction is finally defined by the self-offering of Jesus Christ, and all other concepts are subordinated to that one.

A person who has disobeyed God, then, owes God not just renewed and continued obedience, but some measure of satisfaction for the failure to obey. The level of satisfaction is determined by the level of the offence of human sin, which, Anselm argues, is infinite. God, as creator, is infinitely above his creation in honour and dignity, and so the demand to honour him is of infinite weight. Therefore, any failure to obey or honour God is an offence of infinite weight, and so, finally, an infinite satisfaction is needed. Thus Anselm sweeps aside Boso's offering of 'repentance, a broken and contrite heart, self-denial, bodily sufferings, pity ... and obedience' (I.20) as not answering to the cause at all. It is not original to comment that in this Anselm is decisively relativising the penitential system of the Church of his day,[13] but he is still so regularly accused of having based his theology on the practice of penance that it does need repeating. We need to hear the criticisms of their context that writers of the past make, not just the assumptions of it.

At this point in the argument, towards the end of the first book, Boso expresses a degree of despair. Having been made to see what a serious thing sin is, and so what level of satisfaction is necessary, he can see no way for this satisfaction to be made. His despair, however, as Anselm points out, is misplaced: not only the seriousness of sin has been proved, but also the impossibility of God not providing some way for satisfaction to be made and so for sin to be forgiven. Anselm is even so bold as to claim that his point has been proved, by a version of a *reductio ad absurdum* (I.25): having agreed to argue *remoto Christo*, Anselm now finds, that with Christ out of view, both the absolute necessity, and the absolute impossibility, of satisfaction being made for human sin are established. Therefore, satisfaction must be made through Christ.

Anselm is not, I think, particularly serious in advancing this argument, and he immediately accepts the necessity of demonstrating how Christ's making satisfaction is rational. His argument is not, however, so weak as it may seem. The obvious criticism is that the *reductio* only establishes that there is a flaw in the premises somewhere, and the *remoto Christo* condition is not the only premise with which he is working. So, it may be that one of the other axioms, the assertion of God's aseity for instance, is flawed. However, this criticism lacks much of the force it appears to have: Anselm has undertaken to prove the rationality of the Christian account of how atonement is made; that atonement

---

[13] For instance, Hart, 'A Gift Exceeding Every Debt', p. 340.

needs to be made – *i.e.* that human beings are sinful, and that this is a problem –
is in the class of shared premises. Equally, the existence of God and his
greatness is not in doubt; nor, presumably, is his love, or the basic alternative
position that Boso has urged, that God could and should simply forgive sin
without need for satisfaction, would have little force. It seems, then, that the
logical problem that Anselm uncovers is one that he expects his opponents to
feel to be difficult. This is not, yet, an exercise in logic internal to the Christian
faith; Anselm is, however, discoursing within a theistic community whose
doctrine of God has been decisively affected by Christian faith, and he seems to
think that the logic thus far will be common to all within this community.

Equally, however, he sees the need to demonstrate the rationality of the
gospel story, and so he turns to do that in the second book. This starts with
a rehearsal of the necessity of satisfaction and salvation, and an important
discussion of how something can be said to be necessary for God, essentially
indicating that God is not free to be less perfect in any way than he is, and so if
he has once purposed a thing his constancy demands he see it through, and so
on (II.5). This discussion is, I think, a genuine theological advance made by
Anselm, but it is not central to the flow of the argument at this point, and I
have already assumed the results of it in talking about Anselm's doctrine of
God earlier.

Anselm then states the argument for which this work is perhaps best
known, which answers precisely the challenge of the title 'Why there should
be a God–man'. None but God can make satisfaction, since an infinite satisfaction is demanded; none but humanity ought to make satisfaction, since it is
humanity's sin that is being atoned for, so 'it is necessary for the God-man
to make it' (II.4). Anselm is not quite so ready as some of those who have
borrowed this argument to write QED with a flourish at this point, and turns
immediately to a discussion of Christology to establish that a God–man is a
rational possibility within the hypotheses that have been agreed (II.7). Mere
transformation will not answer the case, as if God just becomes man, without
remaining God (or, indeed, vice versa), we do not have a being who is able
to make satisfaction under the terms laid down. Again, we cannot have a co-
mingling to create a *tertium quid*, or we are faced with a being who is neither
God nor man, and so who neither can nor should make satisfaction. Finally,
there must be genuine union of the two natures in one being, or that being will
not answer the case.

St Anselm's logic here is dense, but of great significance. This is an attempt
to establish the necessity of each of the clauses of the Chalcedonian definition
from the nature of the atonement. If atonement is to have happened, then the
One who made atonement must have been like this. If 'our Lord Jesus Christ'
is not 'perfect in Godhead', 'truly God' and 'consubstantial with the Father',
he cannot make satisfaction; if he is not 'perfect in Manhood', 'truly Man' and

'consubstantial with us', he should not make satisfaction. To do what he has done, he must indeed be and have been both 'begotten of the Father before the ages as to the Godhead' and 'like us in all things, sin apart'. Indeed, even the famous strings of negatives all find their place in St Anselm's arguments: 'in Two Natures unconfusedly, unchangeably, indivisibly, inseparably ...' – so he must be, to make satisfaction for the sins of humanity. Anselm quietly but decisively aligns himself here with the Christian tradition as it had been handed on to him.

I have suggested already that Anselm's apologetic purpose demands he reverse the normal order of theological logic, in that he is not arguing from the gospel story to a doctrine of God so much as from the Christian doctrine of God to demonstrate that it is not inconsistent with the gospel story. These chapters on Christology are perhaps the most striking example of this, as Anselm seeks to reconstruct the gospel narrative in its most precise theological detail on the basis of a doctrine of God and a doctrine of satisfaction for sin.

In the next two stages of this argument, the common opinion is that Anselm overreaches himself somewhat. He attempts to prove that both the virgin birth (II.8) and the Incarnation of the Son, rather than the Father or the Spirit (II.9), are rationally necessary. These arguments are interesting not because they work – bluntly, they don't – but because they show the level of detail at which Anselm was prepared to assert the rationality and fittingness of the gospel story: this is not, as so often presented, a trivial argument that God must have become human to make satisfaction; it is an attempt to derive an entire doctrine of the person of Christ, in its narrative as well as dogmatic aspects, from the work of Christ. That it fails should not blind us to the importance of the attempt.

So, there is a God–man. Anselm does not pause to argue why there should be a God–man rather than a God–woman; that detail, at least, never occurs to him as a celibate in a single-sex community in the Middle Ages. This man, too, owes God the honour of perfect obedience, but he lives the perfect life and so gives God the honour due to him. Anselm does not make much of the perfection of Christ's life, but it is both clearly stated (II.10) and crucial to the argument. There is a broadly Irenaean account of recapitulation here; by living human life as it always should have been lived, Christ changes the possibilities available. In particular, he is not subject to death, since death is only a result of sin, the fundamental sign of a disordered universe, perhaps.

Anselm's logic is nearing completion. There is a need for satisfaction to be made, for a gift to be given to God of infinite worth. The God–man, through the perfection of his life, owes nothing more than perfect obedience to God, and so is in a position to give a gift, and is not subject to death. Through his own being as the Incarnate Son, his life is of infinite value; so to give up his life for God's honour is a gift of genuinely infinite value. Anselm is emphatic that his death is voluntary, a freely offered gift to God (I.8–9; II.11). It is not that he needed to die, or that he was killed (could he not call down twelve legions of angels?); emphatically, it is not that the Father was looking for someone to punish and lighted upon the God–man. He offered his life as a gift to the Father.

The obvious question is why should this gift be pleasing to the Father? It demands, however, careful phrasing. Anselm's repeated insistence on God's aseity demands that God is impassible: nothing done by a creature can affect him, so this death cannot please him. It is not God who has been damaged by sin, but the creation, which has been warped and ruined by humanity's failure to give proper honour to the creator. This is the damage that must be restored. God is honoured in a way that he could not demand to be honoured, and so God's honour is satisfied. Christ gives up his life for God's honour, and, since this is so much greater than all human sin, in his death the creation is fulfilled; after this, God is honoured by the creation as he always should have been, and there is a genuine reordering and renovation of the beauty that is proper to creation.[14]

I have a theory that any appropriately Christian soteriology will struggle more with universalism than its opposite: if the work of Christ is properly understood, the question must always be 'how can any human person not be affected and transformed by this work?' On this test, Anselm scores highly; his logic has a strong tendency to universalism. Boso asks questions about the extent of Christ's salvation, which Anselm answers with strong affirmations of its universality: Boso raises the question of those who put Christ to death, since their sin is greater than all others, and Anselm replies that it is lessened by ignorance: they can be forgiven, because they know not what they do. Again, Boso asks about Adam and Eve, and Anselm strongly affirms their salvation: God's purposes for humanity are for their happiness and so salvation; there should never be a generation of humanity born in vain, so at every moment of human existence there must be some who are being saved. This universalising tendency only stops with Origen's limiting case, as the salvation worked by the God–man can only avail for sinful humanity, and not for the fallen angels or their chief, the Devil (II.14–16, 21).

However, this seemingly provides a problem: why are some not saved? Anselm's only answer is to return to the continued debt of obedience owed by

---

[14] Anselm expresses this in semi-feudal terms, which are perhaps misleading today, as he talks about the Father rewarding the Son, but the Son already calling all that the Father has his own, and so offering his deserved reward as satisfaction for the sins of many. The sense of the re-ordering of the beauty of the world is clear, however, in all that Anselm says.

all humanity; not that Christ's death is not sufficient for this, one assumes, but that to show indifference or despite towards God when offered forgiveness, and with the magnitude of Christ's sacrifice in view, is a further outrage that is intolerable (II.19). This sort of reasoning has led some to criticise Anselm for teaching a merely passive righteousness, that we are not so much saved as given the chance to save ourselves. This, I think, is to miss the point of the text once again; Anselm is not arguing about the salvation of individual human beings: he is asking why the Incarnation was necessary for the salvation of all humanity. His answer to this line would no doubt have been to invoke a doctrine of predestination, learnt from Augustine and from the relatively recent disputes and synods involving Gottschalk's teachings. That he does not mention theological concepts that were common in his particular historical location is no reason to suppose he did not accept them. Indeed, arguably it is evidence in the other direction, as a prolific writer who disagreed with commonly held views on this or that point might be expected to have made his reasons for disagreement clear.

In creating and preserving the universe God can only be himself; he is – let me use the language – not free to be less perfect than in fact he is. From this premise, and the fact of human sinfulness, Anselm argues that the only way the creation can be the beautiful, rational place that it must be, as *this* God's creation, is for the God–man to offer up his life for the sins of the world. The argument is fanciful, flawed in places, time-bound in what it assumes, and sometimes irritating in what it omits. It remains a profound piece of theology that does not deserve to be trivialised by one-sentence Christologies leading to two-sentence accounts of the Father taking pleasure from punishing his Son. The book, like the world it describes, is far too beautiful for that.

Chapter 4

'Something Much Too Plain to Say':[1] Towards a Defence of the Doctrine of Divine Simplicity

The doctrine of divine simplicity is both ubiquitous and important in the theological tradition.[2] None the less, I suspect that it is possible, indeed even normal, today for someone who is qualified to master's level in theology to have never heard of it. When I mentioned my intention of writing on divine simplicity to one or two people, I was met with either blank incomprehension or incredulity. To say, as one introduction does, that this doctrine has a 'public relations problem'[3] is to understate the issue considerably: divine simplicity is today either already forgotten or regarded as best forgotten, or so it seems.[4] Even amongst those who have learnt from Barth's dictum that 'not merely the most important but also the most relevant and beautiful problems in dogmatics begin at the very point where the fable of "unprofitable scholasticism" and the slogan about the "Greek thinking of the Fathers" persuade us that we ought to stop'[5] divine simplicity is regarded as one idea that is best left in the arid

---

[1] From G. K. Chesterton, 'The Wise Men'.

[2] This paper first appeared in an issue of *Die Neue Zeitschrift für Systematisch Theologie* presented to Professor Colin Gunton on the occasion of his sixtieth birthday. It is a pleasure to have a further chance to record publicly my debt of gratitude to Colin, who as teacher, colleague and friend has influenced my thinking and living as a theologian greatly.

[3] R. H. Nash, *The Concept of God: An Exploration of Contemporary Difficulties with the Attributes of God* (Grand Rapids, Michigan: Zondervan, 1983), p. 85.

[4] In a book-length, and avowedly philosophical, discussion of the divine attributes, Edward Wierenga's entire treatment of simplicity is contained in one sentence, asserting that the idea originates in Greek philosophy, and announcing that he has nothing to say about it. *The Nature of God: An Inquiry into Divine Attributes* (London: Cornell University Press, 1989), p. 173.

[5] *Church Dogmatics* I/1, p. xiv.

wastelands of scholastic philosophy. Barth himself, after all, claimed that it 'was ... exalted to the all-controlling principle, the idol ... devouring everything concrete',[6] and if now that idol lies broken and forgotten, then there it may be left, with a sigh of relief on the part of the theological community, or so many today seem to think. I am not sure, however, that this is the case. The doctrine of simplicity seems to me be a casualty of a failure to listen to the tradition, and as such a fine example of my contention that this need is a live one in current theological work.

I begin with an observation: the supposed logical problems and inconsistencies that have led the doctrine to be regarded as so problematic in recent discussions were not even noticed by a wide swathe of the Christian tradition. It seems to me there can only really be three explanations for this. One would be the suggestion that earlier writers who invoked the doctrine, and their readers, were all so dull as to be blind to logical problems which we now expect undergraduate students to spot. This seems utterly implausible. A second would be the suggestion that there was a key argument, valid or invalid, which all earlier writers accepted, and which undermined all the now standard objections to the doctrine of simplicity so effectively that they did not need to be rehearsed even. The third possibility is that the earlier writers meant something different when they spoke of 'divine simplicity' to what modern critics assume they meant. I will suggest that there are elements of truth in both the second and third arguments.

Alongside this suspicion of modern criticisms of this doctrine, I also, when I came to consider it, had an intuition that, despite its regular appearances in the tradition, the doctrine of divine simplicity was not invoked regularly enough. Some, at least, of the problems I saw were not a result of following this 'all-consuming idol', but rather a result of not following it rigorously enough. In this chapter I want to argue first that the doctrine of divine simplicity is theologically comprehensible by suggesting that many of the apparent problems raised in recent years are based on misconceptions, and second that it is theologically useful, in that it allows us to say certain things about God which are difficult to say without holding to this doctrine. On the basis of these two points, I will suggest that with only a few minor repairs this idol may become for us an icon, a way of approaching the One True God who is Father, Son and Holy Spirit.

At the outset I ought to note that there has been an interesting and moderately vigorous philosophical debate over this doctrine in recent years, concerning the question of coherence.[7] Is it at all meaningful to talk about

---

[6] Ibid., II/1, p. 329.

[7] A sample: C. J. Kelly, 'Classical Theism and the Doctrine of the Trinity', *Religious Studies* 30 (1994), pp. 67–88; W. E. Mann, 'Divine Simplicity', *Religious Studies* 18 (1982), pp. 451–71; W. E. Mann, 'Simplicity and Properties: A Reply to Morris',

'divine simplicity' in something approaching the classical sense, or is this the linguistic equivalent of saying 'a four-sided triangle'? More pointedly, can a personal God be simple – is it possible to talk about God's personality and simplicity without contradiction? The debate is important, but I intend to bracket it here, and to assume that this language can, in some sense, be coherent. I do this partly because I think that the philosophical debate has reached a stage where we might be entitled to presume that this is at least a possible position, and partly because I think the doctrine of divine simplicity raises different questions for Christian theologians, which deserve to be addressed, questions, for example, of theological use. As will become clear, however, my major reason for bracketing this debate is that I suspect that the forms of the doctrine being debated do not necessarily relate in any straightforward way to what 'divine simplicity' has been used to mean in the Christian tradition.

It seems appropriate, then, to begin by offering a definition, and a sketch of an outline of the perceived problems that have led this doctrine to recede so far into the background of recent dogmatic endeavour. To describe God as 'simple' means that God is ontologically basic. Any attribution of ontological complexity, any postulation of distinction or division into ontological parts, is excluded by this doctrine. If we accept the linked scholastic account of God's nature as dynamic, as pure act, then this doctrine means that God does one thing, and that is to be God – perfectly, eternally and incomprehensibly

   Now, this definition immediately raises the central issue: the problem, as I see it, of almost every recent discussion of the doctrine of simplicity lies in an assumption that we all know what it is to be simple. That is, some ontology is assumed, which is supposed to be common to us all, and being basic according to this ontology is identified with simplicity. From this, a set of characteristics that are held to be necessary to any postulation of simplicity is derived, and the question is asked as to whether it is possible to ascribe these characteristics to God in a general theist, or specifically Christian or Jewish or Islamic tradition.

---

[7] (continued) *Religious Studies* 22 (1986), pp. 343–53; W. E. Mann, 'Simplicity and Immutability in God', in T. V. Morris (ed.), *The Concept of God* (Oxford Readings in Philosophy) (Oxford: Oxford University Press, 1987), pp. 253–67; T. V. Morris, 'On God and Mann: A View of Divine Simplicity', *Religious Studies* 21 (1985), pp. 299–318; K. Rogers, 'The Traditional Doctrine of Divine Simplicity', *Religious Studies* 32 (1996), pp. 165–86; E. Stump and N. Kretzman, 'Absolute Simplicity', *Faith and Philosophy* 2 (1985), pp. 353–82; N. Wolterstorff, 'Divine Simplicity', in J. E. Tomberlin (ed.), *Philosophical Perspectives V: Philosophy of Religion* (Atascadero, California: Ridgeview, 1991), pp. 531–52; W. F. Vallicella, 'Divine Simplicity: A New Defense', *Faith and Philosophy* 9 (1992), pp. 508–25 (see also the responses to this article in *Faith and Philosophy* 11).

It seems to be regularly assumed that a monad, perfectly actualised, without extension, without duration, without composition, and so on, is ontologically basic, and so that to call God simple is to identify him with such a monad.[8] This, it must be said, seems difficult from a Christian perspective: the God who reveals himself in Scripture is active rather than actualised, is triune rather than a monad, repents on at least two occasions, which seems a difficult thing for a being lacking duration to do, and becomes incarnate, which raises more problems than there is space to list here. Following this procedure, we are regularly faced with on the one hand a philosophically derived definition of God's being and on the other an exegetically derived description of God's acts, and a serious problem: how could this God do those things?

Now, I happen to believe that this whole procedure is fundamentally wrong-headed theologically, because this is just not what any important part of the Christian tradition meant when they confessed God's simplicity. The most compelling piece of evidence I have to support this is the observation that a dogmatic tradition stretching from at least as early as Basil in the fourth century to at least as late as François Turretin in the seventeenth and from as far east as John in Damascus to as far west as Jonathan Edwards in Stockbridge, Massachusetts, never had any of these problems. Indeed, for much of this tradition a standard form of dogmatics could deal with the doctrine of Scripture in the first locus, God as he is simple in the second,[9] and the doctrine of

---

[8] Wolterstorff, 'Divine Simplicity', recognises that the modern problems are due to a different ontology, but does not take that insight very far. By contrast, and more in keeping with the modern tradition, Alvin Plantinga, in his 1980 Aquinas lecture *Does God Have a Nature?* (Milwaukee, Wisconsin: Marquette University Press, 1980), claims that the same idea of simplicity is operative 'all the way back to Parmenides … [and] has been embraced by thinkers as diverse as Duns Scotus and Louis Berkhof' (p. 27). As a result, Plantinga thinks it is rather easy to demonstrate that a simple God must be either non-relational or non-personal (pp. 42, 53). These demonstrations proceed from a discussion of Aquinas's account of simplicity; St Thomas, of course, was rather insistent that God was to be understood in terms of persons who are properly described as 'subsistent relations'. Assuming Aquinas was not utterly blind to trivial logical contradictions in his own theology, something must have gone wrong with Plantinga's argument – which he indeed tacitly acknowledges when he says '[p]erhaps when he argues that God is [simple], he doesn't mean to identify God with a property or a state of affairs at all, but with something quite different. If so, it is not easy to see what sort of thing it might be' (p. 53). That it is 'not easy to see what' the simple essence of God 'might be' is precisely what the tradition (including Aquinas) insisted in asserting God's incomprehensibility.

[9] The second locus classically describes the One God, and contains a discussion of God's attributes. Simplicity is often placed first or last in such lists to emphasise its centrality amongst the attributes (I will explore the theological reasons for this centrality later).

the Trinity in the third. Now, if the problems of reconciling the concept of simplicity with the triune God of Scripture are as obvious as we have been led to think in recent years, someone in this tradition should have noticed, and the apparent fact that nobody did suggests that the modern problems are a result of a misunderstanding of the tradition somewhere.

If it is in the area of ontology, as I have suggested, then there should be a traditional ontology with which divine simplicity is compatible, and it should be rather easy to point to this ontology. The problem is there is no traditional account of God's being or, rather, there is a strong witness to a refusal to give such an account throughout the Christian tradition. In discussions of what God's essence actually is, there is a standard assertion that God is pure actuality (which is, I think, already incompatible with the perfect unchanging, eternal monad of recent tradition),[10] and beyond that a strong insistence on ignorance. The positive form of this ignorance is the standard dogma that the essence of God is incomprehensible. Why, after all, should we suppose that our minds might be capable of understanding God's essence or existence? The confusion generated by quasi-philosophical discussions of the physical realities that lie behind the equations of quantum mechanics attest that we are unable to comprehend our own (physical) essence at a basic level; there should be little surprise, then, if we are unable to understand God's essence. Instead, there are certain things that we know must be true of God: things revealed in the gospel narrative; things that must be true for the gospel history to make sense; things (perhaps) that we can demonstrate are true of God by reasoning about who God must be. We can talk about these things, and reason about them, whilst maintaining that we do not comprehend the totality of what is meant when we say 'God'. As a result, certain things will remain mysterious to us but, unless one or another can be shown to be illogical, mystery is not a sufficient reason to reject a position.

I do not think that such a strong apophaticism is in any way an abdication of responsibility here, but I believe a slightly more positive case can be made. The recent suggestion that underlying much of the most creative Christian theology is a relational ontology of personhood offers us a way to talk slightly more positively about God's being without claiming to have comprehended him. Whatever God's essence is, and that we still refuse to pretend to know, he is

---

[10] As Thomas Weinandy has pointed out in discussing the related doctrine of impassiblity recently, '[w]hat must be grasped and remembered [when God is described as *ipsum esse*], something which Aquinas' critics never seem to do, is that *esse* … is a verb' (*Does God Suffer?* [Edinburgh: T&T Clark, 2000], p. 122). I suppose that it may be possible to demonstrate that a perfect, unchanging monad can at the same time be so purely active as to be a verb, but it would seem that the onus of proof is on those who claim such a thing, not on those who deny it.

not improperly called 'personal', and personal relationships are central to who he is. Alongside the traditional apophaticism, I hope in this paper to illustrate how such an ontological proposal offers a way of thinking about divine simplicity which appears not to be subject to any of the commonly discussed problems.

Any statement about God is, amongst other things, an ontological statement, a claim that is made about God's essence. The problems – all the problems, I think – raised by the doctrine of divine simplicity are results of an improper assumption that we can understand God's essence. If we import an ontology, an account of God's essence, from (say) neoplatonic philosophy to inform our understanding of what it means to say that God is simple, but then make biblical and credal confessions that are not based on that account, we will very probably be faced with incoherence. I mentioned earlier that almost every recent account of the doctrine of simplicity I have read tacitly assumed that we all know and agree on what it is to be simple, that ontology is commonsensical. This is just not the case. In Plotinus, for instance, the concept of simplicity that is operative is rather different from that which is asserted and used by (say) John of Damascus; in fact Plotinus is rather closer to the visions of the recent writers. Plotinus starts with the One who is beyond description and certainly beyond personhood, and can only be described as eternally and perfectly generative, as the various degrees of being emanate from it. John, by contrast, interweaves language of simplicity, Trinity and incarnation in ways that demand that, whatever concept of ontology may be underlying, simplicity is a property of the tri-personed actor of gospel history.[11]

Here we can return to the way the perfections of God were derived in the tradition, and learn from it: as I have indicated, the attributes were often discussed in the *second* locus, concerned with the being of God. This came after a discussion of prolegomena, usually asking about the nature and possibility of theology and so including statements on the doctrine of Holy Scripture. This arrangement happily protected the discussions of the perfections from a disastrous logical reversal – coming *after* the doctrine of Holy Scripture, these could only be read as saying 'God is simple', rather than 'the simple is God'. Could only be read, that is, as insisting that 'this God, the God who is talked about in these Scriptures, is simple' and never as a suggestion that 'we identify God as the one who fulfils this abstract construction of simplicity'.[12]

---

[11] I will discuss this account in more detail below.

[12] This, incidentally, raises my major criticism of Hughes's account of Aquinas's theology (C. Hughes, *On a Complex Theory of a Simple God: An Investigation in Aquinas' Philosophical Theology* [London: Cornell University Press, 1989]): QQ. 2–13 of the *Prima Pars* do *not* describe 'The God of the Philosophers', as Hughes entitles his interpretation. This should be obvious from Q.1, which begins by insisting that 'It was

The question that must be answered, then, is what sort of accounts of simplicity were offered in the tradition. There is in fact a fairly standard formulation. In the Aristotelian logic of the schoolmen, it was asserted that there is nothing accidental in God, and so everything that is predicated of him must be predicated substantially. Nor is God composite – made up of different parts. Another regularly repeated formula is to say that God's existence is his essence – that God could not be in any other way than he is without ceasing to be himself. Such positions may, for instance, be found in Aquinas's classical formulation of the doctrine.[13] To illustrate these three positions, God's love is not something that God could still be himself without; that would make it an accident. Nor is it one part of his nature; that would make God composite. Nor, finally, is it a way God happens to be which could be different; that would mean that his essence and existence would be separate. Rather, God is his love.

Thus far, the formulation might seem unobjectionable, but the same argument can be applied to God's holiness, God's omnipresence and so on. If God is identical with his love, however, and God is identical with his holiness, and God is also identical with his omnipresence, the normal rules of logic suggest that God's love, holiness and omnipresence are identical with each other. Thus, fairly early on in a certain sort of modern discussion of divine simplicity one finds assertions of the form 'God's love is his holiness is his omnipresence' – assertions that do not appear to be especially useful or indeed comprehensible either philosophically or theologically.[14] So, the doctrine of simplicity as constructed according to this tradition appears to be forcing us to say things about God that are incoherent.

I have focused on this particular scholastic formulation of the doctrine because most of the recent writers claim to be following and exploring Thomas Aquinas's account. Already, however, at this early stage in the exposition, positions are being asserted that Thomas never asserts and indeed explicitly denies, and that on the basis of an assumption that we understand God's simple essence sufficiently to be able to reason about it. I imagine that it is just incoherent to say that God's love is identical with his omnipotence, but

---

[12] (*continued*) necessary for man's salvation that there should be a knowledge revealed by God besides philosophical science built up by human reason' (art. 1 *responsio*) and ends with a brief treatise on hermeneutics (art. 10). In this context, the God of QQ. 2–13, and the rest of the *Summa*, is the God of the Bible, the only God that St Thomas, incidentally one of the great biblical commentators in the Christian tradition, was interested in. Hughes's careful and rich exposition of Aquinas's arguments contains much of value, but it seems to me that this basic hermeneutical flaw damages his conclusions in a whole series of ways.

[13] *Summa Theologica* Ia q.3, &c.

[14] See, e.g., Mann, 'Divine Simplicity', p. 453; Morris, 'On God and Mann', p. 300.

St Thomas, at least, never says this. Rather, he insists that it is meaningful to assert that there is a foundation in God for our distinct conceptions of him, whilst insisting that this foundation is not any real division within his essence.[15] Indeed, Thomas does not even appear to regard this as a difficult or problematic position, and, whilst he spells it out in his *Commentary on the Sentences*, he apparently assumes that it is obvious enough not to need inclusion in the *Summa Theologica* – the equivalent, perhaps, of the need to include standard arguments in a PhD thesis that can be left out of later monographs. So, how can it be said that, without any real division in God, there are nevertheless good reasons to assert that talk of God's love and God's justice and so on has genuine foundation?

This is a mystery; a full answer to this question would involve an account of God's essence that is not available to us. Illustrations may help us, however, to feel that this position is not as counterintuitive as it may seem: wine-tasting notes, for example, often contain a number of words and phrases, some of them apparently in tension if not simply contradictory, which are the attempt of the taster to express a single, but immensely rich, experience, viz., the taste of a fine wine. Could this serve as an analogy of what we mean when we talk of God's simplicity in relation to his various attributes?

We might be able to take a step further than this if we follow the intuition that whatever God essentially is, he is personal. If we were to take a small set of attributes and apply them to a human person, we might argue for coherence: that she is 'good', 'merciful' and 'loving' suggests a single character trait which is not precisely covered by any one of these words. We might even include 'just' in this list and still be able to see a coherence in her character. Were we to add that she does enjoy poisoning pigeons in the park, there is an apparent incoherence, but until this point we might conclude that the various different names we give refer to different aspects of a coherent nature – but so refer in an accurate, if partial, manner. Just so, we might assert that the various perfections of God are names we give to various facets of God's utterly simple personal

---

[15] In the *Commentary on the Sentences* Lib.1 Dist.2 q.1 art.3 *responsio* point 4. The text can most conveniently be found in Timothy McDermott (ed.), *Selected Philosophical Writings: Thomas Aquinas* (Oxford and New York: Oxford World's Classics, 1998), pp. 236–8). See also Copleston's summary of Aquinas's position: '… we know that God is actually a simple Being, but we conceive in a composite manner the object which we know to be non-composite. This means simply that our intelligences are finite and discursive and that they cannot apprehend God save by means of His different reflections in creatures. Our knowledge of God is thus inadequate and imperfect, but it is not false. *There is indeed a certain foundation in God for our composite and distinct concepts…*' F. Copleston, *A History of Philosophy*, vol. 2, pt II: *Mediæval Philosophy: Albert the Great to Duns Scotus* (Garden City, New York: Doubleday, 1962), p. 80, my emphasis.

nature. The coherence of his nature is what is being affirmed and, although how all these different attributes can be coherent might be incomprehensible to us, I can see no straightforward argument that this is a logical problem instead of a merely noetic one – and, as I have said, noetic problems are not really problems here, as we should not expect to understand.

I think, therefore, that the doctrine is more robust, if less ambitious, than recent philosophical discussions have suggested. There have also, however, been a number of theological criticisms of the doctrine: I now want to show how these criticisms can be answered in some measure by the suggestion that what is at stake is an assumed ontology. The doctrine of divine simplicity is only one of a complex of apophatically derived and philosophically determined statements about God that are inimical to more basic Christian doctrines, or so some recent writers have claimed.[16] Usually with the example of impassibility to the fore, it is argued that simplicity, as a part of the standard Neoplatonic apophatic account of who God is, should not be used of the God who became incarnate in Jesus Christ. The doctrine of God is to be determined by Trinitarian and incarnational categories, which are about revelation, and so by positive affirmations, not by apophatic negatives. Further, it is regularly suggested that simplicity, along with immutability and impassibility, is clearly a difficult thing to postulate of the God who is known only in the gospel account of the Son become incarnate, suffering, being forsaken by the Father, and dying.

The objection that has been made is that a God who is simple cannot become incarnate. Let me first note that this objection has problems of its own if it is thought through: a moment spent considering the surpassing majesty of God, as well as being a moment well spent, will convince us of the need to say things about the God who became incarnate in Jesus Christ which are in flat contradiction to human being, and to face the tension. Thus God is ubiquitous, Jesus Christ is (or at least was) localised, and so on. This tension is surely precisely what lies behind the acceptance of such orthodox positions as the *extra calvinisticum* or, indeed, diphysitism. We confess two natures in one person without confusion just to enable us to say things about God that we cannot say of any human being. And if this leads to a series of apparently paradoxical statements, then so has all orthodox Christology – the Chalcedonian Definition, for example, teaches both that Christ suffered and that the only-begotten is

---

[16] Indeed, Robert Jenson claims that '[r]ejection of the dominant tradition just at this point is endemic in contemporary theology'. 'The Triune God', in Robert W. Jenson and Carl E. Braaten (eds), *Christian Dogmatics*, 2 vols (Philadelphia, Pennsylvania: Fortress Press, 1984), vol. 1, p. 166.

impassible, and the orthodoxy of the Christology of Chalcedon is hardly to be questioned![17] The Incarnation must decisively affect how we confess such things as impassibilty and simplicity, of course, but, unless we are monophysites, we cannot form a straightforward argument from the Incarnation to a refusal to attribute such things to God.[18]

The common division of God's perfections into those which are communicable and those which are incommunicable was central to the Christological and eucharistic debates that separate the Reformed and Lutheran traditions. Within the Reformed discussions, a series of careful distinctions sought to define what could and could not be said of the communication: there was a real and concrete communication of properties to the person of Christ, but the abstract communication of the properties of one nature to the other was denied. Reading the reasons given for this in a standard manual, Turretin's *Institutes of Elenctic Theology*,[19] we discover the following: communication cannot occur from one nature to the other because the divine nature cannot be communicated; because all the properties of the divine nature must be communicated if any one is, since that nature is simple; because there cannot be a communication of human attributes to the divine nature; because the natures cannot be confused. This is perhaps a rather good illustration of the first claim I made in this essay, concerning the unproblematic nature of the doctrine of simplicity in much of the tradition: Turretin had an acute mind, but seemed quite happy to argue a controversial point on the basis of simplicity. He saw no problem at all with one person of a simple God becoming incarnate: this was so trivial that it was something to be argued from, not for.

How can this be so? Once again, it is a question of the ontology that is adopted. If Turretin's doctrine of simplicity were built on an ontology that

---

[17] The suffering of Christ is affirmed in the Council's text of the creeds agreed at Nicea and Constantinople, both of which state that he '... was crucified for us under Pontius Pilate, and suffered (*pathonta*), and was buried...' (the original Creed of Nicea seems to have stated only that he 'suffered, and rose on the third day', but the text in the Chalcedonian Definition contains the fuller form). His impassibility is affirmed later in the definition, where those are condemned who 'introduc[e] a confusion and mixture, shamelessly imagin[e] the Nature of the flesh and of the Godhead to be one, and absurdly [maintain] that the Divine Nature of the Only-begotten is by this confusion passible (*pathētēs*)'. Translations are from T. H. Bindley's *The Oecumenical Documents of the Faith*, F. W. Green (rev.) (London: Methuen, 1950⁴).

[18] Weinandy's discussion of the *communicatio idiomatum* with reference to impassibility makes this point admirably, and far more fully than I can here. *Does God Suffer?*, pp. 173–206.

[19] XIII.8.ix–xiii. An English translation is now available in three volumes: G. M. Giger (tr.) J. T. Dennison (ed.) (Phillipsberg, New Jersey: Presbyterian and Reformed, 1992–7). Quotations are taken from this translation.

regarded an eternal unchanging monad as basic, then I think there would be a serious problem with holding to the Incarnation, but it seems that it is not. Although Turretin never discusses ontology specifically, the account of God's being that lies behind his invocations of simplicity must be straightforwardly compatible with the Incarnation if we are to make sense of what he says without supposing that he was totally oblivious to basic philosophical contradictions in his theology; the texts make no sense otherwise.[20]

Turretin's account of simplicity is couched in terms of an affirmative reply to the question 'Is God most simple and free from all composition?'[21] The divine nature/essence, he affirms, is not only free from composition and division, but incapable of these things. Distinction, however, is said to be different from division, and the Son is distinct from the Father (III.7.xvi; Turretin does not say so, but we may assume that the Spirit is distinct from both Father and Son). The difference here is that the Father, Son and Spirit have one common essence, which is in no way divided, but subsists in the three hypostases.

With regard to the Incarnation, Turretin says only that

> The Son of God is God–man not by composition properly so-called, but by hypostatical union (by which the Word indeed assumed human nature in one hypostasis, but was not compounded with it as part with part, but stood to it in the relation of perfecter and sustainer to make perfect and sustain an essential adjunct, so that the human nature indeed did thence receive perfection, but nothing was added by it to the divine nature).[22]

There is no assertion here of any particular account of the ineffable divine nature, merely assertions of some particular things that may properly be said, or must be denied, of that nature. Assume for a moment that the traditional position is correct, and that we cannot know what it is to be ontologically simple, but can merely make certain assertions about what may not be said of a simple being: is anything Turretin says about the Incarnation illogical? It seems to me that the answer is no: there are several points in the account where we might say that we cannot understand how a position might be so, but there is no point where any form of contradiction is visible. One person of a simple God may become incarnate without any loss of simplicity.

Again, however, an ontology of personhood offers a way of understanding the point: God is ontologically simple, which is to say (amongst other things)

---

[20] Turretin's polemic against the Lutherans includes a demand that reason, which is to say logic, is a valid route to theological inferences (*Institutes of Elenctic Theology*, Dennison [ed.], I.9–10). This might suggest that other parts of that same polemic would be rather carefully logical.

[21] Ibid., III.7.

[22] Ibid., III.7.vii.

that his nature, his *personal* nature, is basic and unchanging. Applied to the Incarnation, the ontological simplicity for which I have been arguing would insist only that the personal character displayed by the man Jesus Christ is an accurate revelation of the personal character of God – an important point, but hardly an original or difficult one. I am not making claims concerning the precise ontology that Turretin held; I am suggesting that firstly the texts make no sense unless we postulate that he assumed an ontology under which the problems which are often seen in recent discussions were absent, and secondly that an ontology which makes personhood basic to reality will serve as an example which demonstrates that such a position is not impossible. On the basis of these two claims I suggest that the recent assumptions that the doctrine of simplicity is incompatible with the Incarnation are no more than the result of a failure to work with the same doctrine of simplicity as the Christian dogmatic tradition.

What, however, of the doctrine of the Trinity? To deny division or composition to a three-personed God looks remarkably difficult. Again, however, this is a modern problem: the most basic knowledge of the tradition will demonstrate that the doctrine of the Trinity and the doctrine of simplicity have gone hand-in-hand for much of Christian history. In the post-Reformation Protestant tradition, it is the Socinians who attack the doctrine of simplicity, not the Trinitarians, and divine simplicity is regularly invoked as a support for Trinitarian doctrine, at least in the understanding of the time.[23] Classically, of course, divine simplicity is associated with Aquinas and a Western tradition that has often had its commitment to Trinitarianism questioned (usually somewhat unfairly, in my opinion). This doctrine, however, is apparently more decisive still for a tradition deriving from Athanasius and the Cappadocians. A letter traditionally attributed to Basil defends the doctrine stoutly, and even if the current consensus ascribing it to Evagrius Ponticus is correct,[24] he is still a close friend of Gregory Nazianzus, who shows his own familiarity with, and acceptance of, this doctrine in his second *Theological Oration*.[25] Gregory of Nyssa holds to divine simplicity firmly, not least one suspects because his Trinitarianism is so robust that he feels the need to find arguments to defend against tritheism.[26] Most strikingly, I think that the fullest

---

[23] For an example of this see again ibid., III.7.i.

[24] See Letter 8, and the attached notes, in *St Basil: Letters*, vol. 1 (*The Fathers of the Church* vol. XIII), Sr Agnes Clare Way, C.D.P. (tr.) (Washington, DC: Catholic Universities of America Press, 1951), pp. 21–40.

[25] 28.7.

[26] Most obviously, of course, in *That We Should Not Think of Saying There are Three Gods*.

use of simplicity I have seen in a dogmatics text is in John of Damascus, whose *Exposition of the Orthodox Faith* follows several earlier Greek Fathers extremely closely, and interweaves simplicity, Trinity and Incarnation so thoroughly that one must assume that he regarded them as necessarily linked doctrines.[27]

These examples do not establish anything, of course, but do rather suggest that the opposition between simplicity and orthodox Trinitarianism is not as devastating as has recently been generally assumed. The Damascene will use a phrase like 'indivisibly divided', which is not, I think, simple obscurantism but a conscious echo of the paradoxical epigrams of the earlier Fathers, such as the famous Cyrilian *apathos epathen*, 'the impassible One suffered'.[28] One of the great merits of John's exposition is that he will not talk of the being of God before talking about the Trinity, and so his account of God's being, in which assertions of simplicity are almost a leitmotif, is determined through and through by Trinitarian dogma. His argument begins with standard positions: the Son and Spirit possess all properties from the Father, with the exception of the personal, or hypostatic, properties in which the three differ: un-begotteness, begotteness and procession. These are the 'distinguishing marks' of the proper and peculiar subsistence of each. John then argues that the perfection of the hypostases prevents division of the *ousia*. First, three imper-fect hypostases would necessarily be expressions of a compound nature, '[f]or all that is composed of imperfect elements must necessarily be compound'. This is, I think, a reasonable assertion. John wants, however, to assert the converse also: 'from perfect subsistences [hypostases] no compound can arise'. So the divine *ousia* is not compound, but 'one, simple essence, surpassing and preceding perfection, existing in three perfect subsistences'.

The argument at this point is somewhat dense, but clearly turns on the defi-nition of perfection: it is the surpassing perfection of Father, Son and Spirit that ensures that the God who is Father, Son and Spirit is simple, not compound. John asserts 'we speak of those things as imperfect which do not preserve the form of that which is completed out of them. For stone and wood and iron are each perfect in its own nature, but with reference to the building that is completed out of them, each is imperfect: for none of them is itself a house.' So the perfection of Father, Son and Spirit consists in the standard position that each is in himself fully God, and the doctrine of perichoresis safeguards the simplicity of God.

---

[27] John of Damascus, *On the Orthodox Faith*. Quotations are from the Nicene and Post-Nicene Fathers (2nd series, vol. IX) S. D. F. Salmond (tr.) (Oxford: J. Parker, 1899).

[28] Despite the common and long-standing attribution, it seems that this precise phrase does not occur in any extant text of Cyril's. For similar phrases which do, and a defence of regarding it as 'Cyrilian in tone and meaning', see Weinandy, *Does God Suffer?*, pp. 202–3.

At this point it is worth reflecting on the methodology: John does not offer an ontology to make sense of this, but he has no need to. He is attempting to expound the orthodox faith; to the extent that these positions are orthodox, then there is no need to show how they could be held – rather, someone who objects to such positions must demonstrate that they are either unscriptural or illogical. The defender of perichoretic unity may assert 'this I know, because the Bible tells me so', and rest her position on that until an adequate challenge is made. We may seek to understand how orthodox positions work for our own edification, but there is no need to do so in order to hold and teach them.[29]

So, the argument advanced by John of Damascus is that divine simplicity may be derived from standard Trinitarian positions. Each person expresses not a part of God's nature, but the fullness of the *ousia*; each person indwells the other two, without confusion; each person differs from the others only in one relational property that is of the hypostasis, not of the divine *ousia*. If all this is true, then it follows that God can properly be described as simple. Any explanation of how such positions might hold together, any attempt to discover the underlying logic, is a work of supererogation – beneficial and praiseworthy, but not necessary to the maintenance of the faith.

I said at the start of this chapter that I wanted to argue two things: that the doctrine of simplicity was firstly available and secondly useful for Christian dogmatics. I hope that at this stage I have at least sketched an argument for the first of these positions, and so I shall now turn, more briefly, to the second. I shall argue this by way of two steps: first I shall argue that there are good theological reasons to hold to this doctrine; and then I shall suggest that it is useful in enabling us to solve at least one dogmatic problem.

So my argument thus far has, I hope, established that there are no good reasons not to believe in divine simplicity; is there any good reason why we should, however? I have already indicated that the standard derivation of simplicity is via apophaticism, and noted that this method seems unpopular in recent dogmatics, but I hope that I may use it nonetheless without defence.

---

[29] This methodology is not as obscurantist as it might seem, as an analogy with a fairly naïve methodology of the natural sciences will show. Data is acceptable in science if it is observable repeatedly in controlled conditions; it does not need to be explained by any scientific theory to be acceptable, although the task of science is to generate theories that suggest how the different data that has been gathered is coherent. Equally, positions may be established theologically by appeal to revelation – to Scripture; whilst it is the task of theology to seek to explicate the fundamental coherence of all such positions, the failure at any point to do so does not invalidate the position; it merely points to the partial and provisional state of our theological understanding.

Some apophaticism, after all, is surely necessary for any adequate account of God's greatness and majesty.

Alongside the way of negation, we may also proceed by means of fulfil-ment, as when we understand divine omnipotence by thinking about human potency and removing all imperfections from our conception. This is the *via eminentiae*, the way of pre-eminence, the coherence and use of which depends on a method of analogy. So, although human love is only a broken and partial analogy of God's love, analogy it is, and by extrapolating the good things of that love to their highest possible level, we may conclude that God is, pre-eminently, love.[30] This distinction between those human realities we deny of God and those we ascribe pre-eminently to God is only another way of speaking of the standard Reformed distinction between communicable and incommunicable perfections of God, which I have already had cause to mention. There are those things which are true of God which cannot, even analogically, be predicated of created beings; these we necessarily speak of using the *via negativa*. Other perfections, for which we use the *via eminentiae*, are analogically communicable to creatures, and so we say that God is like this, but more so, indeed pre-eminently so, instead of saying that God does not suffer from this limitation.

The particular human realities that we deny or extrapolate, of course, can only be discerned through a hearing of God's revelation: God denies his own mutability or transience in Scripture, but affirms that he is love, and so we may speak with confidence concerning these matters, at least. When we turn to simplicity, the basic affirmation of the oneness of God is certainly scriptural, and most dogmatic treatments of simplicity find in the affirmation 'I am who I am' an assertion of God's identity with his essence. I am not sure that the position can be established quite so simply by exegesis, however.

It would be possible to argue that some of those things that have tradition-ally been subjected to negation should instead have been attributed to God pre-eminently – one might, for example, see Barth's much-praised revision of the doctrine of eternity[31] as starting in an exercise in fulfilling, rather than negating, the creaturely experience of time; as starting, that is, in the assump-tion that here, where the *via negativa* has traditionally been employed, a mistake was made; this experience of creaturely reality is ripe for the applica-tion of the *via eminentiae*, and so we speak of God not as timeless, but as having true time, of which ours is only a poor shadow. When we focus on divine simplicity, and a cluster of related negative doctrines such as aseity, however,

---

[30] The direction of this analogy is, of course, crucial: God's love is basic, human love is derived. To reverse this is merely to embrace atheism, albeit in a characteristically modern form that likes to think of its own confusion as sophistication.

[31] *Church Dogmatics* II/1, pp. 608–40.

this does not appear to be a useful move: the vicissitudes and weaknesses of human ontology are surely not concepts to be ascribed pre-eminently to God: God does not come into being and pass away much more purely and radically than we do, he simply does not come into being or pass away ('all flesh is like grass, and its glory like the flowers of the field, the grass withers, and the flowers fall, but the word of our God stands forever ...'). It is not at all clear what a reversal at this point would look like, but it seems safe to assume that it would not be appropriately honouring to God, whose everlastingness and constancy are, after all, biblical doctrines before they are Neoplatonic ones. So, we cannot, I think, rule out the doctrine of divine simplicity on the basis that its derivation is questionable.

Let me, however, return to Barth. What he does in his discussion of eternity is perhaps more complicated than my brief mention allowed for: he distinguished between the vicissitudes and limitations of time and the roominess, and so liberative nature, of time, and the one he denied of God whilst ascribing the other pre-eminently to God. A similarly complex account of simplicity may perhaps be offered: we deny composition, change and ontological limitation of God, whilst acknowledging the freeing and positive aspects of the condition of being many that are summed up in the concept of relationship. With Barth's account of eternity as the model, we may speak of God fulfilling the positive aspects of plurality in his ontologically basic and so simple life as Father, Son and Holy Spirit, whilst denying the alienation and division that are the negative aspects. At the root of many of the problems of Platonisms in Christian theology, after all, is a denial of the particular resulting from an ontology which sees the One as prior to the many. The Christian answer to this must be, as Colin Gunton more than any other has shown, to build a rival ontology on the doctrine of the Trinity, and so celebrate both the one and the many.[32]

So finally I turn to a classic form of the problem of the one and the many, in order to show how the doctrine of simplicity is of use in offering a solution to at least one dogmatic problem. The issue is a philosophical question that was prevalent in later medieval discussions, and was decisive in some of the problems that were faced by the Reformed tradition some centuries later. In the creation myth in Plato's *Timaeus*, the Demiurge takes eternally existing matter and shapes it according to the eternally existing Forms. Whilst Christian doctrine rapidly did away with the concept of pre-existent matter, the Forms proved more resilient: there are good reasons for believing in some sort of universals, and to describe these universals as the creation of God is to embrace

---

[32] See, for instance, his 1992 Bampton Lectures, *The One, the Three and the Many: God, Creation and the Culture of Modernity* (Cambridge: Cambridge University Press, 1992), *passim*, but especially pp. 11–40, 210–31.

a form of moral relativism that has usually been considered unacceptable. If God creates the concept of justice, then we may not usefully call God 'just' or 'unjust' – he is beyond such things. The *via eminentiae* becomes a difficult road to walk, and God may only be described negatively; he is even, in Nietzsche's phrase, 'Beyond Good and Evil'. However, Plato's own view that the Forms exist eternally apart from God is also unacceptable: God is then limited, and judged by a standard other than his own character, and we must look elsewhere than God if we wish to understand what 'goodness' and 'love' mean.

This much is standard and, as a result, the Forms remain in the Western tradition that stretches from Augustine to Thomas, but in a Christianised form: they exist eternally 'in the mind of God'.[33] Gunton has described such a position as 'only half-way to the doctrine of creation out of nothing', and goes on to say in an attached note that 'we … must take extreme exception to a theology that speaks of entities other than God which are *"stabiles atque incommutabiles … formate non sunt … aeternae ac semper eodem sese habentes"*'.[34]

So we must – but are these 'entities other than God'? Augustine, Aquinas and this entire tradition, after all, held to the doctrine of divine simplicity, and if these entities exist in God's mind then they are, by the logic above, simply God.[35] This position is theologically attractive in that it cuts through the nominalism–realism debate with some ease. God is neither above the standard of justice as its creator nor alongside it as one subject to it just as we are. Rather, his very being is the standard of goodness, and so on.[36]

Now, in the Western theological tradition at least, such a position has always been asserted – we might think of the condemnation of Gilbert de la Porrée by Bernard of Clairvaux at the Synod of Reims in 1148. Gilbert had taught that the fullness of the divine attributes, the Godhead, was distinct from God, and that God was God through this Godhead; Bernard insisted that this was unacceptable, that God was not distinguishable from his Godhead, and so the perfections of God were indeed identical with God himself.[37] What I am

---

[33] Augustine, *Eighty Three Different Questions* (The Fathers of the Church, vol. LXX), David L. Mosher (tr.) (Washington, DC: Catholic Universities of America Press, 1982), question 46. This is cited by Aquinas in the *sed contra* of *Summa Theologica* Ia 15.2.

[34] Colin E. Gunton, *The Triune Creator: A Historical and Systematic Study* (Edinburgh: Edinburgh University Press, 1998), p. 78 and (latter quotation from the Augustine text referenced above) n. 29.

[35] As indeed Aquinas argued in the *responsio* to *Summa Theologica* Ia 15.2.

[36] Plantinga calls this view 'the sovereignty-aseity intuition', traces it in Aquinas, and asserts its importance in traditional accounts of divine simplicity. *Does God Have a Nature?*, pp. 28–34.

[37] For some details, see Edward H. Landon, *A Manual of Councils of the Holy Catholic Church*, 2 vols (Edinburgh: John Grant, 1909 [revised ed.]), vol. II, pp. 74–5. See also

suggesting is that the doctrine of divine simplicity, by means of precisely the counterintuitive and philosophically difficult propositions I have referred to, is a way of asserting this point robustly and straightforwardly. Barth's long historical discussion of the point in *Church Dogmatics* II/1[38] suggests strongly that a robust and straightforward way of insisting on this has long been needed in the Church.

I have argued that the confusions and problems that seem to accompany recent discussions of the doctrine of simplicity are the result of an ontological confidence that is foreign to the Christian tradition. The strongest evidence for this thesis is the initial and apparently trivial observation that the doctrine of simplicity was not a problem for most of that tradition; if it is for us, then something must have changed. If it is accepted that God's essence is incomprehensible then, as I have tried to show in this chapter, most of the theological problems that divine simplicity apparently raises can be side-stepped. Further, recent attempts to uncover the assumed personal and relational ontology of the patristic tradition demonstrate that there are indeed ontologies under which simplicity is much less problematic than it has recently been assumed to be. I have also argued that at least one serious theological issue is more amenable to solution if we accept the doctrine of simplicity. I suggest, therefore, that in the absence of any other theological reflections, this doctrine, in the form in which it was discussed in the majority Christian tradition, remains both available and useful for dogmatic endeavour.

---

[37] *(continued)* Barth, *Church Dogmatics* II/1, p. 331. As Barth notes, the opposite result obtained in the East, under the tutelage of Gregory Palamas, in whose theology the eternal light was developed to encompass all the divine perfections, and said to be separated from God's being. This was declared orthodox in the face of Western-supported objections at a series of synods in Constantinople between 1341 and 1351. For the history, see John Meyendorff, *A Study of Gregory Palamas*, G. Lawrence (tr.) (London: Faith Press, 1964), pp. 42–101; for the theology, see ibid., pp. 202–27, and Vladimir Lossky, *The Mystical Theology of the Eastern Church* (Cambridge: James Clarke, 1957), pp. 76–80.

[38] pp. 323–41 (throughout the small-print sections).

Chapter 5

Calvin against the Calvinists?

I think that the first book of Paul Helm's[1] that I ever read was his mono-
graph in response to R. T. Kendall's *Calvin and English Calvinism to 1649*,
which was entitled simply *Calvin and the Calvinists*.[2] With this, he entered a
discussion concerning the Christian tradition that could be traced back to
Schleiermacher's heirs,[3] but which was then in the process of becoming both
widely and hotly debated amongst Anglophone theologians and historians, at
least. The question underlying this debate is a deceptively simple one of
assessing the continuities and discontinuities between the thought of Calvin
and those in the later tradition whom we identify as 'Calvinists', particularly
in the two centuries after his death. When we listen to the tradition, we may
disagree about what we hear, and the only way forward is then sustained,
careful and patient listening. This chapter is an attempt to demonstrate how
giving attention to the particular historical locatedness of a particular writer
might offer evidence to resolve such conflicts.

---

[1] This chapter is a revision of a paper prepared for a day conference on 'Calvin and the
Calvinists' held in Professor Paul Helm's honour to mark his retirement from King's
College, London. It is a privilege to record publicly my own debts of gratitude to Paul
over the time we were colleagues at King's, and also to thank Paul himself, Professor
Anthony Lane and Professor Carl Trueman for helpful comments they made on the
paper on that occasion.
[2] R. T. Kendall, *Calvin and English Calvinism to 1649* (Oxford Theological Mono-
graphs Series) (Oxford: Oxford University Press, 1979); Paul Helm, *Calvin and the
Calvinists* (Edinburgh: Banner of Truth, 1982).
[3] On which see various discussions by Richard A. Muller: *Christ and the Decree:
Christology and Predestination in Reformed Theology from Calvin to Perkins* (Grand Rapids,
Michigan: Baker, 1988[2]), pp. 1–13; 'Calvin and the "Calvinists": Assessing Continu-
ities and Discontinuities between the Reformation and Orthodoxy', *Calvin Theological
Journal* 30 (1995), pp. 345–75; 31 (1996), pp. 125–60, 345–59; *The Unaccommodated
Calvin: Studies in the Foundation of a Theological Tradition* (Oxford Studies in Historical
Theology) (Oxford: Oxford University Press, 2000), pp. vii–viii, 3–4.

One of the classic statements of the charge that Calvin is noticeably different from the later Calvinistic tradition can be found in Basil Hall's paper,
'Calvin against the Calvinists'.[4] Although old, this illustrates most of the points
that are still regularly urged, so I will glance at it. On Hall's account, the final,
1559, edition of the *Institutes* shows a profound balance between the various
doctrines treated, which is distorted and finally lost after Calvin's death, as a
result of the work of Beza, Zanchius, Perkins and others. Beza's work in
Geneva led to Calvin's emphasis on biblical exegesis being downplayed, and
even 'subordinated to a restored Aristotelianism' as the young Reformed
churches were being defeated by the Counter-Reformation, and borrowed
the apparently superior armaments of their opponents to defend themselves.[5]
Beza himself is accused by Hall of being dogmatic about things that should be
regarded as indifferent, such as patterns of church order; of introducing the
concept of propositional revelation, and so a literalistic approach to Scripture
that is foreign to Calvin's thought; and of systematising those things that his
teacher left unclear, with disastrous effect. The example of the last is naturally
limited atonement; according to Hall, Calvin's refusal to teach this 'may have
been illogical', but is 'typical of his refusal to be too systematic, too logical and
too precise …'.[6]

William Perkins's distortion of Calvin's doctrines took another form, or so
Hall suggests. Most importantly, he was responsible for the introduction of
casuistry, and with it the characteristic Puritan attempt to find evidences
for one's election in one's own life. Perkins's account of the decree is
'determinist', in contrast to the 'qualifications and balance of doctrines' that
Calvin had offered.[7] Finally, Perkins fails to place proper emphasis on
the Church and the sacraments. Beza and Perkins are both thus accused of
distorting the tradition that was handed on to them.

Calvin's successors, then, hardened and systematised his theology. Where
he had refused to follow logic, as in predestination, they pressed the logic to its
last extreme; where he had steered a careful middle way, as on the Church,
they rushed to one side or the other, Beza insisting on presbyterianism, Perkins
failing to notice the Church at all. This form of criticism is recurrent in discussions of how Calvin differed from his followers,[8] but is not often adequately

---

[4] This can be found in G. Duffield (ed.), *John Calvin: A Collection of Distinguished
Essays* (Grand Rapids, Michigan: Eerdmans, 1966).

[5] Ibid., p. 25.

[6] Ibid., p. 27.

[7] Ibid., p. 29.

[8] For a recent example, if anything less nuanced than Hall, and certainly more
culpable, because written in apparent ignorance of so much of the careful scholarly
discussion that has followed Hall, see Alistair E. McGrath's *A Life of John Calvin: A Study*

explained. In particular, to make a distinction in good scholastic manner, such criticisms appear to conflate complaints about methodology with complaints about content, and that in a most unhelpful manner. If the tradition, what has been handed on, has been distorted in the process, then there is a need to be clear about precisely what distortions have been introduced.

Either or both of these charges might be fair: all I am pointing out at the moment is that they are different. A criticism about theological method is about the proper presentation of shared doctrines; a criticism about content is about the fact that doctrines were not shared. Now, it is certainly the case that methodology and doctrine are intertwined: to anticipate a later discussion, we might note the tendency for theologians influenced by Ramist method to find a series of bifurcations when others might seek a different account. None the less, we may ask, I think, whether the fundamental charge is methodological, with unfortunate material consequences, or whether the problem is actually material – or indeed, whether there are problems in both areas.

Starting, then, with problems of method, I want to make a further distinction, between what the schools would have called rhetoric and dialectic. Dialectic consists of the construction of arguments from premises, rhetoric the appropriate and persuasive presentation of those arguments. Calvin's humanist and legal training inducted him into a particular rhetorical tradition, rather different to that which he might have discovered if he had been trained in the Sorbonne theological faculty, for instance. We might compare the different ways a moral philosopher and a human rights lawyer would present the same argument today: in the one case, the rhetorical values are precision and clarity; in the other there is a conscious attempt to engage and persuade. The point is, however, that the same argument may be presented in either rhetorical mode.

Just so, to notice that Calvin's theology does not look scholastic, in the sense that there are not carefully arranged lists of positions, objections and responses, is not sufficient to establish that the basic dialectical or logical forms underlying the text are not identical to scholastic forms of argument.[9] When

---

[8] *(continued)* in *the Shaping of Western Culture* (Oxford: Blackwell, 1990), where Calvin's own work is described as 'opposed to scholasticism in general, and Aristotelianism in particular' and Beza's work is described as 'an Aristotelian scholasticism' with a great emphasis on predestination (p. 212). Again, '[w]here Calvin adopts an inductive and analytical approach to theology, focusing upon the specific historical event of Jesus Christ and moving out to explore its implications, de Bèze adopts a deductive and synthetic approach, beginning from general principles and proceeding to deduce their consequences for Christian theology …' (p. 213).

[9] A trivial point that is nonetheless entirely sufficient to answer the several pages of rather overblown rhetoric offered by McGrath, samples of which appear in the previous note.

we start looking, Calvin's dialectic is quite clearly heavily influenced by scholasticism: he makes regular use of standard distinctions,[10] and will give long lists of objections and responses in classic *quaestione* fashion,[11] albeit arranged in a slightly more attractive, and so less obvious, manner than was traditional in scholastic rhetoric.

Now, a difference in rhetoric is not insignificant: the 'warmth' or 'piety' that has regularly been noticed in Calvin's theology might well stem directly from this.[12] Neither, however, is such a difference in any sense basic; if the totality of the charge against Beza is that he was not such a golden-mouthed expositor of the Calvinian theology as his teacher, then the charge does not justify the opprobrium that has been thrown in his direction.[13] Calvin himself will point to the widely varying rhetorical styles of the biblical writers, insisting that the majesty of the doctrine will be clear, regardless of whether it is the beautiful poetry of David or the plain speech of Amos that conveys it.[14]

Is there, however, more to the methodological charge than this? Is it in fact the case that there are specific and identifiable methodological moves which Beza or Perkins made but which Calvin resisted? The charge that there are usually relies on a suggestion that Calvin was more 'humanistic' and less 'scholastic' than the tradition on either side of him. This leads, we are told for instance, to a different attitude to Scripture, as in Hall's suggestion that in Beza biblical exegesis was subordinated to Aristotelianism. This, however, is most unclear. 'Aristotelianism' in this context seems to refer to little more than a method of logic, in which case the charge looks like a category mistake: one cannot play off a method of study against an object of study (the text of Scripture), at least not without showing that the method is necessarily inadequate to the object. There was nothing in Aristotelian method, however, that was inimical to disciplined biblical interpretation, as the example of one of Calvin's

---

[10] On which see Muller, *The Unaccommodated Calvin*.

[11] For example, in *Institutes* III.21, where §§2–3 state three objections, to which one response is given to the first, and two to the other two. Again, in IV.6, §2 states a *quaestio*, contains a first objection and two responses, §3 contains the second objection, again with two responses; and so on through, with Calvin's own opinion finally stated in §17.

[12] As might the common sense that Barth's theology 'feels' closer to Calvin's than much of the orthodox tradition; whatever technical differences there may be in rhetorical method, it seems beyond argument that Barth, like Calvin, writes inspiring and compelling prose.

[13] Equally, the criticism sometimes offered of certain forms of modern theology, that they are 'rhetorical', is utterly uninteresting: if rhetoric is conveying bad arguments, then the piece should be criticised for its logical failures, not its rhetorical successes; if the logic is sound, then surely it is to the writer's credit that he or she presents good arguments in a persuasive and attractive way.

[14] *Institutes* I.8.2; cf. I.8.11.

few serious rivals as a commentator in the Christian tradition, Thomas Aquinas, surely demonstrates.

This complaint is sometimes explained by a suggestion that humanism was displaced by Aristotelianism in the tradition following Calvin, which was a bad thing. Why so? Renaissance humanism might be argued to have placed more emphasis on the source texts (*ad fontes!*) as centrally authoritative, and less on the importance of a continuing tradition, in which these texts are placed, albeit pre-eminently, but if that is an appropriate standard for passing judgement, then we should be championing the cause of Balthasar Hubmaier, Conrad Grempf and other representatives of the radical wing of the Reformation over Calvin and the Calvinists alike. Calvin was not a straightforward biblicist, in the sense of regarding the testimonies of others in the Christian tradition as unimportant or even necessarily flawed – that is surely clear, not least from nearly five hundred direct references to Augustine in the 1559 *Institutes*.[15] Like any late medieval theologian, in polemical debate Calvin calls on the *auctorites* to support his position. The most that can be gained from this line of argument, then, is a suggestion that the precise balancing between respecting the witness of the tradition and subordinating that witness to the biblical texts was slightly different in Calvin as compared to Beza, Perkins and others. No doubt that is true, and no doubt this precise balance is different in Beza and Perkins as well, but there is surely no room for a historical account that pits 'Calvin against the Calvinists' in such slight differences of emphasis.

In any case opposing 'humanism' and 'scholasticism' like this is merely a failure to understand the historical situation.[16] That these terms are useful shorthand to describe broad intellectual currents present in the sixteenth century is undeniable; this does not mean, however, that we may cheerfully go through sixteenth-century history asserting that A is a humanist and B a scholastic, and that the twain shall never meet. Calvin, as I have briefly indicated, was able to frame scholastic theology in humanist rhetoric without being aware of any fundamental incompatibility, and if he found no problem we will need very good evidence indeed to demonstrate that he was wrong. To quote Paul Helm's analysis of *Calvin's Defence of the Secret Providence of God*, 'Calvin is by no means averse to using some of the standard conceptual distinctions of medieval scholasticism.'[17]

---

[15] See particularly Anthony S. Lane, *John Calvin: Student of the Church Fathers* (Edinburgh: T&T Clark, 1999). The whole work discusses Calvin's use of earlier writers in many interesting ways, summed up in the eleven theses of the first chapter. The direct citations from the Fathers in the 1559 *Institutes* are listed on pp. 54–61; I count 463 references to Augustine there.

[16] Muller, *The Unaccommodated Calvin*, pp. 174–7.

[17] Paul Helm, 'Calvin (and Zwingli) on Divine Providence', *Calvin Theological Journal* 29 (1994), pp. 388–405, 400. Helm goes on to give four clear examples.

It is true that Calvin attacks 'scholasticism' in several places in his writings, but careful attention is needed to what is meant. As Richard Muller has recently pointed out,[18] those attacks on scholasticism that are found in the Latin *Institutes* are regularly translated into French as attacks on the *Sorbonistes*; this indicates that the target is not some all-encompassing idea of the pre-modern theological method, but a rather specific theological school, holding to an extreme nominalism, that was opposing the cause of Reform in France.

Having said all this I must acknowledge that there were some technical differences between humanist and older scholastic approaches to dialectic. Humanism, for instance, tended to understand the role of dialectic as establishing probabilities rather than offering proofs, and so placed correspondingly more emphasis on the method of persuasion, rather than demonstration. Again, the distinctively humanist concern for respecting literary genre is evident in Calvin's work, in a way that it is perhaps less evident in some of his successors. It is not inconceivable, I suppose, that in such *minutiae* may be found a horseshoe nail which will, just as in the old nursery rhyme, lead finally to the loss of the Kingdom if left out; until this is demonstrated, however, we surely cannot regard the minor technical differences which no doubt existed between the methodologies of Calvin and Beza or Perkins as in any way decisive. Within this debate, after all, we might note that the rather more fundamental divide between broadly Ramist and broadly Aristotelian methodologies in English Puritanism did not appear to lead to two different theological traditions.

What other forms of the charge are there? In Hall, and elsewhere, there is a regular suggestion that Calvin refused to be 'too systematic', 'too logical' or 'too precise'. It is difficult to know what such charges mean, particularly when they are usually either unsupported by evidence or supported only by a sense that Calvin's theology *feels* different, a sense that may be entirely explained by the rhetorical difference I have noted, but I will none the less try to do them what justice I can. The last may, I think, be dismissed very rapidly: it surely should not even need arguing that Calvin strove to be as clear and as definite as possible in his use of words and his formulation of theologumena and, further, that any writer in any age who did not so strive would be a worse theologian for it. If evidence is needed, however, consider Calvin's teaching on the one point where this charge is most often made: predestination. Calvin begins his account of predestination by stressing how important clarity – let us say 'precision' – is in discussing this doctrine. Proper – precise – knowledge of it is useful and necessary in promoting God's glory and true Christian humility, and also offers the 'sweet fruit' of assurance of salvation.[19] He then turns to

---

[18] Muller, *The Unaccommodated Calvin*, pp. 56–61.

[19] *Institutes* III.21.1. I have argued in another place as to whether Calvin's doctrine succeeds in offering the assurance he desires to offer; whether it does or not, he thinks it does, and so this point stands.

oppose two sorts of people: those who would speculate too much about God's decrees; and those who would say nothing at all. In response to the first he acknowledges, famously, that there is a *docta ignorantia*, a 'learned ignorance', in refusing to go beyond certain bounds.[20] Is this evidence of a refusal to be 'too precise'?

Well, if it is, it would appear to be a thoroughly scholastic refusal. The phrase is originally Augustine's,[21] and had a long history, notably as the title of an important treatise by Nicolas de Cusa in 1440. If what Calvin says about the use of this 'learned ignorance' is taken seriously, however, it becomes clear that it is a way of insisting on precision. Those who fail to cultivate this ignorance will be lost in a labyrinth,[22] or will find themselves in darkness, where they can only stumble and slip,[23] or will be wandering in a pathless wasteland.[24] These, surely, are not images of a too-precise theology, but of one that has lost all precision. Calvin's middle way between speculation and silence is to say as precisely as possible what the Scriptures say and then to stop.

Again, we must ask what can possibly be meant by Hall's assertion that later Calvinism was 'too logical', a fault which Calvin avoided. It is true that later Reformed theology, as a part of its polemic against the Lutherans, stressed the place of reason in theological argument,[25] but it is not clear that there is anything contained in such comments which is different to what Calvin might have said. None the less, let us look further. Those passages from the *Institutes* that are regularly quoted as establishing that Calvin thought reason to be an unreliable guide in theological matters are actually directed to narrower points: II.2.18–21, for example, argues, to quote, that '[h]uman reason … neither approaches, nor strives towards, nor even takes a straight aim at, this truth: to understand who the true God is or what sort of God he wishes to be towards us'. Quite so, but this does not deny the use of reasoned argument in theology, only that theology is a different science to what we now call philosophy. Calvin is rather sceptical of the ability to discover any-thing with any certainty by arguing from necessary truths.[26] He also believes that propositional revelation is not enough, as there is much in these passages about an appropriately affective response to God. He will not, however, deny

---

[20] Ibid., III.21.2 and III.23.8.

[21] *Epistles* cxxx.15.28 (Migne, *Patrologia Latina* 33.505).

[22] *Institutes* III.21.1.

[23] Ibid., III.21.2.

[24] Ibid., III.21.2.

[25] See, for instance, Turretin, *Institutes of Elenctic Theology*, Dennison (ed.), I.ix–x.

[26] And who, reading the history of philosophy since Descartes' day, will now say he was wrong?

the narrow point that the form 'all a are b; all b are c; therefore all a are c' is as valid when speaking of divine things as at any other time.[27]

The editor of the standard English translation of the *Institutes* has inserted an unfortunate footnote at one point which asserts that '[l]ogic is … subordinated to Scripture, and, characteristically for Calvin, is rejected as a device for understanding what is beyond the limits of the revealed mysteries' (I.18.3, n. 6). Calvin certainly believed Scripture to be true in all that it affirmed, and that in a fairly sophisticated manner, but 'logic' is only subordinated to 'Scripture' in believing this if it is assumed that on at least one point Scripture asserts two contradictory things. Calvin, however, stresses 'the beautiful agreement of all the parts with one another',[28] thus removing any need to oppose reason to the biblical testimony like this. Further, the texts cited to prove that this is his practice turn out in each case to be about something different. We may concede, for example, that there are arguments that appear to be logically valid, although they are not if considered carefully, as Calvin says in III.18.10 without accepting the suggestion that Calvin rejects logic. Calvin's successors are not 'too logical', whatever that may mean; Calvin and his successors alike strive to be carefully logical in all that they say, neither making unwarranted claims nor refusing to make warranted ones. This, again, should not need arguing.

So, finally, we have the suggestion that Calvin's successors fall away from his theological method in being 'too systematic'. Again, it is not obvious what is being claimed here, but assuming that by 'systematic' we mean the giving of attention to the connectedness of doctrines, then being too systematic must involve finding a connectedness between doctrines that is not in fact there. Again, this charge might take several forms: it might, for example, be another way of saying 'too logical', claiming that Calvin's successors drew systematic connections which were logically required by his theology but which he refused to draw. In this form, arguments already presented show the charge to be straightforwardly false. It might be taken to mean something like a 'central dogma' account of the work of the Reformed scholastics, whereby one doctrine (usually predestination) was seen to be elevated to a decisive place and used as the key to unlock all other doctrines. The question here is whether such a 'central dogma' picture is an accurate portrayal of seventeenth- or eighteenth-century theology, which seemed to understand itself as offering a series of interconnected loci, or common-places, which did affect one another but

---

[27] In a discussion of a brief work of Calvin's in response to Pighius on providence, Paul Helm helpfully distinguishes between Pighius's appeal to reason as 'common sense' – in essence, a natural theology – and Calvin's appeal to reason only as a way of arguing. See 'Calvin (and Zwingli) on Divine Providence', pp. 401–2.

[28] *Institutes* I.8.2.

were not heirarchically ordered, and were generally presented following the credal order. Even in Ames who, under the influence of Ramist logic, does offer an account of the connectedness of theological loci,[29] the decree in general is one of four topics on the third level down, and predestination in particular is buried on the ninth level. In any case, Ames's picture is clearly heuristic, and no metaphysical implication can or should be read into it.[30]

Another way of understanding the charge that those who followed Calvin erred in being 'too systematic' might be to borrow some recent analysis of the nature of 'mystery' from Jacques Maritain.[31] In this account, non-trivial questions susceptible to human enquiry can be divided into two general classes: problems, which may be solved; and mysteries, which may only be elucidated. Whether Fermat's last theorem could be proved was a problem: it was open to a final solution, which has been offered and, assuming there are no errors in the proof, the question is now closed. The nature of beauty, by contrast, might well be a mystery: different investigations close off certain lines of enquiry, perhaps, and explore others more carefully than they have been explored before, but it is not unreasonable to suppose that there will never be a definition of what makes a thing beautiful so final that the question will be closed.

Maritain used this analysis largely to explain why philosophical and theological problems were not of the same sort as scientific ones, but, assuming that there is some truth in it, we have a further possibility for what the gnomic phrase 'too systematic' may mean: Calvin, conscious that God's nature is fundamentally mysterious on this understanding, did not attempt to foreclose questions that by their very nature should remain always open; his too-systematic successors, by contrast, did. Here is an assertion which is at least not ridiculous, and which we can test by recourse to the texts.

Let me again use the obvious, if tedious, example of predestination: it is clear that, for Calvin, there is a fundamental inscrutability here; certain things may and must be affirmed, but there is also a proper 'learned ignorance', a wisdom in knowing that the mystery may be elucidated thus far and no further. Is it the case that this learning and wisdom were cast aside by those who followed, and that a fully explicated doctrine of predestination, which collapsed the mystery into a too-easily-solved problem, was the result? The

---

[29] The chart on pp. 72–3 of Eusden's translation of Ames's *Marrow of Theology* (Grand Rapids, Michigan: Baker, 1997), which is based on charts in seventeenth-century editions, and gives an accurate picture of the contents of the work in my estimation, is a convenient source for these connections.

[30] The work, and the chart, describe 'theology', which is immediately defined as 'the doctrine or teaching of living to God' (Ames, *Marrow of Theology* I.1).

[31] Jacques Maritain, *A Preface to Metaphysics* (London: Sheed and Ward, 1939).

answer must be no. Consider a central text: the Westminster Confession. Chapter III clearly stresses the proper limits to knowledge of 'God's Eternal Decree'. The initial statement in particular bears witness to the mystery involved, asserting as it does that:

> God from all eternity did, by the most wise and holy counsel of His own will, freely, and unchangeably ordain whatsoever comes to pass: yet so, as thereby neither is God the author of sin, nor is violence offered to the will of the creatures, nor is the liberty and contingency of second causes taken away, but rather established.

Again, at the end of the chapter we read that '[t]he doctrine of this high mystery of predestination is to be handled with special prudence and care ...'.

The mystery and inscrutability which must be present appear to be properly respected here; there is no attempt to solve the basic mysteries of predestination (God decreeing sin without approving of it, predestination not incompatible with the true freedom of creatures, etc.), but a sober naming of them. This is standard in the tradition, and so we cannot accept that Calvin's followers were too systematic in this sense. We might also comment that the willingness to accept two schemes which are fundamentally divergent theologically, the infralapsarian and the supralapsarian, demonstrates the awareness of the general tradition that here we are dealing with mysteries that cannot be finally solved. Here again, there seems to be no form of the charge that the theology of Calvin's successors was decisively different methodologically from his own work that can be supported by the evidence.

Where have we got to so far? Firstly, I have acknowledged that there is a clear rhetorical difference between the way Calvin wrote theology and the practice of most of his successors, and I have tried to take that seriously, but denied that it can be a serious enough charge to warrant the suggestion that one may place 'Calvin against the Calvinists'. Secondly, I have sought to demonstrate that certain forms of the charge, notably those suggesting that Calvin himself refused to be bound by standards of logical precision or coherence, and that this was somehow a good thing, can be rapidly dismissed by recourse to the texts. Thirdly, I have noticed certain technical methodological differences between Calvin's more humanist dialectic and the various more Ramist or Aristotelian writers who came after him. However, in the absence of an argument demonstrating otherwise, which has not been offered to the best of my knowledge, these differences do not appear to be enough to substantiate the picture of a Calvinist tradition that decisively departed from Calvin's own best insights. In any case, the differences in dialectic within the later Reformed tradition were at least as great as those between any particular later writer and Calvin. Thus, I suggest that there is no methodological justification to pit Calvin against the Calvinists as a certain recent tradition of theological historiography has wanted to do.

All of which leaves the other side of the distinction I made early on: are there material differences sufficient to justify this accusation? Before investigating particular possible candidates here, it is worth making clear the criteria any given candidate will have to fill: if 'Calvinism' as a lump differed so markedly from Calvin that the two may be set 'against' each other, there must be one identifiable move, or perhaps a cluster of related moves, that was nearly universally adopted, and that can be shown to make a decisive change. This is not, it seems to me, implausible: at various points in the history of theological enquiry, there is indeed such a near-universal and decisive move, as perhaps in Schleiermacher's reorientation of theological method in nineteenth-century Germany or, rather differently, Augustine's linked vision of the doctrines of grace and the mixed Church at the start of a distinctively and exclusively Latin theological tradition.

Within these criteria, then, are there even any plausible candidates? There are indeed: several, in fact, which will each merit further discussion. In no particular order, they are: what has become known as the federal theology; the linked questions of the extent of the atonement, the nature of faith, and assurance; and a perceived shift in the doctrine of Scripture.

Starting with the federal theology, the response is in a sense quite straightforward. There appears to be general agreement that full-blown federalism, teaching both the covenant of works and the covenant of grace, and using the two to provide an overarching schema for Christian theology, is a development first found in the work of Johannes Cocceius, who was born four decades after Calvin died. The first Reformed symbol to interpret theology in federal terms was the Westminster Confession, first published in 1647. Even assuming that federalism was a fairly unified theology and was a substantial and dangerous departure from Calvin's own thought (and I think both points could and should be contested), this does not allow us to set 'Calvin against the Calvinists'; it might allow us to set the early Calvinists against the later Calvinists, with (certainly) Beza and (perhaps) Perkins here on the side of the angels, so to speak. As it happens, this opposition seems to me to be as simplistic and as erroneous as the one we are discussing, but that is not the point: it is a different opposition, and so the federal theology will not do as a substantial and fatal difference that allows Calvin and the Calvinists to be opposed.

Turning to the idea of limited atonement and the linked questions of faith and assurance, we are faced with R. T. Kendall's thesis that Helm wrote to oppose. The contention here is that Calvin believed assurance to be of the essence of faith, and taught an unlimited atonement, although a definite election. His followers, beginning with Beza and Perkins once again, restricted the scope of the atonement to the elect only, which led to worried believers questioning whether Christ died for their sins, or only for others'. The response to this within the Puritan tradition was the *syllogismus practicus*, the argument from my own Christian practice to the fact of my salvation, leading to genuine assurance being regarded as a rare and precious gift belonging only to the most holy saints.

Helm's argument in response to the first point was to suggest that Calvin did indeed teach a limited atonement, and so that the Puritan tradition did not depart from Calvin's theology anything like as thoroughly as Kendall had suggested. I think Helm has the best of it here. The account of limited atonement given by the Synod of Dort and by the later scholastic writers relies on an old scholastic distinction, that pre-dates the Reformation, between the universal sufficiency of Christ's death and the limited or particular efficiency.[32] There is clear textual evidence that Calvin not only accepted this distinction, but regarded it as something unexceptional and uncontroversial: in his commentary on 1 John 2:2, he says this:

> Here a question may be raised, how have the sins of the whole world been expiated? I pass by the dotages of the fanatics, who under this pretense extend salvation to all the reprobate, and therefore to Satan himself. Such a monstrous thing deserves no refutation. They who seek to avoid this absurdity, have said that Christ suffered sufficiently for the whole world, but efficiently only for the elect. This solution has commonly prevailed in the schools. Though then I allow that what has been said is true, yet I deny that it is suitable to this passage …

Although the comment is made in passing, it seems clear: Calvin accepts the old scholastic distinction. He did not use it to teach that there is a sense in

---

[32] So in the Canons of Dort we read that '[t]he death of the Son of God is … abundantly sufficient to expiate the sins of the whole world', but that 'the sovereign counsel and most gracious will and purpose of God the Father [was] that the quickening and saving efficacy of the most precious death of his Son should extend to all the elect …' (2. 'Of the Death of Christ…': the translation cited is Gerald Bray's, from his *Documents of the English Reformation* [Cambridge: James Clarke, 1994], pp. 453–78). Turning to the later writers, we might select almost at random: only a few years after the Synod, William Ames asserts that 'it is rightly said that Christ made satisfaction only for those he saved, though in regard to the sufficiency in the mediation of Christ it may also be rightly said that Christ made satisfaction for each and all' (I.xiv.9); at the beginning of the next century, Turretin speaks approvingly of 'the distinction used by the fathers and retained by many divines – that Christ "died sufficiently for all, but efficiently for the elect only" ' (*Institutes of Elenctic Theology*, Dennison [ed.], XIV.xiv.9). Similar statements can be found variously in Cocceius, Olevianus and Riisenius (see Heinrich Heppe, *Reformed Dogmatics*, Ernst Bizer [rev. and ed.], G. T. Thomson [tr.] [London: George Allen & Unwin, 1950], pp. 475–9) – and, no doubt, dozens of other writers.

which the atonement is limited, but that is a necessary implication of the position. The point may be asserted: the distinction that was the basic content of the post-Dort scholastic doctrine of limited atonement is one that Calvin not only explicitly accepts, but apparently regards as so obvious and trivial that it may be mentioned in passing without argument. Whatever the details may be, there is no fundamental divergence between Calvin and the later tradition on the question of a limited atonement; the later teaching is no more than a making explicit of what was implicit in Calvin's theology.

What, secondly, of faith? Kendall's suggestion was that, whereas for Calvin faith is a passive intellectual persuasion, through the influence of Beza, Perkins and Dort faith came to be seen as fundamentally an act of the will, what Kendall calls 'voluntarism'.[33] This is a gross over-simplification of the evidence: whilst Calvin did indeed call faith 'knowledge', he stressed that this knowledge necessarily 'makes us rely on [God's] goodness', and is 'sealed on our hearts through the Holy Spirit' (III.2.7). He will even say later in his discussion of faith that 'the heart's distrust is greater than the mind's blindness' (III.2.36). Clearly, Calvin saw faith as involving both mind and will, although he appears to give priority to knowledge.

In the later tradition, the same desire to stress both intellectual and volitional aspects of faith is everywhere present. The Canons of Dort, which Kendall accuses of voluntarism, stress both aspects: '[God] powerfully illuminates their minds by his Holy Spirit, that they may rightly understand and discern … by the efficacy of the same regenerating Spirit he … opens the closed and softens the hardened heart … infuses new qualities into the will … that like a good tree, it may bring forth the fruits of good actions' (I.11). Conrad Cherry sees a constant attempt in the Puritan tradition to hold these two realities together, which was none the less defeated by an assumed anthropology which regarded the will and the intellect as separate entities (the 'faculty psychology'). The result of this, however, as Cherry shows, was not a lurch to voluntarism as Kendall claims but resolutions in both directions by different writers.[34]

In the continental Reformed tradition, it seems that the attempt to hold together the intellectual and volitional aspects of faith was more successful: Wollebius (I.xxix.7) divides faith into three parts: *notitia*, or knowledge; *assensus*, or assent; and *fiducia*, or trust. It is true that he regards *fiducia* as the only part unique to saving faith – this is what the demons, who believe there is one God and shudder, lack – but *notitia* and *assensus* are still necessary components of saving faith, if not sufficient. Turretin follows the same division (XV.viii.3),

[33] Kendall, *Calvin and English Calvinism to 1649*, p. 3.
[34] Conrad Cherry, *The Theology of Jonathan Edwards: A Reappraisal* (Garden City, New York: Doubleday, 1966), ch. 1.

acknowledging on the way the diversity of opinion on the matter: 'some place faith equally in the intellect and the will; others only in the intellect formally and in the will only energetically or effectively and consequently (or even principally in the will)' (XV.viii.2). Notice here that the position that Kendall claimed was universal in the later tradition is included only as an afterthought by Turretin, indicating that he thought of it as a minority opinion. It seems difficult, on this evidence, to argue that there is any fundamental change in the understanding of what faith is in the tradition. Rather, there is a witness to a certain confusion, and a series of quite complex positions and differences.

Thirdly, what of assurance? Here the charge, regularly made, is that Calvin believed assurance to be of the essence of faith, and structured his theology to offer this assurance, whereas the later tradition regarded assurance as a rare and special gift of God, attainable only by those who were far advanced in holiness and could apply the *syllogismus practicus* to themselves with no fear of deception. It is further claimed that this move was pastorally disastrous.

Calvin clearly desired Christians to possess assurance of their salvation, but I have argued elsewhere[35] that he attempts to do this through the doctrine of election and that his account of election does not, in fact, allow him to succeed in giving this assurance to worried believers, despite his desire to do so. Whilst it is true, I think, that Calvin does not teach the practical syllogism, it is not so far from some things he does say as some recent writers have suggested,[36] and is in any case not a departure from his theology so much as an attempt to succeed in giving assurance where he failed – a failure due, as Perkins and others recognised, to the concept of temporary faith. Many later writers link the doctrine of election with the desire to give assurance of salvation to believers in just the same way, but try to do it more adequately than Calvin did.[37] Doctrinal

---

[35] Holmes, *God of Grace*, pp. 255–6.

[36] *Institutes* III.21.7.

[37] Dewey W. Wallace's account of the development of Puritan doctrines of grace from Calvin's day to the end of the seventeenth century highlights the desire to give comfort and assurance as a distinctive of this tradition. He argues, for example, that the Elizabethan alterations to the Articles of Religion are 'related to the growing Reformed use of predestination for providing assurance' (*Puritans and Predestination: Grace in English Protestant Theology, 1525–1695* [University of North Carolina Studies in Religion] [Chapel Hill, North Carolina: University of North Carolina Press, 1982], pp. 31–2). Turning to the continental writers, the Leiden synopsis says of election that '[t]he uses of this doctrine are many and outstanding in the Church of Christ. But these uses reach their full effectiveness, only when the elect are made surer of their election' (XIV.41–2, quoted by Heppe, *Reformed Dogmatics*, p. 178). Turretin also insists on the use of election in giving assurance (*Institutes of Elenctic Theology*, Dennison [ed.], IV.xiii; see the statement of the question, and particularly §§ 13, 22 and 27, which last asserts 'this certainty is necessary …'); again, a recent study on the Dutch 'Second Reformation' begins with the assertion 'one of the great struggles of the theologian and pastor of the

development can be seen here, but not the leap required if we are to believe the rhetoric of those who would set 'Calvin against the Calvinists'.

So, and finally, is there a shift in the understanding of Scripture? The standard charge, heard already from Hall, is that Beza introduced a notion of 'propositional revelation' quite foreign to Calvin's concerns into the tradi-tion.[38] What lies behind this seems to be a debate as to whether Calvin drew a distinction between the Word of God, which is revelation proper, and Scrip-ture, which is the record of that revelation. The commentators seem to be completely divided on this issue, with texts and arguments cited on both sides.[39] Two things seem clear: first, that Calvin did indeed make this distinc-tion; it is explicitly taught in various places, most notably in *Institutes* I.6.1–2; second, that Calvin also believed that Scripture is uncomplicatedly trust-worthy in all it affirms. If one assumes that the only possible theological positions here are the nineteenth-century ideas of inerrancy or conversely an account of an authoritative teaching lying beneath the, itself erroneous, plain sense of Scripture, then to believe these two things simultaneously is indeed difficult – but Calvin was not concerned with nineteenth-century debates. The distinction between the Word of God which came to Jeremiah (say) and Scripture which is the record of that is a standard scholastic one, and relies on nothing more than the Scriptures' own account of how most of them came to be written – God spoke to Jeremiah, and Jeremiah wrote (Jer. 36:2) or Baruch wrote at Jeremiah's dictation (Jer. 36:32).

As far as I am aware, Calvin does not discuss the process of the writing of the Scriptures in any significant way; he simply assumes that the Bible is indeed an accurate record of the Word of God. As Joseph Haroutunian has pointed out,[40] Calvin's interest in the trustworthiness of the Bible is to fight the battles he had to fight, so the Bible is an authority which trumps any appeal to the Fathers, the councils, or the mind of the Church. Calvin was not faced with challenges to biblical authority based on the slight discrepancies in certain numbers or chronological orders which appear to exist between various parts of the Bible,

---

[37] (*continued*) post-Reformation churches lay within the area of personal assurance of faith …': Joel R. Beeke, *Assurance of Faith: Calvin, English Puritanism, and the Dutch Second Reformation* (American Universities Study Series VII: Theology and Religion, vol. 89) (New York: Peter Lang, 1991), p. 1.

[38] See McGrath, *A Life of John Calvin*, p. 214, for a particularly blunt version of this.

[39] See particularly the collected papers in Richard C. Gamble (ed.), *Calvin and Calvinism*, vol. 6: *Calvin and Hermeneutics* (London: Garland, 1992), most of which address this issue and indicate the 'great gulf fixed' rather well. Richard Prust's paper there, 'Was Calvin a Biblical Literalist?' (pp. 380–96) suggests that about half the scholars who had written to that point fall on each side of this divide (pp. 313–14).

[40] In his 'General Introduction' to the volume of *Calvin's Commentaries* he edited for the Library of Christian Classics (London: SCM Press, 1958), p. 34.

and so does not develop a response to such challenges. We simply cannot know how Calvin would have responded to questions he was never asked.

All the same arguments could be made for Beza, or any other figure in the tradition. They were no more sub-Warfieldian fundamentalists than Calvin was. They were in different contexts and situations, and so said some different things – to each other, as well as to Calvin. To illustrate by picking up an issue that is sometimes urged as a difference, we might look at what discussion is given of the doctrine of Scripture in a particular text. Calvin in the *Institutes* launches straight into his theology, pausing three times to discuss the Bible: under the knowledge of God, at the start of Book I; in discussing the relationship of law to gospel in Book II; and in discussing authority in the Church in Book IV. In the years immediately following the council of Dort, Wollebius's little compendium starts with prolegomena which discuss the nature of theology and the doctrine of Scripture, not because these are primary doctrines – that place is clearly given to theology proper, at the beginning of Book I – but for heuristic reasons. William Ames, at a similar time, but in complete contrast, deals with Scripture under the doctrine of the Church, towards the middle of his *Medulla*. Wollebius stresses more the authority of the written word, Ames that of the writers, the 'extraordinary ministers of the Church'. There is difference here but, once again, nothing that will justify an account of history that sets 'Calvin against the Calvinists'. Such an account, I submit, cannot be upheld.

One final question to end with: why does any of this actually matter? There are various levels to this question. There is, for instance, the question of fidelity to the virtues we aspire to: within the academy it naturally matters that we give as accurate a portrayal of any period of history as possible, just because fair, accurate and dispassionate reporting is an academic virtue; within the Church, as well, it matters that we are fair to those who are still our Christian brothers and sisters – we will, after all, have to live with them for all eternity. That is not the level I wanted to ask the question at, however.

In his deservedly famous preface to the revised edition of Heppe's *Reformed Dogmatics*, Karl Barth wrote of finding his own way to do theology by working back through the orthodox to the Reformers and thence to Holy Scripture. It is indeed, as I have argued, a part of God's good gift of created particularity that we cannot go straight to Scripture but, like Barth and Calvin before him, must find our way into a tradition, with authorities who will guide us in our reading of the texts. It is clear that much of the heat generated in the arguments over the later writers' relationship to Calvin has been due to a consciousness that for reasons like this the tradition does matter, which has led to attempts to claim that a particular reading of the tradition is more authentic, whether it be McLeod Campbell and the Marrowmen against the Westminster-influenced theology of the Scots Kirk, or the orthodox against the neo-orthodox, to use that objectionable oxymoron.[41] In many ways this is a hopeful sign: that many theologians now care sufficiently about the tradition to argue is surely better than the previous assumption that it really was not important. The one virtue that lies behind the *odium theologicum* is the realisation that theology actually matters.

The question is pressing, however: how, as responsible theologians and historians, do we respond to these debates? Must we fight over the tradition as has been done, seeking to claim it for our own party and opinions? I trust not. It seems to me that not least amongst the many virtues of scholastic theology was the ability to contain divergent interpretations of a tradition. If I may return one last time to the question of predestination, the great example is the Synod of Dort: faced with varying interpretations of the doctrine it is clear that the mind of the Synod was infralapsarian, but they did not simply declare that position right and all others wrong. Rather, they took judgements as to which disagreements were legitimate and acceptable within the tradition, and which must be discarded, and wrote their Canons accordingly. Amongst the basic distinctions it was suggested that to be supralapsarian was to be wrong in a way that was nonetheless acceptable, whereas to uphold the Remonstrance was to separate oneself from the tradition.

In refusing to see any single major disagreement between Calvin and the later Reformed theologians, I have, however briefly, sought to complicate the picture: methodologically and materially, I have not argued for unanimity, but instead have hinted at a plethora of minor differences and developments, at shifting alliances and complex lines of descent. There never was a single Reformed theology, rather there was a family of approaches, with similar parentage and with various divergences, held together by a scholasticism that refused to make hasty judgements. Even in Calvin's *Institutes*, amongst the many scholastic features we find also a distinction made between acceptable errors and unacceptable ones.[42] A rediscovery of this facet of scholasticism might enable us to disagree without denouncing, to argue without anathematising. I hope that the day might come when hasty generalised denunciations of Beza and Barth or, worse, orthodoxy and neo-orthodoxy will be alike treated with contempt by theologians who have learned once more to value precise statement and logical rigour, and who are able to state with some

---

[41] One of the earliest recognitions of this facet of the debate is indeed Paul Helm's Introduction to *Calvin and the Calvinists*, which discusses a tradition of interpretation, and recognises that one of the effects of Kendall's thesis, if proved, would be to break the continuity of tradition between Calvin and later Calvinists.

[42] The obvious example being his desire to unite Reformed and Lutheran teaching on the Eucharist, whilst stringently opposing the sacrifice of the Mass.

exactitude where *Church Dogmatics* II/2 and the Canons of Dort part company, if indeed they do. If the main fault line in the recent discussion has been whether Barth is regarded as a better interpreter of the Reformed tradition than scholasticism was, or vice versa, then perhaps what we need to listen to first are the points of methodological agreement: for thoroughly theological reasons, Barth and the scholastics were alike precise about what they disagreed about and generous toward those they disagreed with. These, surely, are examples we would all do well to follow.

★   ★   ★

I argued in the first part of this book that within the theological vocation is a demand that we listen to the tradition. In this part I have attempted both to indicate why I think the reminder of such a demand is necessary, and to demonstrate that it is possible. There are places where the tradition has been consistently misheard, whether the work of a particular theologian (Anselm, in Chapter 3), the contours of a particular school (Reformed Orthodoxy, in this chapter) or a particular facet of the more general tradition (the doctrine of divine simplicity, in the previous chapter). I do not suppose that my hearing, and so my readings, are perfect in any of these cases; I have, however, tried to indicate corrections of particular failures that I see as general. Such theological work, undertaken by many who can correct each others' mistakes and overemphases, will enable the Church of today to receive what has been 'traditioned', handed on, without addition, diminution or distortion.

Chapter 6

Strange Voices: Edwards on the Will

When we learn to listen to the tradition faithfully, not assuming that we already know what we shall hear, but instead allowing earlier voices their own integrity, we will inevitably be surprised by the strangeness of much of what is said. At that point we will be faced with a choice: we might take the modern way of patronising earlier voices by assigning them to their 'place in history', and so pretending that they have nothing to say to us; or we might believe that, as I have argued in the first two chapters of this book, to listen to these voices in all their strangeness, and to regard their positions as serious, and live, options is actually a theological imperative. Perhaps the two most obvious areas where this will be true are sexual ethics[1] and biblical interpretation,[2] but I intend to look at a different, and perhaps less obvious, question in this chapter.

Of all the various voices in the Christian tradition, the high Calvinism of New England may seem amongst the least likely to be relevant to us today. We have learnt well of the inhumanity of this tradition, its rejoicing in visions of unimaginable torment imposed by a capricious deity on human beings long before their birth. Jonathan Edwards's magisterial examination of the nature of human freedom, *The Freedom of the Will*,[3] was conceived precisely as a defence of this Calvinism: can there really be anything of value here?

---

[1] For one example of an attempt to take the tradition seriously, see Michael Banner, *Christian Ethics and Contemporary Moral Problems* (Cambridge: Cambridge University Press, 1999), *passim*, but especially pp. 269–309.

[2] Again, an example of listening respectfully and seriously to those who have come before might be Hans W. Frei, *The Eclipse of Biblical Narrative: A Study in Eighteenth and Nineteenth Century Hermeneutics* (New Haven, Connecticut: Yale University Press, 1974). Perhaps the most sensitive attempt to do what I am suggesting here that I have encountered is an unpublished paper on Augustine's hermeneutical method, so often patronised, that Dr Mike Higton read to the Society for the Study of Theology in 2001.

[3] I am using the edition in the current Yale series of Edwards's Works: *The Works of Jonathan Edwards*, vol. 1: *Freedom of the Will*, Paul Ramsey (ed.) (New Haven, Connecticut and London: Yale University Press, 1957).

I think that it is a worthwhile text of particular interest because Edwards wrote at a time when two definitions of freedom remained available. One of these, Edwards's own view, has now been lost and almost forgotten, but in its defence he prophesied with some clarity the result of the embracing of the other, what he called the 'Arminian',[4] view, which, I suggest, is now almost universal. What I hope to show in this chapter is that, if only we are prepared to listen to Edwards's diagnosis in all its strangeness, he will enable us to see that positions that go unquestioned in our time, even in our churches, are in fact deeply illogical, utterly inimical to the gospel of Christ, and seriously damaging to any serious ethical reflection. Edwards can speak to us as a shockingly modern prophet, diagnosing the ills of our own time because he saw their roots in his, but that demands that we take him seriously, and do not write him off as a sad anachronism even in his own day.[5]

The task will be easier if the normal order is reversed, so I will start with Edwards's diagnosis of the problems of 'Arminianism', and seek to map these to standard positions in present culture. I recall a cartoon in which a boy stands beside his father's armchair as he reads his son's clearly unsatisfactory school report. The caption reads: 'What do you think the problem is, Dad? Nature or nurture?' This assumption, that human action is not culpable if it can be explained, is a pervasive one in our modern culture, and gets right to the heart of the issue. If both nature and nurture are the responsibilities of a parent, and a child's behaviour is in large part a response to some combination of these, then what culpability the child's actions may give rise to must be charged to the parents' account. To the extent that actions are explicable, they are excusable; the logic is so common as to seem unassailable.

In *The Freedom of the Will* the full powers of a great mind are turned on such positions at the moment when they began to become convincing, and their absurdities are carefully exposed. It has perhaps not been often enough recognised that Edwards's fundamental question in this book is ethical: what conditions must obtain for an action to be worthy of praise or blame? The fault might lie with the modern reader who imposes modern standards on the text,

---

[4] Edwards comments in his preface (pp. 131–2) that he uses 'Arminian' as a convenient shorthand to denote a particular family of views on the subject, whilst recognising that not everyone who holds those views is in any sense an Arminian (Isaac Watts, whose *Essay on the Freedom of the Will*, in *God and the Creature*, is one of Edwards's targets throughout the book, is the example to the fore). With the same caveats in place, I will occasionally use 'Calvinist' and 'Arminian' in my discussion as a shorthand to identify the two opposing views.

[5] I have tried to demonstrate that this has been Edwards's fate far too often in the opening chapter of my *God of Grace*.

and so fails to listen properly to the tradition. Thinking the book is entitled *The Freedom of the Will*, we pass straight on to the first chapters, where we discover Edwards discussing different understandings of freedom, and so we assume that the nature of human freedom is his concern. The book is not entitled *The Freedom of the Will*; it is merely called that for convenience. Its title is *A Careful and Strict Inquiry into the Modern Prevailing Notions of that Freedom of the Will, which is Supposed to be Essential to Moral Agency, Virtue and Vice, Reward and Punishment, Praise and Blame*, and that is what Edwards is interested in. His methodology might be philosophical and/or theological, but his focus is on ethics, or at least on 'meta-ethics'. He is concerned to establish those things that must be the case concerning human decision for such decision to be meaningfully analysable ethically.

There is, however, even more in that title: 'modern prevailing notions' of freedom form the subject matter for the discussion. In listening to this classic text, I will seek to demonstrate that what in 1754 were the 'modern prevailing' notions have now prevailed.[6] The understanding of human freedom that Edwards sought to stop in its tracks is now so pervasive as to be axiomatic everywhere except amongst philosophers, who are aware there is an argument to be had, and those theologians who are prepared to risk incomprehension and dismissal as anachronistic by daring to mention such offensive (but traditional) notions as predestination, special providence and the sovereignty of God. The world may once have 'groaned to find itself Arian', but I suspect that most men and women in the world were rather comfortable with such an accommodation to natural pagan religiosity; today, for arguably the first time in the history of the Church, the 'post-Christian' world, at least, finds itself Pelagian, and its people seem happy that it should be so.

Edwards presents us with two competing understandings of what a choice, an act of will, might be. His own understanding is that all decisions are predictable: sufficient causes may be found within the attitudes and circumstances of the person called upon to choose to account fully for his or her choice. The opposing, 'Arminian', view is a synthesis of the views of a variety of writers including, but not limited to, Chubb, Watts and Whitby, who are his major dialogue partners in the book.[7] Under this scheme, the essence of free human choice is that it is not predictable, that it cannot be reduced without residue to an analysis of motives and situation. There is an old piece of advice when faced with a hard decision, to list 'the pros and cons' in opposing columns; Edwards's

---

[6] In this my reading owes much to Robert Jenson's magisterial account of Edwards's theology: *America's Theologian: A Recommendation of Jonathan Edwards* (Oxford: Oxford University Press, 1988). See particularly the chapter on freedom, pp. 154–68.

[7] For notes on these three, see Ramsey's 'Editor's Introduction', *Freedom of the Will*, pp. 65–118.

assertion is that, if only I could list all the pros and all the cons that were in my mind at the time of deciding, and assign an accurate evaluation of the weighting that I placed on each, that would be an infallible prediction of my decision. His opponents assert that to be able to jump either way even with such a balance sheet in view is precisely what it means to be free.

The importance of this disagreement lies in its implications for the field of ethics. Edwards's opponents claim that any choice that is predictable must be necessary and therefore cannot be considered morally relevant. If I cannot do a thing, I cannot be held responsible for not doing it. The response is twofold: firstly, Edwards insists that the alternative account of freedom that is being urged by his opponents is incoherent: if carefully thought about philosophically, it simply makes no sense; secondly, he argues that a choice that is inevitable may still be morally relevant, provided the causes that make it inevitable are of a certain sort. To illustrate, he argues that I am not culpable if I do not try to save a drowning child because I am unable to swim, but I am culpable if I do not so do because I am unable to *care*. That is to say, there are inabilities and necessities that do indeed remove moral culpability, certain meanings of 'I cannot do so' that do indeed imply that I am not responsible for not so doing, but there is another sort of necessity that does not remove, but instead establishes, moral culpability. The fact that '*I* cannot do so' is precisely what makes me responsible.

If, as Edwards's opponents insist, I cannot be held responsible for anything I cannot but do, what sort of freedom must I possess in order to be regarded as culpable for my actions? Three things are asserted to be necessary: that the will is self-determining; that the mind at the moment of choice be perfectly indifferent to the objects proposed for choice; and that the will's self-determination be perfectly contingent, which is to say uncaused.[8] The demand is that the 'will' must be 'free' – the *liberum arbitrium* of the classical tradition must exist. It seems to me that Edwards's account of the results of holding to this position, thus analysed, resonates quite startlingly well with many of the grosser ethical absurdities that are current in Western society.

The first condition demands that the will, the faculty of choice, is not determined by anything other than itself. The inevitable result of this commitment is perhaps best illustrated by questions of how character mitigates ethical responsibility. Edwards uses at one point the example of a drunkard, who might have reached a condition in which he is unable to resist drink if it be available. Although he does not say so, the implicit judgement in Edwards's comments is that such a person is all the more to blame for having gone so far in depravity. Today the same fact would be pleaded as a mitigating, not a compounding, factor: the attempt is regularly made in our courts to excuse

---

[8] Ibid., pp. 164–5.

someone who admits to a certain crime on the grounds that psychologically his or her character is such that the behaviour could not be avoided. '[I]f we pursue these principles', asserts Edwards, 'we shall find that virtue and vice are wholly excluded out of the world.'[9] Quite so: all that is left is the rule of law, but without concepts of virtue and vice even that is eroded by pleas of mitigation.

The second of the three conditions, the demand for indifference at the moment of choice, implies that 'true freedom' is most purely demonstrated in those situations where my mind is not inclined towards any one of the things proposed for choice, where there is a total lack of motive, and yet I can come to a decision with ease.[10] Two consequences of this demand for indifference may be observed today: firstly, the logical result of such a position is that commitment damages freedom. The more strongly I feel about a decision, the more closely I ally myself with a cause, the less 'free' I am in doing so.[11] To take marriage vows, therefore, would damage my freedom, and so would be inappropriate, unless I am free to renege on those vows for any reason that I might consider sufficient at any point in the future. Thus we see the seemingly unstoppable drive to 'no fault divorces' in Western legal reform, so that it is no longer just in California where, as the old joke has it, 'the only legal grounds for divorce are being married'.

Consider, however, the absurdity of this: every choice, however lightly taken, is an act of commitment on some level. Even if I refuse to contemplate marriage because (the universal excuse) 'I don't want to be tied down yet', my choice to form a relationship with a partner at some level is an act of commitment to that partner, whether it involves the combining of our lives in cohabitation, or merely an implied promise of faithfulness and availability until the connection is formally severed. This must also be true of any friendship, any communal interest or club membership, of, indeed, any social involvement at all. If every act of commitment is a diminution of my freedom, then all social involvement must tend towards slavery.[12] That this (bizarre) position is nevertheless standard in Western societies should be obvious: the regularly heard assertion 'I had to move on, I was getting too involved', whether the referent is a sexual partner, a job or an entire social life in the case of an *émigré*, is a striking example. Again, the iconic figures of freedom point in the same direction: the

---

[9] Ibid., p. 326.

[10] The present author might note that, on this point, his experience is rather different to that of Edwards's targets!

[11] Ramsey (ed.), *Freedom of the Will*, p. 320ff.

[12] Hence Edwards argues that motives and inducements, which is to say the moral discourse of society, must remove freedom according to the 'modern prevailing notions'. Ibid., pp. 328–33.

cowboy, riding empty plains with no history to enslave him, who involves himself for a few days in a situation and then leaves it and its ties behind; the long-distance lorry driver, or solo pilot, whose existence is separated from any society by the nature of the role. Politically right-wing groups regularly define 'freedom' as 'freedom from society', and so argue for 'less government', fewer regulations and less taxation, because these are the things that 'restrict' the 'individual's freedom'.[13]

However, the positions have not yet in this discussion been pushed to their logical extremes. All social interaction inhibits and destroys my freedom, but the choice not to interact socially is surely just as much an act of commitment. The cowboy, or the right-wing libertarian, avoids enslavement by another or by society only to become enslaved precisely by his or her own attempts to avoid enslavement. No choice that results in commitment can preserve freedom and so the only truly free choices are those which result in oblivion. The philosopher with the courage to face this will finally insist that the only authentically human decision is suicide; the adolescents (of whatever age) who lack that courage will link freedom with psychoactive substances. The quest for genuine freedom finally results (not just today, but amongst the early Romantic generation who saw all this for themselves) in massive levels of drug addiction.

Secondly, and even more incoherently, what is surely the most perverse form of modern alienation is exposed and displayed in this formulation of freedom. An obvious contradiction is present in the assertion as Edwards formulates it: no faculty ('mind' or 'will') can be both totally indifferent to the objects of choice and involved in choosing one over the others at the same time. The writers who Edwards quotes avoid this contradiction by separating 'self' from 'will': '*I* am entirely indifferent to either; and yet my will may determine *itself* to choose.'[14] Suddenly, I am a passive observer of my own actions. The refined forms of this in late modernity have heard Edwards's warning (based as it was on Newtonian science) that nothing is uncaused,[15] and yet preserved this bizarre division to insist that, although they are caused, I am not the cause of my own actions. The prophets of this brave new world are Darwin,[16] Marx[17] and

---

[13] 'The end of laws is to *bind to one side* ... But if liberty consists in indifference, then [this] destroys liberty.' Ibid., p. 304 (emphasis original).

[14] Ibid., p. 197 (my emphasis).

[15] Ibid., pp. 180–6.

[16] If not Darwin himself, then certainly his modern disciples: see, for example, S. Jones, *In the Blood: God, Genes and Destiny* (London: Flamingo, 1997).

[17] Or, indeed, the apostles of free-market capitalism, whose accounts of human economic behaviour are just as simplistic, just as deterministic, and no doubt just as wrong as that of Marx. As Colin Gunton has pointed out, *oikonome* is a theological word, and so any account of its processes which ignores the grace of God and the doctrine of creation is inevitably flawed.

Freud, whose followers will tell anyone foolish enough to listen that it was, notoriously, 'not your fault', it was biological instinct, or inevitable social forces, or 'subconscious urges', and so what is needed is more awareness of the 'self' which such themes define. If the first consequence of such positions is to alienate me from the society of which I am a part, the second is to alienate me from my now-isolated individual 'self'. When 'I' am alienated from 'myself', the response is counselling, the new universal liturgical practice of the self-absorbed Western world. As if Narcissus needed to become more 'self-aware'!

With the axioms set for the discussion, however, the cure is worse than the disease. What will happen if I finally 'find' my 'self' in counselling or therapy? I will become fully aware of my self-alienation. Seeing all the causes of my actions, and so knowing why I do each thing I do, I will realise that I am almost totally unfree (according to this definition of freedom). My social background and my parents' failures and my psychic make-up conspire to make me act in this way; I see myself doing it, and I understand why I do it, but I cannot change it; I can merely observe the causes of my own actions.[18] The result under the terms of the argument is the standard one observed in those who have 'successfully' completed counselling or therapy: they have 'learnt to forgive themselves'. Their actions have not changed, but they now understand what causes these actions, see that they are not freely chosen with the definition of freedom that is being advanced, and so do not hold themselves culpable. 'Their doctrine [of freedom] excuses all evil inclinations', says Edwards, 'because in such inclinations, they are not self-determined.'[19] Thus perhaps the one great 'triumph' of Christian pastoral theology this century: we have learnt how to convince sinners with tender consciences that they have no need of Christ's atoning work.[20]

The third thing asserted to be necessary for 'true freedom' to obtain is that a decision is contingent, which is to say uncaused. Continuing a polemic that runs through the text, Edwards shows that those writers who insist that acts of will are contingent nevertheless allow that certain causes influence them. In particular, he mentions 'the dictates of the understanding' and motives: if an object or a course of action appears pleasant or good to me, then I will be disposed to choose it. The point is trivial, but useful precisely in its triviality. Edwards is able to quote passages from those writers he is opposing showing that they believe and teach this, and regard it as important, and so claims once again to have trapped them in inconsistency. More importantly, he is once more able to show the bizarre nature of the ethical claims that are made by his

---

[18] Edwards foresaw even this. See Ramsey (ed.), *Freedom of the Will*, pp. 312–15.

[19] Ibid., p. 421.

[20] If the Christian gospel is true, this is a far crueller practice than Edwards's notorious preaching of hell to scare people into salvation.

opponents: if contingency is essential to freedom, and freedom to moral agency, then it would seem that I am absolved from moral culpability to the extent that what I do (even if it be murder or worse) appeared to be a good or appropriate action to me.[21]

To pick an example from a recent storyline of a British radio soap opera, I might under this scheme justify my decision to break the law, and to cause wilful damage to a relative's property, on the grounds that my own estimation of the morality of the act was carefully considered. In the particular radio programme, this argument was used by a teenage boy to justify criminal damage against his uncle's farm, and was found convincing by his parents, who regarded the action as totally inappropriate, but were prepared to accept it, and to defend him, on the grounds that he had thought hard about it. Such ethical incoherence was dramatically entirely convincing because it is so usual in current Western discourse. Even within the churches, as Robert Jenson indicates whilst making a similar point, policy statements are regularly made to the effect that abortion is a deeply unethical action, which may, however, be right if undertaken with sufficient forethought and (of course) counselling.[22] Abortion may or may not be tantamount to murder (or this may vary from situation to situation), but if in a particular instance it is, then no amount of thinking about it beforehand will change that. An older age saw the inability to distinguish good from evil as the height of moral depravity; now, apparently, it will save us from any accusation of the same. 'Had it not been for the law, I should never have known sin,' says Paul, but he is emphatic in his repeated refusals to follow that up by suggesting 'that the law is identical with sin'. The current age might be less robust.

It is not difficult to demonstrate absurdities and non-sequiturs in recent Western ethical discourse;[23] the value of Edwards's analysis is more in exposing some, at least, of what lies behind the existence of these incoherences. The Arminian demand is that my decisions should be *mine* – not caused or influenced by anything else. Freedom is found only in the interior space that nothing from outside ever reaches; a decision, if it is to be classed as free, must be created *ex nihilo*.[24] Here, perhaps, we are coming very close to the attraction and the danger of the modern notions that Edwards is so concerned about. He claims to have demonstrated the absurdity of the opposing position at several decisive points in this analysis where the explanation that the will (or moral

---

[21] As, once again, Edwards indicated. See Ramsey (ed.), *Freedom of the Will*, p. 337.

[22] Jenson, *America's Theologian*, p. 167.

[23] Alistair MacIntyre has shown this most powerfully in his *After Virtue: A Study in Moral Theory* (London: Duckworth, 1981).

[24] I owe this fine identification to Colin Gunton, 'God, Grace and Freedom', in Colin Gunton (ed.), *God and Freedom* (Edinburgh: T & T Clark, 1995), pp.119–33, 119.

agent) is *a se* (i.e., self-caused or created) would provide a coherent explanation for the difficulties. Edwards was a Christian theologian who understood the doctrine of creation *ex nihilo* very well; it was for him absurd to assume that anything other than the triune God could possibly be regarded as having necessary and hence uncaused existence, as *a se*. In an age which might take as its motto 'I am the master of my fate, I am the captain of my soul',[25] this is perhaps less obvious. 'Ye shall be as gods' is the oldest lie in the Book, but that does not seem to make it any less convincing to each new generation born under Adam's curse.

Modern understandings of freedom, as Christoph Schwöbel has pointed out,[26] are attempts to take for ourselves a vision of God's power that has been borrowed from a time when we still believed in God. Even the vision of God is the wrong one, however: such visions of freedom owe everything to the worst excesses of nominalism, in which the essence of God's existence was naked will, rather than love, goodness and all the attributional language that should describe God's character. So Barth, whose discussion of God's perfections show great concern to avoid nominalism,[27] will not speak of God's freedom without insisting that it is the freedom to love,[28] and at one point speaks of 'the inner necessity of the freedom of God' in contrast to 'the play of some sovereign *liberum arbitrium*'.[29] In the *Two Dissertations* which he left on his desk when he died Edwards made the point: only God can be God without becoming demonic.[30] God is identified with being-in-general in these works; anything else is partial, and to elevate any part to the position of decisive importance is disastrous. In attempting to believe the lie that we can be as gods, we define ourselves against the community and the world, and find our freedom only in alienation from society, reality and finally self.

So to Edwards's response and *The Freedom of the Will*. With astonishingly clear foresight of both the attractions and the incoherences of the Arminian notions of freedom, Edwards set out to demolish them in their infancy. By the end of the book he will have claimed that Calvinist accounts of freedom are philosophically coherent, whereas Arminian accounts are not, and that

---

[25] William Earnest Henley, 'Invictus'.

[26] 'Imago Libertatis: Human and Divine Freedom', in Gunton (ed.), *God and Freedom*, pp. 57–81, 70–6.

[27] *Church Dogmatics* II.1, pp. 322–50.

[28] Ibid., II *passim*, but consider especially how decisively the account of God's election of grace in II.2, pp. 1–506, is affected by this commitment.

[29] Ibid., IV.1, p. 195. The reference is to the inevitability of the Incarnation.

[30] See Paul Ramsey (ed.), *The Works of Jonathan Edwards* vol. 8: *Ethical Writings* (New Haven, Connecticut, and London: Yale University Press, 1989), pp. 550–60.

Calvinist accounts make ethics possible, whereas Arminian accounts destroy the possibility of morality. 'Modern notions' may well be 'prevailing', but Edwards will demonstrate that with such notions one may neither think straight nor live straight. The book very nearly falls into two neat halves: the former two parts address the nature of freedom, and the coherence or otherwise of the competing accounts, and are philosophical in method; the latter two parts are concerned with the ethical ramifications of the different accounts, and are much more theological in character. Two brief sections at the end of Part II spoil this scheme, offering theological arguments in support of the Calvinist understanding of the nature of human freedom. I will use the division for convenience, however, in my exposition of the text.

So, to the first point, and the coherence of notions of freedom.[31] What must 'freedom' (and all the other words: 'choice', 'will', 'necessity', 'contingence' ...) mean if our language about it is not to be incoherent? Edwards claims that there are two discourses here: a normal discourse used in the market square and the town meeting; and a philosophical discourse in which some of these words are given different meanings. This might not be a problem in itself, but he further claims that those who use the philosophical discourse forget sometimes that they have redefined words, and so an argument is constructed in which key terms regularly shift meaning, and which could not be constructed if the terms were to be used univocally in either sense.

In normal discourse, then, the 'will' is 'that by which the mind chooses any thing' and so an act of will is very simply a choice, and nothing more mysterious or metaphysical than that. What 'determines the will'? Rephrasing, what makes us choose one thing over another? Edwards's answer is in terms of 'motives', defined simply as those things that incline the will towards a particular choice. Naturally, then, the will is determined by 'that motive which, as it stands in the view of the mind, is the strongest'. Simply and trivially, we do the thing we want most to do. My 'will' is that part of me which feels the strengths of the various motives and inclines towards the stronger. This is an exhaustive description of the act of choosing.

What of language of 'necessity', 'impossibility' and the like? In common usage, such words merely describe that 'which is, or will be, notwithstanding all supposable opposition'. Thus they admit qualifiers, so we may meaningfully speak of something being 'medically impossible', for example. Again, some things are impossible or necessary in general ('I cannot fly, so I must walk around'), others only with reference to a particular person ('I cannot swim, so I must walk around'). The philosophical use of necessity, however, is the one that is relevant to discussions of freedom, and this does not admit qualifications

---

[31] In what follows I am expounding parts I and II of *The Freedom of the Will*. I will not give detailed references to these parts of the text.

in the same way. Edwards regards it as much more difficult to define than is usually assumed: standard (and still oft-quoted) definitions speak of 'that by which a thing cannot but be' or similar. However, defining 'necessity' in terms of impossibility ('cannot') is question-begging, according to Edwards, since we could as well define what 'cannot but' means by speaking of necessity. His alternative definition is that 'necessity' is a 'full and fixed connexion between the things signified by the subject and predicate of a proposition, which affirms something to be true'.

Edwards suggests three different classes of proposition that might fit this definition: some things, firstly, are necessarily true a priori, in that to deny them would involve contradiction. Edwards offers the standard Enlighten-ment example of mathematical propositions, and also suggests that the existence and character of God fit into this category, mentioning an idiosyn-cratic version of the ontological argument, which he uses at various points in his writings. Secondly, some propositions have a contingent nature, but if once true are necessarily always true. An obvious example would be a certain form of historical statement: the proposition 'King Harold was shot in the eye at the battle of Hastings' might not be true, but it has a form of necessity about it: if it is once true, it must remain true subsequently. Thirdly, there are consequent necessities, of the form 'if x, then y must follow' where x is itself necessary in some way. Clearly, future events, if they are to be described as necessary at all, can be necessary only in the third way: if something is neces-sarily true, then it cannot be not-yet true, and something that is not-yet true has not yet happened, so cannot have the second sort of necessity.

Edwards applies two further distinctions to his discussion of philosophical necessity: firstly, he reiterates the distinction he made earlier between general and particular necessity; secondly, he introduces a distinction between natural and moral necessity, which is crucial to the argument. Moral necessity is the result of causes that are properly regarded as 'moral': duty, desire or habit, for example. Natural necessity is that which results from natural causes: 'I cannot fly, for I lack wings' is an example of natural necessity; 'I cannot fly, for I have such a phobia about it' is moral. That such moral causes can lead to a necessity to act in a certain way is part of the common human experience: 'Here I stand, I can do no other.' Edwards offers examples of his own: 'A woman of great honour and chastity may be unable to prostitute herself to her slave. A child of great love and duty may be unable to kill his father … A drunkard, under such and such circumstances, may be unable to forbear taking strong drink …'

In his final attempt at language analysis, Edwards considers the meaning of 'freedom' and 'liberty'. The common usage is once again simple: 'power … that any one has, to do as he pleases'. Clearly, then, only a being with a 'will' can be free; if I cannot choose, then how can I do as I choose? To be free is to be an agent, to possess the ability to prefer one thing over another; to have, in short, a will. Thus, and trivially, talk of 'free will', the *liberum arbitrium* of the tradition, is incoherent, considered according to the normal meanings of the words. People are agents possessed of wills; wills themselves are not. Thus, people are free, wills are not. This is Edwards's alternative position, established by simple philosophical analysis.

The second part of the book is devoted to exposing the incoherence of the Arminian understanding of freedom against which he is writing. He introduces the three points that I indicated earlier he takes to be central, and he presses each one to show that it is logically untenable. There is as yet none of the ethical analysis with which I began; that comes later. His concern for the moment is merely with philosophical coherence.

Edwards exegetes the first point, the insistence on the self-determining power of the will, as meaning 'the person determines his/her will', as he regards it as meaningless to speak of the will as an agent that determines anything. In Edwards's analysis, therefore, when faced with a choice between two options, those who insist on the self-determining power of the will do not accept his assertion that 'the will is as the greatest apparent good is', but rather postulate an act of will to decide whether to follow the weight of motivation or whether to go another way. This postulation, however, demands that every act of will is determined by a previous choice, which is to say a previous act of will, and so involves an infinite regress, which Edwards demonstrates by use of a *reductio ad absurdum*, positing a first act of will in the chain and asking what determines that. At some point, therefore, there must be an act of will that is determined by something other than a prior act of will, and it matters little whether this is the second or the hundredth; the will is still not finally self-determining. Given this, Occam's razor might encourage us to assume with Edwards that it is indeed the primary act of will which is determined by motives, not some shadowy act of will, which determines the act of will, which finally determines the primary choice.

One often senses when reading Edwards that his victories are too easily won, and that might be the case here. The self-determining power of the will is a philosophically naïve way of defending the position; to speak of a moral agent as self-determining is far more robust.[32] Edwards addresses a position very close to this in the first of the 'evasions' he discusses, that it is not a previous act of will that determines the will, but it is only that either the faculty of the will or the soul through that faculty determines the will. Edwards asks the obvious question: how is this determination accomplished, if not by an 'act' of the will? He suggests that the only coherent way of understanding this

---

[32] This point was made by Edwards's first serious respondent, James Dana, as Ramsey mentions in his 'Introduction' to *Freedom of the Will* (n. 3, p. 10).

would be to say that 'the will or soul determines the act of the will *in willing*; it determines its own volition, *in* the very act of volition ...', and he further claims that there are only three ways of making sense of this claim: firstly, what is claimed might be a logically prior act, rather than a temporally prior one; or secondly, there is no real distinction between the determining act and the determined act; or thirdly, 'that volition has no cause, and is no effect'.

Of these, the first does not remove the problem at all: an infinite logical regress has all the same difficulties as an infinite temporal one. The second is simply nonsensical, according to Edwards: everything is an effect of some cause; here, by supposition, the act of the will is not caused by the will itself; equally, by common supposition of those who hold such positions, the act of the will is not caused by anything other than the will. At best, then, it collapses into the third position, that an act of the will is not the effect of any cause. A 'cause', according to Edwards, is 'any antecedent ... on which an event ... so depends, that it is the ground and reason ... why it is, rather than not ...' On the basis of this definition, he asserts that anything that is not *a se* must be caused, and so each act of will must have in some sense a cause somewhere.

The second part of this construction of freedom is an insistence that the mind should be in a state of indifference immediately prior to the act of will. Edwards, as I have indicated, not only believed that such genuine indifference is an illusion, he also regards this assumption as contradictory: how can I be both perfectly indifferent and yet choosing one thing over another at the same time?

Finally Edwards discusses the demand that the act of will be contingent, which is to say not necessary in any philosophical sense, not even consequently (i.e., having a necessity of the third form that I discussed above, where the decision is necessary because it is an inevitable result of events that have already happened). Edwards has two sets of arguments, that this is an incoherent position, and secondly that even if it were to be tenable, it would not establish the existence of 'freedom' in any useful sense of that word. The first relies on positions already established earlier in the discussion: if no event can occur without a cause, and an act of will is an event, then an act of will must be explicable without residue in terms of prior causes, which is to say consequently necessary. I have already indicated how Edwards demonstrates that his opponents contradict themselves here by allowing that some causes, 'the dictates of the understanding', for example, do affect the act of will.

My exposition of the first two parts of the book is now almost complete. Thus far, Edwards has addressed only the question of the nature of freedom, establishing his own position and seeking to demonstrate the incoherence of the opposing account. He has done this purely philosophically: no theological arguments have appeared, little Scripture has been cited, and the name of Jesus Christ has not been mentioned (other than in a request for prayer in the preface). At the very end of the second part one theological argument is raised: God's foreknowledge of events, including human choices, demands that events are subject to a necessity of some kind. In discussing 'foreknowledge', Edwards focuses on prophecy, thus his arguments are not dependent on a particular understanding of the relationship of God's eternity to human time. Neither do they depend on any doctrine of providence or predestination, in that Edwards is only arguing for the necessity that some things will happen in the future, not that God causes them to happen.[33] Certain future events will inevitably happen, because God has given prophecies that they will happen. This is particularly true of events concerning the coming of the Messiah, his work and his second coming. To the extent that these events depend on free human choices (Mary's response of faith, for example), those choices form a class of human decisions that are freely made, yet necessary. Thus freedom is not incompatible with necessity.

What are we to make of Edwards's philosophy? He is merciless in exposing incoherence in the positions that have been put forward by his opponents, and in this he is also very successful. All that this procedure can result in, however, is an assertion that as yet a coherent account of freedom of the Arminian form has not been offered. Edwards's intention is surely stronger than that: he would convince his readers that no such account could possibly be offered, that the very notion of a freedom defined by contingency is incoherent. To establish this he must depend on the language analysis in the first part, or the theological arguments at the end of the second.

Edwards's method of language analysis must assume that only one language game operates, or at least that one is privileged, or else there is no 'ordinary language' to analyse. After Wittgenstein and MacIntyre, however, it seems difficult to make this assumption. What we call 'ordinary language' is a patchwork of elements of different language games that have become common. Each square of the quilt is itself a partial, and so probably incoherent, subset of a wider game (one might think of the elements of psychological or psychoanalytical language that have passed in to public usage, for example), and the different squares certainly lack coherence with each other. So, even if we could isolate something that we could regard as 'the' common language of our society, Edwards's position relies on the assumption that this language game will produce meaningful and non-contradictory results when subjected to rigorous philosophical analysis. Perhaps Edwards did live in a society where the day-to-day discourse was sufficiently unified and philosophically robust to

---

[33] On which compare Luther: ' ... we act, *and are caused to act*, according to his foreknowledge and action'. *The Bondage of the Will*, J. I. Packer and O. R. Johnston (trs) (Grand Rapids, Michigan: Fleming H. Revell, 1957), p. 217, my emphasis.

withstand such analysis, but, in an age when academic livings are made by deconstructing texts with the intention of showing that even the most significant philosophers use language in demonstrably incoherent ways, this seems a difficult position to regard as axiomatic.

What of the theological argument? On the basis of the existence of God's foreknowledge, and hence of prophecy, Edwards seeks to establish that there exist certain human decisions whose outcome is predictable in advance. Let us for the moment grant this; his argument does not yet establish the freedom of these particular human decisions. He seeks to extend it, to suggest that God's foreknowledge is universal, and so all decisions are foreknown and necessary, and so either there are no free decisions in the world, or freedom is not incompatible with necessity. This disjunction, however, must remain a disjunction: the former option is not yet so incoherent or so irreconcilable with human experience that it may be discarded.[34]

Edwards makes one final comment in this part of the work, asking what contingent freedom might look like. By supposition, a free choice is here not dependent on motive or intellectual evaluation or any other cause. Perfect freedom, then, would be total randomness in action. 'The notion mankind have conceived of liberty', says Edwards, 'is some dignity or privilege, something worth claiming. But what dignity or privilege is there, in being given up to such wild contingence as this, to be perfectly and constantly liable to act unintelligently and unreasonably … as if we … were as destitute of perception as the smoke that is driven by the wind.'[35] Once again, those things which Edwards regards as necessary but ridiculous results of the Arminian view of freedom turn out to be prophecies of modern society. Whether the 'high art' of Jackson Pollock or John Cage or the pop philosophy of 1960s' radicalism, the assumption that perfect freedom is found in randomness has been explored to its nihilistic conclusion. One might also mention the regular attempts to invoke the alleged randomness of the quantum world as the locus for the possibility of human freedom in a scientifically determined universe. As Edwards has said, what freedom is this? Surely there is more dignity in being an automaton that is at least rational in its movements than in such celebrations of randomness.

Edwards does not, then, I think, succeed in finally establishing the incoherence of Arminian accounts of freedom, although he does demonstrate the philosophical difficulty of holding to a concept of 'free will', and the ease with which the alternative can be held. He also demonstrates the undesirability of a concept of 'free will' defined by contingency. It is not difficult to believe that

---

[34] The existence of fatalistic philosophies and religions is sufficient testimony to this point.

[35] Ramsey (ed.), *Freedom of the Will*, II.13, pp. 272–3.

freedom is merely the freedom to do what I want, and so that I can be free at the same time as being subject to necessity, so long as that necessity is moral not natural. Nor is it unusual; Edwards does not make reference to the tradition (except perhaps obliquely in his title: he is questioning '... *modern* prevailing notions ...'), but he could have cited Augustine, Luther, Calvin, even Anselm, in his support.[36] The problem, as the title of the work indicates, is an ethical one: Edwards's opponents think that this account of human freedom is detrimental to morality.

The charge is a standard one, which Calvinists (and indeed Augustinian theologians before the Reformation) have constantly faced: does not a doctrine of predestination, which is to say an insistence that the particular outcomes of human decisions are necessary outcomes, remove any possibility of holding people responsible for their actions, and so inevitably lead to antinomianism? To quote only the first theological treatise to deal with predestination in the history of the Christian Church, 'Should we then say "let's go on sinning so that grace may increase"?' (Romans 6:1). In the terms in which he has been carrying on the argument, Edwards must show that an action can be both necessary and morally relevant.

To establish this, Edwards turns to a series of theological arguments, each of which seeks to establish an instance in which a particular volitional being acts under necessity, but is at the same time held morally responsible for the action. The first of these arguments concerns God: God's actions are necessarily morally perfect, and yet he is to be praised for his moral perfection. If praise is appropriately offered regarding a particular action, it demonstrates that that action is morally relevant, and so an instance of the general point is established. Edwards's opponents will allow that God is necessarily holy, and so must deny the second premise. His sarcasm is sufficiently biting at this point to be worthy of extensive quotation:

> ... the infinitely holy God, who always used to be esteemed by God's people, not only virtuous, but a being in whom all possible virtue, and every virtue in the most absolute purity and perfection, and in infinitely greater brightness and amiableness than in any creature; the most perfect pattern of virtue and the fountain from whom all others' virtue is but as beams from the sun; and who has been supposed to be, on account of his virtue and holiness, infinitely more worthy to be esteemed, loved, honored, admired, commended, extolled and praised, than any creature; and he who

---

[36] Augustine, *Anti-Pelagian Writings* (Nicene and Post-Nicene Fathers, series 1, vol. 5) (New York: Christian Literature Crusade, 1887). See particularly 'On Man's Perfection in Righteousness' 9 and 'On Forgiveness of Sins and Baptism' 30. See also: Luther, *The Bondage of the Will*; Calvin, *Institutes* II.3.5; Anselm, *Cur Deus Homo* I.24.

is thus everywhere represented in Scripture; I say, this being, according to this notion of Dr Whitby, and other Arminians, has no virtue at all … he is deserving of no commendation or praise; because he is under necessity, he can't avoid being holy and good as he is; therefore no thanks to him for it …[37]

That is, Edwards foresaw an age when saying of God 'Of course he will forgive me, *c'est son metier*' would not be counted the most horrible blasphemy; when even the most conservative and 'evangelical' writers would answer questions about the 'use' of worship with comments about human psychological needs, rather than God's overwhelming beauty; and when churches would be empty, or reduced to offering moralistic advice about ways to live well, because they have no convincing reasons to offer people as to why they should worship God ('he is deserving of no … praise … he can't avoid being holy and good as he is; therefore no thanks to him for it …'). Contrary to common rumour, Edwards never suggested that a Christian should be willing to be damned for the glory of God; he did, however, make it a great test of true spiritual experience that a person love God because God is surpassingly lovely, and not because of any selfish gain.[38]

Edwards's second example of necessary acts that are praiseworthy concerns the activity of our Lord Jesus Christ during the period of his humiliation on earth. Again, Edwards argues that his holiness was necessary, and yet also virtuous. The necessity of his holiness is demonstrated in various ways: God had given promises to his Son in Scripture that he would give him the Spirit and so preserve him in holiness (for example, the first Servant Song in Isaiah 42, applied to Christ during his time on earth in Matthew 12:18); again, there are promises of the Messiah's future Kingdom, which depend for their fulfilment on the successful completion of his mission, and so imply a promise that it will be successful; thirdly, the Church was promised a sinless Saviour by God (the traditional Christmas readings from Isaiah 9 and 11 will serve for example); yet again, God's promises to the Blessed Virgin and to Joseph. In each of these cases, Edwards regards it as inconceivable that God's promises should fail, without discussing any sort of mechanism by which they will be infallibly established. He quotes the letter to the Hebrews as saying God 'confirmed it by an oath; that by two *immutable* things, in which it was *impossible* for God to lie, we might have strong consolation' (Edwards' emphasis). More theologically, he argues from the nature of the decrees and covenants: God's eternal decree, as revealed in Scripture, depends for its fulfilment on the perfect obedience of Christ; the eternal covenant made between

---

[37] Ramsey (ed.), *Freedom of the Will*, p. 278.

[38] John E. Smith (ed.), *The Works of Jonathan Edwards*, vol. 2: *Religious Affections* (New Haven, Connecticut: Yale University Press, 1959), pp. 240–66.

Father and Son, which the federal theologians found referred to in Psalm 40:6–8, depended on the same thing; the salvation of the patriarchs and Israelites from Adam to the coming of Christ depended on this being infallibly in the future. Finally, Edwards points to the Lord's own predictions of his Kingdom before his time of trial was complete.

The number of Edwards's arguments (which I have compressed), and the Scriptures he piles up in support of each one, show the importance he placed on establishing this point. 'I look upon it', he wrote, 'as a point clearly and absolutely determining the controversy between Calvinists and Arminians, concerning the necessity of such a freedom of the will as is insisted on by the latter, in order to moral agency, virtue, command or prohibition ...'[39] The echo of the title is surely deliberate: all else has been preamble; the argument turns here on the person of Jesus Christ. I will make two dogmatic comments.

It is a point regularly made in introductory courses on Christology, and too little reflected on, that the person and work of Christ are inseparable dogmatic loci. If this point is accepted, then there is surely a sense in which Christ's work is necessary, in which the outcome of the (genuine) crises that punctuate the gospel narratives, in Jordan river and the desert at the beginning, in the Garden as the end approached, and between, was indeed inevitable. If not, we would be forced to assert that Christ could have been other than he was, which is a difficult thing to say of a divine person. Somehow, the gospel narrative must be described as necessary, without compromising its status as a truly human, and so genuinely contingent, story. Modern dogmatics has responded to this challenge in various ways: one may, with Lutheran theologians such as Jüngel or Jenson,[40] take with full seriousness the implications of the radical Lutheran formulation of the *communicatio idiomatum* and make the gospel narrative a part of the description of God's being (and hence, one presumes, necessary); one may (with Edwards and, very differently, Barth) take a more Reformed route, and locate the necessity, the full force of the little Greek word *dei* which punctuates the gospels, in the decree of God;[41] finally, one could (with, for example,

---

[39] Ibid., p. 289.

[40] Robert Jenson, *Systematic Theology*, vol.1: *The Triune God* (Oxford: Oxford University Press, 1997), pp. 125–45; and see Douglas Farrow's comments in his 'Response' in the *International Journal of Systematic Theology* 1 (1999), pp. 89–95, especially pp. 90–1. For Jüngel, see John B. Webster, *Eberhard Jüngel: An Introduction to His Theology* (Cambridge: Cambridge University Press, 1986), pp. 63–78, and particularly Webster's recognition that 'the role played by Hegel's metaphysics in Jüngel's doctrine of God is ... very closely parallel to that played by Barth's doctrine of election...' (p. 64).

[41] To show that this is an adequate description of what Barth is about in vol. IV of the *Church Dogmatics* would require an exposition of how the intimate relation of Christology and Election in II.2 is mirrored in the narratives of Redemption in IV. I trust that

Moltmann)[42] duck the question, link the being of God to the contingent being of the world, and so end up in a form of panentheism, which is in danger of denying the central Christian affirmation of *creatio ex nihilo*.

Secondly, Edwards offers no mechanism for this necessity (unless the gift of the Spirit to Christ be interpreted as such), but it would perhaps be possible to indicate the lines along which a systematic construction could proceed: central to Edwards's argument is the distinction between moral and natural necessity, with moral necessity being compatible with free agency; the whole purpose of the current arguments is to establish the free and yet necessary nature of the actions of Christ, so the necessity we are looking for must be moral. Jesus Christ is the perfect instantiation of both the human nature (*phusis*) which we all share and the divine *phusis* of the Eternal Son. Playing on the meanings of the Greek word, this could and should imply one character (when we speak of Jesus as revealing God, it is usually a revelation of God's character that is meant: that God is loving, good, merciful ... is what is established this way). God's character is pre-eminent in all the virtues, in love and mercy, and in holiness, which at least includes hatred of sin. If this describes the character of Jesus Christ, then we may certainly argue that being the person he is, it was and is morally impossible for Christ to sin. Thus Edwards's point follows from basic Christological positions and the central distinction with which he is working.

Having sought to establish the necessity of Christ's holiness, Edwards turns to establishing that Christ's acts are free, virtuous and so worthy of praise and reward. The first argument is again on the basis of Scripture promises: 'the man Christ Jesus had his will infallibly, unalterably, and unfrustrably determined to good, and that alone; but yet he had promises of glorious rewards made to him, on condition of his persevering in, and perfecting the work which God had appointed him (Is. 53:10, 11, 12; Ps. 2 and 110; Is. 49:7, 8, 9)'.[43] Again comes the ironic pursuit of the opposing logic: 'According to this doctrine, that Creature who is ... the highest of all creatures in virtue, honor, and worthiness of esteem, praise and glory, on the account of his virtue, is less worthy of reward or praise than the very least of the saints.'[44]

This point is worthy of pursuit: the question is about human freedom, and Edwards, in speaking of Christ the creature, is finding in Christ an example, albeit pre-eminent, of creaturely freedom. In the past century we have learnt from Barth to interpret anthropology (as every other doctrinal locus) Christ-

---

[41] (*continued*) readers who know Barth will be able to see the possibilities (and limitations) of this interpretation.

[42] Jürgen Moltmann, *The Trinity and the Kingdom of God: The Doctrine of God* (London: SCM Press, 1981).

[43] Ramsey (ed.), *Freedom of the Will*, pp. 289–90.

[44] Ibid., p. 291.

ologically; where Edwards finds an example, then, we may find a definition. We only know what it is to be human when we look to Jesus Christ; when we look to him, we see free and praiseworthy acts that are nonetheless necessary; therefore, human freedom is in its definition not incompatible with necessity. Edwards's instinct, that the centre of the argument was here, and turned on Christological dogma, was sound. The necessity of Christ's holiness may be established from Scripture, and from theological arguments; the praise-worthiness, and so freedom, of his behaviour may be established in the same way; I have suggested a dogmatic mechanism for holding these two together that relies on standard Christology and Edwards's key distinction, and so I suggest that Edwards's position cannot be dismissed as incoherent. The conclusion: in the one place we can look to truly know what it is to be human, we find that freedom is not incompatible with (moral) necessity, and that (morally) necessary actions may deserve praise. The 'Arminian' position against which Edwards was writing is, I suggest, unsustainable within an orthodox Christology.

I have one criticism to make, however: Edwards's account of freedom does not, apparently, regard freedom as a soteriological category. 'It is for freedom, therefore, that Christ set us free' (Galatians 5:1), and so any appropriately theological account of freedom must finally conclude that the fullness of freedom is found only in Christian being, not in any general human being considered apart from the union with Christ brought about by the Spirit that is definitive of redeemed life. The problem here, I suggest, is that Edwards has allowed some of his earlier philosophical arguments to determine his argument throughout. In particular, when we look at what it is to be capable of freedom, to be a moral agent, we find a sense of autonomy: God, we are told, is 'in the highest possible respect' a moral agent,[45] suggesting that our decision making is of the same sort as God's. Edwards is in danger of accepting the basic error of his opponents here: human beings are not 'little gods', possessed of the same autonomy as the Triune Lord. Rather, we are creatures of the living God, fundamentally contingent, and created with and for a purpose. We are determined to serve God, to live as children of God. This is an ontological assertion, and so should be decisive for every part of our lives, and so – my point – for the nature of the 'freedom' that we claim.

Edwards has argued that true freedom is simply the ability to be the person you are, nothing more complex or abstruse than that. If this is the case, then, as creatures of the Living God, determined to live with him and to serve him, we are finally less than free if we are living any other way than this. Before conversion, however, we do not know this; we do not know what is 'good' and what is 'bad', what is appropriate action for us as creatures.[46] Edwards had

---

[45] Ibid., p. 364.

argued in a very significant sermon that the work of the Spirit in conversion is precisely in enabling us to see the aesthetic and hence moral[47] quality of God's actions as recounted in the gospel story, and so to understand the nature of true virtue, which lies in total commitment to God.[48] To attempt to live apart from Christ is finally to attempt to live as something other than we are, a creature of the Living God, and so is unfree. Human beings can only be free when they give up the impossible attempt to live as little gods.

Edwards's alternative construction looks beyond the modern claim that 'men will be like gods' to a time when 'men will be like men'. It depends on what would now be called a virtue ethic, and even perhaps a narrative construction of that. It is because, and only because, our actions demonstrate who we are, the virtues (or 'habits' in Edwards's terms) that are present in our hearts, that our actions are praiseworthy or culpable. 'From inside, from the human heart, come evil thoughts, acts of fornication, theft, murder, adultery, greed and malice ... all these evil things come from within, and they are what defile a person' (Mark 7:20–3). Our actions are caused, we are not gods, but they are caused by our personalities, our 'hearts', and so are morally relevant because morally necessary. It is precisely because *I* cannot do such and such that I can be held responsible for not so doing. This is narratively constructed because it is a necessity that springs from personal history: events that have happened, and so have necessity of Edwards's second sort, combine to create the third sort of necessity, inevitable human decisions. The things that I have done, the things that have been done to me, are what make me the person I am, and being the person I am results in the actions for which I am morally culpable.

Thus, I am caused by the community in which I live; it is the community that is the source of the things that have made me to be who I am. This is neither fatalistic nor necessitarian (in fact it is far less so than most modern scientific accounts of human agency: because Edwards refused to reduce all being to material being in his doctrine of creation, he is able to separate moral

---

[46] This is not to say that we cease to be moral agents in Edwards's terms. We retain the ability to judge good and evil; we just judge wrongly, because our understanding of what is good and bad is flawed. Calvin, characteristically, puts this with considerable clarity: 'free will', he says, following Origen, is 'a faculty of the reason to distinguish between good and evil, [and] a faculty of the will to choose one or the other' (*Institutes* II.2.4), but later points out that our reason is ruined by the fall (*Institutes* II.2.12), so that 'we are not deprived of will' – we remain moral agents – 'but of soundness of will' (*Institutes* II.2.5).

[47] For the linkage of these two categories, see Edwards on *True Virtue*, in *Ethical Writings*.

[48] 'A Divine and Supernatural Light ...', in *The Works of Jonathan Edwards* vol. 2 (Edinburgh: Banner of Truth, 1974), pp. 12–17.

causes from natural or physical causes,[49] and it is precisely because I am a moral agent and not a machine that moral causes affect me; my computer has never done anything because duty, love or fear constrained it). It is, however, predestinarian: the community of moral agents in which we 'live and move and have our being' exhaustively defines each one of us. Edwards's view can be predestinarian without being fatalistic only because of the greatness of his vision of God: the Triune God is, in a sense, a part of this community but, as Edwards never tired of reminding anyone who would listen or read, he is so much greater (both in terms of naked being and in terms of virtue) than all the rest put together that he may be described as 'being-in-general' without residue. All moral causes, then, come to us in the community which God is so much the greatest part of that the rest may be discounted. Each of us is formed by the community that God orders for his good pleasure, and Edwards's view of the end towards which God orders the community of creation was constant: God is at work creating a bride to be united with his Son.

'Prevailing modern notions' of freedom are one more way human beings have attempted to live as gods. We are not gods, and so, necessarily, such notions are absurd. Their final result is alienation from society and from self, where the only escape from our angst lies in escape from reality. There are a limited number of alternatives to such views: we may believe in chance, the 'freedom' derived from quantum indeterminacy, but what freedom is that? We may believe in fate, whether it be the inevitable historical march of Marx or the genetic determination of Darwin's successors, and so become passive observers of our own actions. Or we may believe in God, who orders all things according to his infinite wisdom, and calls us, as members of the community of morally responsible creatures, to true freedom, which is found only in relationship with him. Jonathan Edwards saw these stark alternatives with more clarity than most, and sought to expose them in his book on *The Freedom of the Will*. It is a book which, precisely because of its strangeness, we need to take seriously once more today.

---

[49] Famously, Edwards developed an idealism similar to Bishop Berkeley's. There are, however, important differences, and I suspect that, in invoking some important Trinitarian categories, Edwards did more to guarantee the relative permanence given to the world by God in his gracious work of creation.

Chapter 7

Baptism: Patristic Resources for Ecumenical Dialogue

This chapter owes its origin to a theological consultation of Baptists, mostly ministers, that was held in Oxford in 1999.[1] Various papers there considered questions of Christian initiation: a particular baptismal practice is, after all, fairly central to Baptist identity. I was surprised by one facet of the discussions surrounding those papers: it appeared that, almost without exception, thoughtful Baptist pastors wanted to differentiate between those who had never been baptised and those who had received infant baptism and later confirmation. Although baptist[2] tradition (and, indeed, the Declaration of Principle of the Baptist Union of Great Britain) insists that baptism can only be administered to believers, and so suggests that whatever rites one may have undergone as an infant one remains unbaptised, there seems to be a widespread intuition that we should treat with due seriousness the consciences of those who believed themselves to be baptised.[3]

My surprise resulted from the universality of this attitude: it is my own fixed opinion, but I had supposed myself to be unusual in this. It raised again a pressing ecumenical question: how can Baptists be open and accommodating to their Christian brothers and sisters whilst remaining faithful to their own

---

[1] Some papers from this consultation were published in S. R. Holmes (ed.), *Theology in Context*, vol. 1 (Oxford: Whitley, 2000). The paper behind this chapter was read at a follow-up consultation, held in Manchester in 2001.

[2] I use the uncapitalised word in a similar, although not identical, manner to James McClendon, to indicate all those who hold to an understanding of ecclesiology and baptismal practice which would accord with traditional Baptist ideas, including, for example, Mennonites, the Churches of Christ and various new churches alongside self-identified 'Baptist' churches.

[3] In a sense, the question here is the relative importance attached to two Baptist principles; it appears that many Baptist pastors believe that respecting the conscience of those who have received infant baptism is at least as important as upholding our particular understanding of the proper mode and subjects of the sacrament.

convictions and best insights? I am committed to the idea that to be properly ecumenical is precisely to be serious and open about our own particularities, those gifts God has been pleased to entrust to our tradition until such time as his Church may again be one, whilst being open to the gifts of others, and charitable to what we see as their mistakes.

By looking back behind the debates, to a time when the Church had not divided, over baptismal practice at least, and indeed was containing within its life varying baptismal practices, it may be that resources from the tradition can be found that speak powerfully to a problem that is pressing for at least some of us in the Church today. This chapter is an attempt to uncover, and explore, such resources, and so to show how listening to the tradition can be directly relevant to the work of theology in the present. For a significant portion of the first five centuries of the Church's life varying baptismal practices, and indeed theologies, coexisted in an undivided Church. As one recent Lutheran treatment of the sacrament puts it, 'It is important to note that the ancient decision was not that the children of Christian parents *should* be baptised as infants, only that they *could* be. Many pastors of the ancient church recommended postponement, and many parents postponed.'[4] That is to say, a situation obtained whereby many pastors and people believed infant baptism to be proper, and many others believed it to be improper, but not invalid, and yet the Church (and, as far as we can tell, the churches) did not discern any need to divide over the issue.

Now, it is possible that the Fathers were suffering a simple failure of discernment: this may be an issue that should have divided the Church, but no one could see this. When we consider, however, just how widespread this peaceful coexistence was, and the calibre of the theologians who failed to challenge it (Athanasius, Basil, Chrysostom, Jerome, Augustine ...), this begins to seem unlikely. It is also the case that the present divisions are sharper than the patristic ones: most baptist Christians and churches will not allow that infant baptism is 'improper but not invalid'; rather, they insist that it is invalid.

Individual attitudes, however, as described in the anecdote with which I began, and the ecumenical practice of baptistic churches, suggest that beliefs are at some variance to confession. It is not the case that people baptised as infants are treated as if they were simply unbaptised. There may be room here for some form of ecumenical rapprochement, and the Fathers may be able to point us towards it.

---

[4] Robert W. Jenson, 'The Means of Grace: Part Two – The Sacraments', in C. E. Braaten and R. W. Jenson (eds), *Christian Dogmatics*, 2 vols (Philadelphia: Fortress Press, 1984), vol. 2, pp. 289–389, 318. Jenson cites the obvious example of Augustine.

'Patristic' covers a wide time span: my interest here is particularly in a series of debates in the fourth and fifth centuries. This was the time when infant baptism began to become normal, although there are witnesses to the practice in the earlier tradition.[5] At the same time, in both West and East, there were controversies over the status of heretical and schismatic baptism. It is a time, then, when the Church was faced with a wide variety of baptismal practice, and with hard questions about possible rebaptisms. It is the reflections of the Fathers on these themes that I wish to explore.

The *Baptismal Instructions* of St John Chrysostom[6] (given in Antioch sometime between 386 and 398) witness to the variety of baptismal practice that a single church could tolerate. Interestingly, John does not refer to two sorts of baptism, but to three: adult baptism following catechesis; infant baptism; and clinical baptism (that is, the baptism of those who are on their death beds [*klínē*]). The norm for baptism, according to John, is adult baptism at Easter following a catechetical period during Lent. 'Norm' here does not necessarily mean the most common form – John gives us no information to determine that – but the form that makes the meaning and results of baptism most clear. If we want to understand the sacrament, this is where we look; other forms are not improper, but derive their meaning from this basic form. This is clear even with regard to the timing of believers' baptism: John did not believe that there was anything magical or necessary about being baptised at Easter; in another place he points out that the apostles, the three thousand who responded to Peter's Pentecost sermon, and others in Scripture were not baptised then.[7] However, Easter is the right time to be baptised, for a series of reasons: first, Easter is the day we celebrate the victories Christ won, over the demons, sin

---

[5] Most famously, Origen's *Commentary on Romans* V. Johannes Warns has challenged the authenticity of this text (*Baptism*, G. H. Lang [tr.] [London: Paternoster, 1957], pp. 331–5). This is a fairly tendentious book, however, and I am not aware that the challenge has been taken up seriously within Origen scholarship. For a thorough account of references to baptism in the second century, see André Benoit, *Le baptême chrétien au second siècle: La théologie des pères* (Paris: Presses Universitaires de France, 1953).

[6] The texts are most conveniently available in English translation in the Ancient Christian Writers series, no. 31, *St John Chrysostom: Baptismal Instructions*, Paul W. Harkins (tr.) (London: Longman, Green, 1963). Only two of the originals appear in Migne (*Patrologia Graeca* 49, pp. 221–40); eight others can be found, with a French translation, in Antoine Wenger, *Jean Chrysostome: Huit catéchèses baptismales inédites* (Sources chrétiennes 50; Paris: 1957). The original text of the final two, according to Harkins, is to be found only in a Russian series published at the beginning of this century. For an exhaustive discussion of these texts, see Thomas M. Finn, *The Liturgy of Baptism in the Baptismal Instructions of St John Chrysostom* (Washington, DC: Catholic University of America Press, 1967), which is also the source for the date and location I indicate (p. 9).

[7] See *St John Chrysostom*, Harkins (tr.), pp. 305–6, for this quotation and a reference.

and death. It is fitting, argues John, that there are those waiting to receive a reward from the King on the day of his victory feast, and that we share in Christ's death and resurrection in baptism at the season of his death and resurrection (10.5–7). So baptism should take place at Easter not because it is wrong or ineffective at other times but because at Easter all that baptism is and does and symbolises is made most luminously clear.

So, the normal pattern of baptism in Chrysostom's day began at the beginning of Lent. It seems that this was a response to the threat to Christian values posed by the influx of the semi-converted after the Constantinian settlement.[8] Those who sought baptism would be taught the discipline required of members of the Church, and would be expected to live according to it. 'I shall say it again and again', insists Chrysostom, 'unless a man has corrected the defects of his character and has developed a faculty for virtue, let him not be baptised. For the bath can do away with sins previously committed; but there is no small fear or insignificant danger that we may fall again into the same sins ... For those who sin after baptism, the punishment is proportioned to the greatness of the grace we received in it' (12.21).

Those about to be baptised, then, must understand both the doctrines and duties of the faith. The former are summed up in the great credal points of Trinity and Incarnation (1.20–3), with particular warning against the major heresies of the day, Arianism and Sabellianism (1.22). The duties of the faith are more varied: on the negative side, John borrows lists of sins from Scripture that are to be avoided ('if one is a fornicator, or an adulterer, or effeminate, or unnatural in his lust, or has consorted with prostitutes, or is a thief, or has defrauded others, or is a drunkard, or an idolater ...' [1.25]); positively, the 'yoke of Christ' is easy and light (1.27–9), and can be summed up by meekness and humility, which is spelt out in rules concerning anger, envy, theft, unnecessary adornment and so on (1.30–8). False religious practice, endemic in the society still in the form of reading omens and similar, is nonetheless to be avoided (1.39–40), as is the lewdness of the theatre and the arena (1.43). 'Avoid, then', finishes John, 'all these wicked snares of the devil and hold nothing in greater honour than your entrance into the Church. Let us have great zeal for virtue' (1.46).

Alongside such instruction, the catechumens also underwent exorcisms. Their minds and souls are to be cleansed (2.12), and they are to be made aware of their present captivity to the devil, so that they may be more sensible of the great deliverance and salvation which baptism represents (2.14). In the rite of baptism itself they will be required by the priest first to declare, 'I renounce thee, Satan, thy pomps, thy service, and thy works' (2.20), and next, 'I enter into thy service, O Christ' (2.21). The sense of one life and one service ending

---

[8] So Finn, *The Liturgy of Baptism*, p. 44.

and of another beginning, close to the heart of the understanding of baptism here, is made very clear by these declarations, which were made at 3 p.m. on Good Friday, the hour that Christ died (11.19). The catechumens are then immediately anointed with the sign of the Cross to protect them from the devil between their renunciation of him and their baptism. The oil, says John, 'is a mixture of olive oil and unguent; the unguent is for the bride, the oil is for the athlete' (11.27).

During the Easter vigil, on the Saturday night, the candidates were anointed a second time. They were stripped of their old clothes, and covered all over with olive oil, representing the Holy Spirit under whose protection the candidates now were, and who was about to come upon them. Their old covering of sin and shame now gone, they are to enter the waters, naked and unashamed ('Do not, then, feel shame here, for the bath is much better than the garden of Paradise ...' 11.29). Chrysostom's own description of the moment of baptism is sufficiently powerful to warrant quotation:

> [T]he priest makes you go down into the sacred waters, burying the old man and at the same time raising up the new, who is renewed in the image of his Creator. It is at this moment that ... the Holy Spirit descends upon you. Instead of the man who descended into the water, a different man comes forth, one who has wiped away all the filth of his sins, who has put off the old garment of sin and has put on the royal robe ... As soon as they come forth from those sacred waters, all who are present embrace them, greet them, kiss them, rejoice with them, and congratulate them, because those who were heretofore slaves and captives have suddenly become free men and sons and have been invited to the royal table ... Since they have put on Christ Himself, wherever they go they are like angels on earth, rivaling the brilliance of the rays of the sun (2.25–7).

This, for John, is what baptism should be, but it was not always thus. Baptism provided full entry into the Church, and with it full exposure to the Church's discipline, and for some this was too much. John borrows a powerful image from boxing or wrestling matches: '[u]p to now', he says, 'you have been in a school for training and exercise' where failures were winked at and for-given. 'But from today on, the arena stands open, the contest is at hand, the spectators have taken their seats...' (3.8; the same image is repeated elsewhere, e.g. 9.28–9). He goes on to offer great encouragement: 'In the Olympic combats the judge stands impartially aloof from the combatants, favoring neither the one nor the other ... But in our combat with the devil, Christ does not stand aloof but is wholly on our side ... He anointed us as we went into the combat, but He fettered the devil ...' (3.9). Clearly, John believed that there was nothing to be feared from the conflict with the devil which began at baptism, and he went on to emphasise this point, describing all God's gifts to the Christian, and particularly the benefits of the Eucharist ('a food which is more powerful than any armour ... If you show him [the devil] a tongue stained with the precious blood, he will not be able to make a stand; if you show him your mouth all crimsoned and ruddy, cowardly beast that he is, he will run away' [3.12]). Nonetheless, even John acknowledged that the demands made upon the baptised were real, borrowing Jesus' words about the easy yoke and the light burden to protest that, though a burden, it is not onerous (9.4).

As a result of this perceived burden, the practice of delaying baptism arose. (We might draw a comparison with the class of 'hearers' in many early Baptist churches, who were a part of the congregation but did not feel able to enter into membership, and with it the church's discipline.) Baptism, however, was seen to be necessary to salvation, and so those who had delayed being baptised and were then taken seriously ill would seek emergency, or clinical, baptism before they died. John was most scathing about this practice, arguing that everything about it opposes the sacrament: what should take place in 'the bosom of the common mother of us all, the Church', takes place in a bed; it is accompanied not by rejoicing and gladness but by tears and groans (9.5). Finally, the appearance of the priest is the confirmation of impending death, and so 'he who is an argument for eternal life is seen as a symbol of death' (9.8). Despite all of this, John nonetheless recognised this as a valid baptism ('the grace is the same for you as for those who are initiated on their deathbeds' [9.5]). Importantly for what follows, it remains a valid baptism even if the candidate is unconscious and unable to make the appropriate commitments, renouncing Satan and confessing Christ (9.9).

Alongside those baptised at Easter after preparation, and those to whom clinical baptism was administered, John notes that children are also baptised: '[w]e baptise even infants' (3.6). Why so? Origen, it appears, wanted infants baptised to wash away the stain of original sin. John, by contrast, thought that children are born innocent ('free from sins'; Augustine and Julian, the Pelagian, argue over what Chrysostom meant by this in their debate on original sin),[9] but nonetheless he saw many benefits which baptism conveys apart from the forgiveness of sins:

> Before yesterday you were captives, but now you are free and citizens of the Church; lately you lived in the shame of your sins, but now you live in freedom and justice. You are not only free, but also holy; not only holy, but also just; not only just, but also sons; not only sons, but also heirs; not only heirs, but also brothers of Christ; not

---

[9] For Augustine's side of the argument, see his *Answer to Julian* I.21–8. The best current translation is found in John E. Rotelle (ed.), *The Works of St Augustine: A Translation for the 21st Century*, pt I, vol. 24: *Answer to the Pelagians II*, Roland J. Teske (tr.) (Hyde Park, New York: New City Press, 1998).

only brothers of Christ, but also joint heirs; not only joint heirs, but also members; not only members, but also the temple; not only the temple, but also instruments of the Spirit (3.5).

John saw no good reason to deny these benefits to children born within the family of faith, and so followed earlier practice in allowing them to come to baptism. They were unable to make the appropriate renunciations and confessions, but in that they did not differ from some who underwent clinical baptism, and so that could be no bar.

What is interesting here is John's theological account of the variety of practice. Baptism, for John, is understood to be the rite of entry of new (believing) converts into the Church after a period of instruction and preparation. Having understood baptism this way, however, John is prepared to admit a variety of practice into what he has understood. We might compare some current Baptist and Congregationalist thinking about ordination: ordained ministry is understood to be the ministry of Word and sacrament within the context of a local church; reflection on that role, however, allows us to regard other callings as proper to this ministry, albeit derivatively. We would not seek to understand what ministry means by looking at the role of a tutor within a theological college, or a translocal *pastor pastorum* (a Regional Minister, in British Baptist terms), but we do not deny that these are proper ways of exercising the ministry that we understand from elsewhere. Just so, John will not understand baptism by looking at infants, but having understood it as the baptism of believers, he finds room in that understanding for infants.

This analysis might give pause to controversialists on both sides of more recent debates: the paedobaptist might claim John's support for his practice, but not, surely, for his theology, which assumes the normative status of that practice. The baptist, by contrast will find in John ample support for her theology, as he could agree to the BUGB Declaration of Principle when it claims '[t]hat Christian Baptism is the immersion in water into the Name of the Father, the Son and the Holy Ghost, of those who have professed repentance towards God and faith in our Lord Jesus Christ ...' However, on the basis of precisely this understanding of baptism, John baptised infants, a practice almost any modern baptist would object to.

What resources might we find here for contemporary ecumenical dialogue, then? Firstly, and in a sense negatively, John's account of baptism should further convince those of us[10] who hold baptistic convictions that the account

---

[10] As will no doubt be clear by now, I write as a baptist Christian, indeed, as a minister accredited by the BUGB. The convictions I am discussing here are my own, and deeply held.

of baptism we hold on to is important for the Church, and so that our witness is an important one. John would teach us that if baptism is not understood through the baptism of believers, then it is simply not understood. Further, the practice of catechesis in the post-Constantinian Church witnesses to a fear that baptism in a mass Church will become detached from Christian discipleship and so meaningless, another aspect of baptist complaint against the paedo-baptist state churches that we might find surprising support for in John Chrysostom.

Secondly, however, this account should challenge the exclusive theology of baptistic Christians. John Chrysostom, it seems, believed as fervently as any baptist that 'Christian baptism is the immersion in water into the Name of the Father, the Son and the Holy Ghost, of those who have professed repentance towards God and faith in our Lord Jesus Christ', but he would not deny on that basis the possibility that those unable to profess repentance and faith (whether through age in the case of infants or infirmity in the case of clinical baptism) could not be validly baptised.

I began this chapter with an anecdote which suggests that there is some desire amongst Baptist pastors to find a way of recognising the seriousness of the faith of those who believe their infant baptism to be valid without compromising our own convictions. It may be that John offers the theological resources to do that, by showing us space within those convictions that we had not realised was there. Baptist Christians will certainly, as he did, want to hold strongly to the confession that Christian baptism is the baptism of believers; they may – I certainly would – want to speak much more strongly than he did about the failings and faults of infant baptism; but if they can acknowledge with him that there is yet room for a strange and inappropriate, but not invalid, form of the sacrament, refusing to condone the practice, but refusing to let it divide the Church either, we might have begun to heal a wound in the Body of Christ.

To do this there is a need to find a practice similar to John's clinical baptism, which allows extension of the sacrament of baptism to those unable to make the appropriate professions. Such a practice is in fact available within British Baptist life, at least: often at the Baptist Assembly, members of the Baptist Union Initiative on Learning Disabilities (BUILD) share in leading the worship. Their literature regularly offers moving accounts of the baptisms of people who are unable to make the normal professions by reason of disability. Baptists will surely want to insist that these baptisms are valid much more strongly than John was prepared to in the case of clinical baptism; in doing so, however, the same theological space is opened.

A way forward might, perhaps, be to adopt and adapt John's rhetoric concerning clinical baptism in discussing infant baptism. Baptists would then enlarge upon how the practice obscures the meaning and denies the symbolism of the sacrament; they would insist that what goes on is a travesty of true Christian baptism; rhetorically, they may even want to ask, 'what benefit does [the infant] get from his initiation?' (9.9). If, however, alongside this they are still prepared to say, as John was of a practice he objected to, 'the grace is the same for you and for those ...' (9.5), then something of value will have been accomplished.

However, it might seem that this move would involve an unacceptable sacrifice on the part of baptist Christians, as it would involve our giving up of the practice of 'rebaptism' so-called, of offering Christian baptism to those who were brought to infant baptism by their parents but who have since come to baptistic convictions. Even the World Council of Churches Lima text, *Baptism, Eucharist and Ministry*, which is everywhere so careful to view charitably the differing convictions and practices of the churches seems to lose patience with this aspect of baptist witness: '[a]s the churches come to fuller understanding ... they will want to refrain from any practice which might call into question the sacramental integrity of other churches or which might diminish the unrepeatability of the sacrament of baptism'.[11]

The question of rebaptism was a live one in the early Church as well. Various heretical and schismatic groups baptised their followers, and so the question naturally arose of what to do when someone who had undergone such a baptism sought membership of the Church. Basil of Caesarea outlines one approach in a letter to Amphilochius, dated to AD 374.[12] 'The old authorities', asserts Basil, 'decided to accept that baptism which in nowise errs from the faith.' Irregular baptisers, then, should be assigned to one of three groups: heretics, who differ from the Church on matters of faith; schismatics, who differ on matters of church order; and those who meet in irregular assemblies, as when a bishop who has been removed from his see nonetheless continues to celebrate the Eucharist. Baptism administered by the last two groups was, according to Basil, to be considered valid, whereas heretical baptism was invalid, and so those coming to the Church from heresy would need to be (re)baptised. The heretics, after all, differed 'concerning the actual faith in God' and so were baptised in a different name to that of the Triune Lord.

This all seems simple enough. The problem was in discerning to which group a sect belonged. Amphilocius has asked Basil about Montanists (here

---

[11] World Council of Churches, *Baptism, Eucharist and Ministry* (Faith and Order Paper 111, Geneva: 1982), 'Commentary' on section B13.

[12] *Letters* 188. All quotations are from the Nicene and Post-Nicene Fathers translation of Basil's works (second series, vol. VIII: *St Basil: Letters and Selected Works*, Blomfield Jackson [tr.]). An edition of the original is most conveniently found in Migne.

called Pepuzeni), pointing out that they appear to be heretics, but that Dionysius of Alexandria had apparently accepted their baptism, and about Cathari, who Basil teaches him to regard as schismatics. What is interesting about this letter, however, is the flexibility Basil is prepared to show on such questions: 'it is right to follow the custom obtaining in each region, because those, who at the time gave decision on these points, held different opinions concerning their baptism'; 'since it has seemed to some of those of Asia that, for the sake of the management of the majority, their baptism should be accepted, let it be accepted'; 'in the case of any one who has received baptism from [the Encratites],[13] we should, on his coming to the Church, baptise him. If, however, there is any likelihood of this being detrimental to general discipline, we must fall back upon custom ...'

Now, these pronouncements are not the *realpolitik* of some ecclesiastical manager who was uninterested in the theological rights and wrongs; Basil is one of the greatest theologians of the Eastern Church, and in large part responsible for the settlement of the Trinitarian controversies that was achieved at Constantinople in AD 381. In the interests of charity and the unity of the Church, however, he was prepared to take a fairly ad hoc line on questions of irregular baptisms, leading inevitably to situations where some within the Church would have been baptised twice, if strictly judged, and others not baptised at all.

A similar flexibility is found in what is perhaps the fullest single treatment of heretical baptism in Patristic literature, Augustine's *On Baptism, Against the Donatists*.[14] Augustine is (in)famous amongst baptist Christians, at least, for championing the practice of infant baptism, which he did, although mostly in order to emphasise the necessity of God's grace in salvation – a noble end, however unhappy some may feel the route.[15] In this book Augustine bears regular witness to the practice of clinical baptism,[16] and does not pause to condemn it. The omission is explicable when we note that his interest is only in using the limiting case of emergency baptism to explore precisely what is necessary for baptism, and what is achieved by it. The witness, however, only confirms the variety of practice found within the early Church, and

---

[13] A fairly imprecise term used to refer to various Docetic and Gnostic sects.

[14] Quotations are from J. R. King's translation, published in Marcus Dodds (ed.), *The Works of Aurelius Augustine, Bishop of Hippo*, vol. 3: *Writings in Connection with the Donatist Controversy* (Edinburgh: T&T Clark, 1872). A new English translation of Augustine's entire output is in process, which will probably become standard. Various Latin editions of Augustine are available; there is nothing wrong with Migne's, and it has the advantage of being found in most good libraries.

[15] See his *Answer to Julian* for many of the arguments he advances.

[16] See, for example *On Baptism, Against the Donatists* I.21.

when writing this work, before the Pelagians had questioned the reality
of original sin and so the need for God's gracious salvation, Augustine, like
John Chrysostom, accepts infant baptism without recommending it, and
sees it as a legitimate extrapolation from true baptism, rather than a self-
evident practice.[17]

In discussion with the Donatists, however, the question was only of the
rebaptism of schismatics. Following similar traditions to those to which Basil
bears testimony, the North African churches had not insisted on rebaptising
Donatists who came out of schism and into the fellowship of the Church; the
Donatists, however, insisted that there was no true baptism other than their
own, and so would rebaptise Catholic Christians who sought to join them.
Augustine goes further than Basil or the earlier traditions, and refuses to
differentiate between heretical baptism and schismatic baptism.[18] A number of
reasons are offered for this opinion, which essentially reduce to Augustine's
belief that God cannot be prevented from doing the good he desires to do in
baptism by the vain prattlings of heretics. So, for instance, Augustine regards
the attempt of the Donatists to separate themselves from the Catholic Church
as a serious sin, but refuses to accept that they succeed in the attempt ('their
party … is severed from the bond of peace and charity, but it is joined in one
baptism. And so there is one Church which alone is called Catholic; and
whenever it has anything of its own in these communions … which are
separate from itself, it is most certainly in virtue of this which is its own …'
I.14). Again, he insists that baptism belongs to Christ, and that 'evil men'
cannot seize it from him (IV.5).

What, however, of the earlier practice of the Church, to which Basil bears
witness? The Donatists had, it seems, appealed to this practice, as upheld by the
Saint and martyr Cyprian. If, after all, this was the appropriate practice, and the
Church refused to rebaptise Donatists, then the Church was acknowledging
that the Donatists were not heretics. Augustine offers a long and detailed
discussion of Cyprian's writings on the subject, beginning with an appeal to
the same variety of practice that Basil noted, and noting that Cyprian explicitly

---

[17] Augustine does offer the standard argument from circumcision in ibid., IV.31, but
the argument that follows, where he claims that both faith and baptism are necessary,
but that God in his goodness makes up the lack of baptism in the case of the penitent
thief and the lack of faith in the case of baptised infants, demonstrates that at this point at
least Augustine does not regard infant baptism as normative. It is interesting to notice,
in this connection, that, in his *Retractions*, Augustine wondered whether the thief
might not in fact have been baptised at some earlier point (II.18).

[18] He insists only that baptism is performed in the Triune name, and explicitly states
that he would accept a baptism so performed by Marcion, Valentinus, Arius or
Eunomius (ibid., III.20).

refused to break communion with anyone who differed on this point (II.3). Augustine unsurprisingly makes much of this example of 'holy humility, catholic peace, and Christian charity' (II.4).

The rights and wrongs of the case need not detain us, but there are two points in the argument of great interest. Firstly, Augustine is prepared, in Cyprian's defence, to claim that the issue might be difficult and obscure. What then should someone do, if coming from heresy to the Church? She is faced with a choice of being in danger of being unbaptised, and being in danger of being twice baptised. Augustine thinks the latter is the lesser evil, on the basis of two dominical statements: the one who has not been 'born of water and the Spirit' 'cannot enter the kingdom of God' (Jn 3:5); to Peter Jesus says, 'whoever has been washed has no need of a second washing' (at least in the Vulgate version of Jn 13:10: *qui lotus est, non indiget ut lavet*); the former is a grave danger, the latter merely unnecessary (*On Baptism* II.19). So, Augustine thinks that there have been those in the Church who were twice-baptised, and is fairly sanguine about it, just as Cyprian was about the thought that there might be some unbaptised in the Church. The mercy of God and the unity of the Church will triumph in either case (II.19–20).

Secondly, this stress on the unity of the Church comes through even more strongly towards the end of Augustine's argument, where he again follows Cyprian in believing that charity, maintaining the bond of peace in the Church, is more important than even the baptismal status of some of the Church's members, priests and bishops. Rebaptism, for Augustine, is only a serious matter if it is done with the intention of creating schism; the bond of unity and charity that marks Christ's Church can cover over improper practices, provided they do not serve to sever it (V.2–3).

There are two areas, I think, where all this witness to the confused and messy nature of baptismal practice in the tradition might be of help to us in modern ecumenical debates. Firstly, and less importantly, Basil and Augustine might teach us very simply not to worry too much about our disagreements: both (Basil implicitly and Augustine explicitly) accepted fairly readily that within their churches there would be those who had been baptised more than once and those who had not been baptised at all. Neither course was a good idea, naturally, but neither was anything to worry unduly about either. I stress again, these are not ecclesiastical administrators anxious to preserve the peace at any cost, and entirely unaware of the theological significance of the sacraments; they are amongst the greatest theologians of the Eastern and Western churches, respectively. Both, clearly, believed in the importance of right baptismal practice: that is why they took the time to write about it (in Augustine's case, at some length). Neither, however, and crucially, thought that this was the most important thing. If the unity and good order of the Church is best served by trusting that irregularities in this area will be forgiven by God, then so be it – only preserve the bond of love.

Which raises the second, and much more important, point: the unity of the Church, like the unity of our Triune Lord, is fundamentally and irreducibly a unity of love, not of shared sacrament. *Pace* the Lima text, which seems to link the oneness and catholicity of the Church with baptismal unity (B6), the Church was once and may again be one and catholic without agreement on the proper administration of baptism, containing within it some whom some of its members believe to be unbaptised (so Cyprian of schismatics received without rebaptism) and some whom some of its members believe to be twice-baptised (so Augustine of those Cyprian rebaptised), if only these divisions are covered by mutual charity and a commitment to unity. For Augustine, the sin of schism, the refusal to live in charity with fellow-Christians, is so great a failing that he would rather people were idolaters (II.9); he even says at one point, 'on the question of whether we ought to prefer a Catholic of the most abandoned character to a heretic in whose life, except that he is a heretic, men can find nothing to blame, I do not venture to give a hasty judgement' (IV.27), so serious is the guilt of failing to love.

In identifying Church unity with a particular form of sacramental unity the Lima text went beyond the testimonies of the Fathers. Rather, for Augustine and Basil, sacramental unity is to be preserved, even in the face of grave difficulties, only because there is a prior and underlying unity of charity. This insight, borrowed from Augustine particularly, surely may help us to move forward in ecumenical debate. I conclude with some practical suggestions as to how it might:

1. We must accept that a variety of baptismal practice is not an insuperable bar to Church unity, provided we respond to each other in charity. That charity will even involve us accepting that dearly held positions concerning the right ordering of the Church must be – not discarded, but constantly regarded as secondary to the demand to love.
2. Following Augustine, Basil and Cyprian, we ought even to accept that baptismal practices we consider to be deeply irregular – a refusal to be baptised 'properly', or an act of rebaptism – should not be a bar to charity, unity and communion, provided always they are not done with any intention of promoting schism.
3. This might involve Baptists, for the sake of charity, choosing not to query the baptismal status of those who have undergone infant baptism. Equally, it might involve others accepting the conscientious decision to seek rebaptism of one they consider baptised, and the conscientious decision of certain ministers to perform the rite.

Once again, let me stress that these suggestions are not made on the basis of any belief that baptismal theology or practice is not important, but out of the belief that there is something yet more important. That the foundation of the (local) church is Christian love and fellowship is a baptist belief; that the fundamental nature of God is loving fellowship is a Christian dogma; that, then, the relationships of Christians together throughout the world should be fundamentally marked by the same distinctive is surely not a difficult point, but it is one that, if taken seriously, might enable us to find ways to break through unfortunate polarisations in our discussions about baptism with our Christian brothers and sisters.

Chapter 8

Karl Barth's Doctrine of Reprobation

The doctrine of election that occupies the first five hundred or so pages of *Church Dogmatics* volume II.2 (hereafter *C.D.* II.2)[1] has been more generally noticed than much else in that massive work,[2] and is widely regarded as both original and successful – a rare combination, perhaps, in theological work. I want to argue three theses in connection with that discussion in this chapter: first, that a crucial distinction between Barth's account and that of the earlier Reformed tradition is that Barth has a doctrine of reprobation, whereas the tradition did not; second, and similarly, that as a consequence of this Barth teaches a symmetrical double decree, whereas the Reformed tradition could not;[3] and third, that the perceived success of Barth's account of election has much to do with these two points.

To argue these theses I am not going to talk very much about Barth; rather, I want to attempt to tell a historical story which will illuminate what is distinctive about Barth's doctrine, and so enable us to draw some theological conclusions.[4] As in Chapter 5, this is an exercise in tracing lines of argument

---

[1] I am using the English translation of Barth's *Church Dogmatics*, G. W. Bromiley and T. F. Torrance (trs and eds) (Edinburgh: T&T Clark, 1956–77).

[2] So, for instance, Hans Urs von Balthasar suggests that this doctrine 'promises to give us the key to Barth's entire theology' (*The Theology of Karl Barth: Exposition and Interpretation*, Edward T. Oakes [tr.] [San Francisco: Ignatius Press, 1992], p. 173). Colin Gunton says that the 'way in which the old ... doctrine of predestination is changed' is 'at the heart' of Barth's project (see his preface to John E. Colwell, *Actuality and Provisionality: Eternity and Election in the Theology of Karl Barth* [Edinburgh: Rutherford House, 1989], p. 1). Geoffrey Bromiley asserts that 'in these chapters [on election and the command of God] he establishes in God the foundation of his later volumes ...' (*An Introduction to the Theology of Karl Barth* [Edinburgh: T&T Clark, 1979], p. 84).

[3] I am grateful to Colin Gunton for the fine formulation of this point, although the development that follows is mine.

[4] This chapter is thus an expansion of a theme I first discussed in the final chapter of my *God of Grace*.

and descent through the tradition in order to test modern accounts of what was going on; here I want to also suggest that what we hear when we listen in this way may speak powerfully to modern problems. More of that later, however, the listening must come first.

Let me start with the position I am arguing against. The adjective that has become almost clichéd when Barth's doctrine of election is mentioned is 'christological',[5] and it seems widely assumed that, whatever else might be argued about Barth's account of reprobation, this is unquestionably the decisive factor in the development of the doctrine of election in *C.D.* II/2. Everybody, surely, by now, knows that, prior to Barth, Reformed theologians had always taught an abstract, hidden symmetrical double decree of election and reprobation, and that Barth, by talking about election only in the context of Jesus Christ, made the whole doctrine Christian. There is only one problem with this: it is not true – it may be, I think is, accurate in what is said about Barth, but with regard to the tradition it is simply wrong, or so I hope to argue here.

There is, I think, a broadly coherent tradition of Reformed theology in the area of predestination – when, early in the twentieth century, Lorraine Boettner wrote a book under the title *The Reformed Doctrine of Predestination*,[6] the criticisms, even from Barth, with his encyclopedic knowledge of the Reformed tradition, were directed at the content, not the assumption that Reformed accounts could be presented in such a monolithic way.[7] There is also, it seems, now a broad agreement that this tradition does not work. Criticism is common enough within the tradition, whether the complaints come from the Remonstrants, Amyrauldians, eighteenth-century Arminian evangelicals or nineteenth-century liberals. The welcome given to Barth's recasting of the doctrine, however, suggests that these various attacks on a still-orthodox position have been replaced by a near-universal rejection of this way of formulating the doctrine, amongst mainstream theologians at any rate. Whilst particular groups still defend five-point Calvinism, there is wide agreement that what Boettner called 'The' Reformed doctrine is unsatisfactory. Where there is less agreement is in the nature of the problem.

---

[5] 'The flaw in most of the previous doctrines of election was a failure to contextualise election as part of God's relationship to Christ. Previous theologians misconstrued the chistological basis …' von Balthasar, *The Theology of Karl Barth*, p.175. See also Bruce McCormack's discussions of the development of Barth's 'christocentrism' in the context of the doctrine of election: *Karl Barth's Critically Realistic Dialectical Theology: Its Genesis and Development 1909–1936* (Oxford: Clarendon Press, 1997), pp. 453–63.

[6] Presbyterian and Reformed, 1968 (14th printing; originally issued 1932).

[7] For Barth's criticisms see *C.D.* II/2, pp. 13, 36–8.

Barth and a series of scholars broadly following his critique have focused on Christological issues, claiming that the Decree ousts Christ from his rightful place as the index of all God's acts. Barth made this criticism of Calvin, as well as the tradition that followed him;[8] later scholarship has tended to revise this judgement by suggesting that Calvin was appropriately Christological, but that the tradition went wrong soon afterwards – Beza often being blamed.[9] Although it has been done before, it will be instructive to review, very briefly, a response to this charge as levelled against Calvin.[10]

The standard criticism of Calvin concerns the 'hidden decree'; if this stands, then there is no assurance in Calvin's account – election and rejection are alike secret decisions of God, and I cannot know which applies to me. Certainly the idea that election belongs to the eternal, secret, absolute will of God is a leitmotiv in Calvin's account; the question remains, however, whether this eternal, secret and absolute will can be revealed. The placement of the doctrine under the work of Christ, and the Christological focus of Calvin's understanding of revelation, suggest that this may be the case. Further, if, as seems clear from the text,[11] Calvin's aim in treating election is to give assurance to believers, then, making the assumption that he was not blind to the most glaring contradictions in his own theology, it seems likely that this will is indeed revealed.

---

[8] 'All the dubious features of Calvin's doctrine result from the basic failing that in the last analysis he separates God and Jesus Christ ...' *C.D.* II/2, p. 111.

[9] So, for instance: James Torrance, in a series of articles on federal theology in the *Scottish Journal of Theology*; Basil Hall, 'Calvin against the Calvinists', in G. Duffield (ed.), *John Calvin: A Collection of Distinguished Essays* (Grand Rapids, Michigan: Eerdmans, 1966), pp. 19–37; Kendall, *Calvin and English Calvinism to 1649*. These examples could be multiplied.

[10] Many studies of Calvin's understanding of predestination have appeared – indeed, a disproportionate number, related to the importance of the doctrine in his own theology, if not in relation to that of those who followed him. Those I have found most instructive include: R. A. Muller, *Christ and the Decree: Christology and Predestination in Reformed Theology from Calvin to Perkins* (Grand Rapids, Michigan: Baker, 1986²); Wilhelm Niesel, *The Theology of Calvin*, Harold Knight (tr.) (London: Lutterworth Press, 1956); J. K. S. Reid, 'The Office of Christ in Predestination' *Scottish Journal of Theology* 1 (1948), pp. 5–19, 166–83; F. Wendel, *Calvin: The Origin and Development of His Religious Thought*, Philip Mairet (tr.) (London: Collins, 1963). In addition, Barth's interactions with any scholar in history are instructive, and he carries out a long and rich (if slightly misconstrued, in my opinion) dialogue with Calvin throughout *C.D.* II/2.

[11] See particularly *Institutes* III.21.1, III.24.4; I am using an English translation, vol. XX of the Library of Christian Classics series, John Baillie, John T. McNeill and Henry P. van Dusen (eds), 2 vols, F. L. Battles (tr.) J. T. McNeill (ed.) (Philadelphia: Westminster Press, 1960).

All revelation, for Calvin, is revelation of the Word, Jesus Christ, who is with God and is God (I.13.7, echoing John 1). Thus, for Calvin as for Barth,[12] revelation is God revealing himself by means of himself. 'For this purpose the Father laid up with his only-begotten Son *all that he had* to reveal himself in Christ so that Christ ... might express the true image of his glory' (III.2.1, my emphasis). There is nothing of God that is not in Jesus Christ.[13] This gives content and force to Calvin's repeated insistence that we look to Christ for assurance of our election: 'If we have been chosen in him, we shall not find assurance of our election in ourselves; and not even in God the Father, if we conceive of him as severed from his Son. Christ, then, is the mirror where we must, and without self-deception may, contemplate our own election' (III.24.5).

Election, for Calvin, is in Christ, and known only in Christ. Calvin goes further than this, however: in III.22.7, Christ is called the *auctor electionis*. *Auctor* (the word carries such senses as 'creator', 'maker' and 'founder', not just 'author') implies that Christ for Calvin is something more than the decree, not less, as his critics imply. In this same section Christ is represented as claiming, with the Father, 'the right to choose'. Christ is the source of the decree, not just its channel, the one who elects elects himself to be the means by which others are elected. Calvin does not spell this out, and so perhaps leaves himself open to misunderstanding, but the conception is nevertheless there.

Given this, I would contend that the standard criticism of Calvin's account, that the decree of election is separated from Christ and so hidden, is unfair. Calvin is straining hard to offer as clear a view as he is able of the certainty of perseverance and final salvation for all who have come to Christ in faith. It is not the case, if one pays careful attention to what Calvin has to say about election, that it is in any way separated from Christology.

However, as I indicated earlier, the standard form of the criticism now accepts that this is true of Calvin, but asserts that the tradition went wrong in this area soon afterwards. Calvin might have been appropriately Christological, but those who followed him were not. Under Beza's influence, a hard system with predestination placed and the head and Christ subordinated to this decree grew up, which infected all Reformed theology of the scholastic period. Barth sets us free from this, and opens our eyes to see that it was never meant to be like this in the *Institutes*, and so, after burning Beza in effigy, we are able to return *ad fontes*, to recover those in the tradition who saw through all this, like John McLeod Campbell, and so to attain the promised land. It is an

---

[12] *C.D.* I/1, pp. 295–347.

[13] Calvin's statement (at least) of the *extra calvinisticum* is clear in asserting that there is nothing of the Son that is not incarnate, although the Son cannot be limited to the humanity of the incarnation. See *Institutes* II.13.4.

attractive and plausible reconstruction of the history. Once again, however, it will not stand up to examination.

Richard Muller's textual scholarship, at least, is always impressive, and in an early but still significant book he traces the connections between Christology and the decree of election in the development of Reformed theology after Calvin.[14] After detailed attention to the writings of Bullinger, Musculus, Vermigli, Beza, Ursinus, Zanchi, Polanus and William Perkins, he finds no evidence of a separation of Christ from the decree of election, or of a subordination of Christ to the decree of election, in any of them, and sums up as follows: 'the concept of "Jesus Christ electing and elected" which overcomes the threat of a *deus nudus absconditus* appears not as a theme barely hinted at but as a fundamental interest, indeed, as a norm for early orthodoxy'.[15] He also indicates, in passing, that at least four accounts of Reformed theology from the first half of the seventeenth century, including the important Leiden Synopsis, chose to locate the doctrine of predestination under the head of Christology, which makes it rather difficult to accept that there was either a separation between Christology and election or a subordination of Christology to election.

Until Muller's work is challenged by someone with an equally impressive grasp of the textual evidence, I think we must say that we cannot assert that there was any widespread failure to be appropriately Christological in discussing predestination before about 1650. This, however, offers a further suggestion: in at least some forms of the complaint, it is the federal theology that is accused of this failing, particularly as represented by the Westminster Confession, and this theology was developed by the work of William Ames and Johannes Cocceius at around that time.[16] Is there a movement to separate the decree from the person of Christ there?

Well, I am unfamiliar with the work of Cocceius, but in his *Marrow of Theology* Ames treats predestination under the heading of 'The Application of Christ', which is asserted to be 'the making effectual, in certain men, of all those things which Christ has done and does as mediator'.[17] In discussing the decree itself, Ames will assert 'God made only one election in Christ,

---

[14] Muller, *Christ and the Decree.*

[15] Ibid., p.173.

[16] For this form of the criticism see two papers by James Torrance: 'Covenant or Contract? A Study of the Theological Background of Worship in Seventeenth Century Scotland', *Scottish Journal of Theology* 23 (1970), pp. 51–76; and 'The Contribution of McLeod Campbell to Scottish Theology', *Scottish Journal of Theology* 26 (1973), pp. 295–311. Also M. Charles Bell, *Calvin and the Scottish Theology: The Doctrine of Assurance* (Edinburgh: Handsel, 1985).

[17] I.xxiv.1; p. 149 of Eusden's translation of Ames's, *The Marrow of Theology.*

mystically considered, i.e. pertaining to Christ and those who are in Christ ...
Yet a certain distinction may be made according to reason whereby Christ may
be considered as first elected as head and then some men as members in him,
Eph. 1:4.'[18] He goes on to distinguish ways in which Christ is properly said to
be the object of election and ways in which he is properly said to be its subject
or 'cause'.[19] There is hardly a radical separation of the decree from Christ here;
it may be that, in the development of these themes, Ames introduces or
assumes a position which fundamentally undermines his more basic assumptions, but, until that is demonstrated, Ames must be seen as following the best
instincts of the earlier tradition.

What about the Westminster Confession? Well, my first comment is a
point about placement: if we start reading at Chapter 3, 'Of God's Eternal
Decree', we might, for a moment or two at least, think that here we are talking
about some putative God who is separate from Christ. Reading the work
through, however, from the last paragraph of Chapter 2, we read this:

> In the unity of the Godhead there be three persons, of one substance, power and
> eternity; God the Father, God the Son, and God the Holy Ghost. The Father is of
> none, neither begotten, nor proceeding: the Son is eternally begotten of the Father:
> the Holy Ghost eternally proceeding from the Father and the Son.

> [Chapter 3] God from all eternity did ... freely and unchangeably ordain whatever
> comes to pass ...[20]

It does not seem to me that the Assembly could have made it much clearer that
they believed the God who decreed all things to be Father, Son and Holy
Spirit. Further, when the Confession turns to the decree of election, there are
four sentences, and four times in them election is said to be either 'in Christ' or
'by Christ'.

For the first century or more of the Reformed tradition, then, the charge
that there is a fundamental separation of the decree of election from the Person
of Christ within that tradition seems to be unfair. There are still, however, the
great systems of the end of the sixteenth and beginning of the seventeenth
centuries; these represent the high point of orthodoxy, and if the tradition fails
here, then there may be said to be some truth in the charge.

The most accessible of these systems, because in English translation, is
Turretin's *Institutes of Elenctic Theology*,[21] and here it seems is the first hint of

---

[18] Ibid., I.xxv.27; p. 155.

[19] Ibid., I.xxv.29; p. 155.

[20] I am using the Free Presbyterian Press edition: *The Westminster Confession of Faith*
(Glasgow: Free Presbyterian Press, 1994²).

[21] Turretin, *Institutes of Elenctic Theology*, Dennison (ed.).

success: Turretin asks, 'Is Christ the cause and foundation of election?' and replies, 'We deny, against the Arminians and Lutherans.'[22] However, when we read his explanation of what he means by this assertion, he explicitly teaches that the eternal Word is the efficient cause of election, and that the Incarnate One is the head and sum of election, and indeed its 'objective and meritous cause'; what he is denying is that the sending of Christ is the cause, rather than the result, of the triune God's love to the elect.[23] Again, when expounding Ephesians 1:4, 'God chose us in Christ', Turretin denies that this text can be taken to mean 'chosen by Christ (as God)', asserting 'although it is not to be denied that Christ, as God, is the author of our election, yet it ... cannot be so understood in this place'. Rather, this text must simply mean that election too is a benefit given to us as those redeemed by, and incorporated into, Christ.[24] I might finally note that in another of the great systems of the period, Petrus van Mastricht chooses this key text from Ephesians as the one he will expound in offering a doctrine of election, and asserts as a result that the object of election was *totus Christus mysticus* – Christ, together with all who are elect in Him.[25]

In the middle of the nineteenth century, when the Reformed Orthodox tradition had proved unable to cope with new ways of thinking, Heinrich Heppe wrote one of those magisterial compendia which that century was so good at producing. By means of extensive quotation, he sought to sum up the teaching of the entire Reformed tradition. Concerning election, he said this: 'Of course the person of Christ is the foundation of election. To a certain extent he is the sole object of it...'[26] The Reformed Orthodox doctrine of election simply cannot be accused of a failure to be Christological; I could have presented much more evidence than I have, but even what is here is, I suggest, overwhelming.

We are, however, left with a problem: almost every serious theological commentator on Barth's doctrine of election has asserted that there is something satisfying and convincing here that is lacking in the tradition; if it is not its Christological nature, what is it? There are several other features of Barth's doctrine of election that are also more or less novel, and so are candidates: the placement of the doctrine, as a part of the doctrine of God, is something new;[27]

---

[22] Ibid., IV.x.

[23] Ibid., IV.x.16, for an explicit statement of this.

[24] Ibid., IV.ix.16.

[25] *Theoretica Practica Theologica* III.3.8; see also Barth, *C.D.* II/2, p. 114.

[26] Heppe, *Reformed Dogmatics*, p. 168.

[27] This is a place where Barth was conscious of innovation; see *C.D.* II/2, pp. 76–93, and also Colin Gunton 'Karl Barth's Doctrine of Election as Part of His Doctrine of God', *Journal of Theological Studies* (new series) 25 (1974), pp. 381–92, for a discussion of the implications of this move.

so also is the particular account of eternity that is at work, enabling a move away from visions of decrees enacted before the beginning of the ages;[28] the account of the nature of the elect community, and particularly the place of Israel, is something new, made more powerful when we notice that the date on Barth's preface is 1942. It would no doubt be both profitable and interesting to explore each of these features, but there is not room here, so I will merely give a reason to look beyond these different places for the complete answer, to the doctrine of reprobation.

Barth's great concern in treating the doctrine of election is that it should be gospel – good news. He begins with the programmatic assertion 'The doctrine of election is the sum of the Gospel because of all words that can be said or heard it is the best ...'[29] Given this, a rapid way to an idea, at least, of what separated Barth from the Reformed tradition might be attained by asking what prevented previous Reformed accounts from fulfilling this laudable aim. Why, for instance, did Calvin's presentation of election, certainly intended to offer assurance of salvation to worried believers, not succeed?

Well, the point at which Calvin appears to engage in special pleading in his attempt to give assurance to believers is when he speaks of 'temporary faith' (III.24.7–9). Those with this 'temporary faith', according to Calvin, 'never cleaved to Christ with the heartfelt trust in which the certainty of election has, I say, been established for us'. They may indeed 'have signs of a call that are similar to those of the elect', but lack 'the sure establishment of election' (III.24.7). Such phrases achieve the very opposite of their intention, however, suggesting that there is something that masquerades as true faith, but is not. How can any believer know whether he or she feels a 'sure establishment' or whether it is merely 'signs of a call similar to those of the elect'? The invitation for years of morbid introspection by later believers is surely here – at this point, with these phrases in my ears, that I cannot be sure of my own salvation. There is no assurance, and so the doctrine fails to be gospel, instead informing me that there is a way of being, indistinguishable (to those living it at least) from Christian being, which is nonetheless supremely dangerous. The weakness in Calvin's account of predestination, I suggest, is that the doctrine of reprobation is detached, Christless and hidden in the unsearchable purposes of God. As such it bears no comparison with the doctrine of election, but remains something less than a Christian doctrine. There is, in Calvin's account, a fundamental difference between election and reprobation. Contra

---

[28] John Colwell has pointed out the full importance of this in his book on the subject, *Actuality and Provisionality*, and a paper, 'The Contemporaneity of the Divine Decision', in N. M. de S. Cameron (ed.), *Universalism and the Doctrine of Hell: Papers Presented at the Fourth Edinburgh Conference in Christian Dogmatics* (Exeter: Paternoster, 1991).

[29] *C.D.* II/2, p. 3.

Barth, Calvin's failure is not that he teaches a symmetrical double decree
(Barth speaks of 'the classical doctrine with its opposing categories of "elect"
and "reprobate"'),[30] but that he has almost no room for the doctrine of reprobation in his account.

This difference, this asymmetry, is 'a very amiable fault'; it gives insight into
Calvin the pastor, whose heart and mind were full of the glories of God's gift of
salvation in Christ – so different from the caricature so often painted. Calvin's
doctrine fails not because of a double decree, because the 'No' is equal to the
'Yes', but because the 'No' does not really enter his thinking. It is a logical
result of the 'Yes', and necessary for the 'Yes' truly to be 'Yes', but, whereas
election is bound up in his theology, it is the very fact that he is seemingly not
interested in reprobation, that he has not brought it within the Trinitarian
scope of his system, that makes it such a weak point. That is to say, Calvin's
doctrine fails to be gospel, is not 'of all words … the best', because he gives no
doctrinal content to his account of reprobation and hence has no meaningful
symmetry between the two decrees.

How does this square with Barth's own estimates of where he departed
from the tradition? A cursory glance at *C.D.* II.2 will discover that Barth
regarded a failure of the tradition to be appropriately Christological as the
issue. The opening pages of that volume assert in ringing tones that theology
must begin and end with the name of Jesus Christ if it is to avoid the error of
replacing the knowledge of God with a human construct or reflection. When
we turn to the section on the 'foundation of the doctrine', the criticism of
the tradition there given is summed up in a series of questions: 'Is it the intention of these thinkers that serious theological attention should be paid to the
assertion that election is to be known in Jesus Christ? Does this assertion
contain the first and last word on this matter, the word by which we must hold
conclusively, and beyond which we must not conceive of any further word?
Is it a fact that there is no other basis of election outside Jesus Christ?'[31] Equally,
the section 'Jesus Christ, Electing and Elected' is shot through with the
assertion that a *decretum absolutum* had taken the place of Jesus Christ in almost
every theological account of the doctrine that had been offered in history.[32]

Should we then suppose that Barth was ignorant of the historical data I have
just sketched, and was in fact, without realising it, reproducing traditional
positions? This would not answer the case, as I am exploring the claim that
Barth's doctrine is theologically satisfying in ways that the older dogmatics
were not: but in any case it is not remotely true. Barth was well aware of the
history, knew the assertions and theological employments of Christological

---

[30] Ibid., p. 326.
[31] Ibid., p. 63.
[32] Ibid., pp. 94–145.

election in the tradition and even applauded them in the course of his account.[33] Is there, then, some nuance, some new way of being Christological here that somehow makes all the difference?

Well, not quite: the issue here is one of linguistic confusion. When Barth speaks of election, he is speaking of the totality of the decree of God; when the tradition spoke of election, it spoke more or less universally (from Augustine down) of one side of God's decree, whilst denying, ignoring, or treating differently the other side. Hence, all my arguments about Christological accounts of election in the tradition offer no comment on reprobation, and there, like Calvin, the tradition constantly refused to speak of Christ's presence and work.

For an example of this, one might look to the 'Survey or Table declaring the order of the causes of salvation and damnation' from William Perkins's *Golden Chaine*,[34] which closely follows Beza's similar diagram in his *Summa Totius Christianismi*.[35] Notice first of all that 'The love of God to the elect in Christ' is parallel to 'God's hating of the reprobate' – i.e. election is Christocentric in a way that reprobation is not. This theme continues, as the white line showing the course of election includes 'Christ, the Mediatour [*sic*] of the Elect', whereas the black line, showing the causes of damnation bypasses him, and, most strikingly, in the 'lines A A A', which, Perkins says, show how faith apprehends Christ and his benefits, which have no parallel on the side of reprobation. In these lines, twenty-six different theological connections are traced between the work of Christ and the application of election. There are no connections at all with the reprobate.

Perkins certainly places God, Father, Son and Holy Spirit at the top of his chart. He is orthodox in his theology. The time of Christ's incarnation, however, from his mediatorship to his ascension and heavenly intercession, is only connected to the elect, not to the reprobate. With a doctrine of revelation that focuses on the Israelite man Jesus Christ as the revealer of God, this scheme inevitably removes the possibility of doing any Christian theology about the course and nature of reprobation.

Barth, then, I suggest, differs from the tradition in having a Christological doctrine of reprobation, in refusing to speak of God's 'No' apart from the

---

[33] Ibid., pp. 60–3. Notice particularly '... the Church and theology have always kept before their eyes certain utterances in the New Testament witness which reminded them clearly enough, and not altogether ineffectively, that knowledge of election is only a distinctive form of the knowledge of Jesus Christ' (p. 60).

[34] William Perkins, *A Golden Chaine*, in *Works*, vol. 1 (Cambridge, 1612), pp. 9–114, conveniently reproduced in E. Kevan, *The Grace of Law* (Grand Rapids, Michigan: Baker, 1976).

[35] Theodore Beza, *Summa Totius Christianismi*, in *Tractationum Theologicarum* (Secunda Aeditio) (Anchora: Eustathii Vignon, 1576), pp. 170–205. The table is on p. 170.

name of Jesus Christ. This is not, as I have indicated, the only difference, but I suggest it is an important one. I want now, fairly briefly, to offer an exposition of Barth's account of reprobation, and indicate the theological implications of it.

Famously, Barth will discuss the election of particular human beings only after considering the particular Israelite Jesus Christ as both electing and elected, and considering the election of the community in its twofold form, Israel and the Church. In willing to be gracious in the particular way God in fact wills to be gracious, the Incarnation of the Divine Son, there is both a 'Yes' and a 'No', election and reprobation.[36] God elects for humanity life, salvation, forgiveness, hope; for himself he elects death, perdition, even, as the Creed has said, hell.[37] This self-reprobation of God is indeed the primary referent of the doctrine of election, in that God's determination of himself is formally if not materially more basic than his determination of the creature, and so is considered first by Barth. In the eternal election of grace, which is to say in Jesus Christ, God surrenders his own impassibility, embraces the darkness that he was without – and indeed impervious to – until he willed that it should be otherwise. 'He declared Himself guilty of the contradiction against Himself in which man was involved ... He made Himself the object of the wrath and judgement to which man had brought himself ... He took upon Himself the rejection which man had deserved.'[38] So says Barth. The apostle put it more succinctly: 'He became sin for us.'[39] This is the full content of the divine judgement, of the 'No' that is spoken over the evil of the world and of human beings. God elects for himself the consequences of that 'No', in saying 'Yes' to, that is, in electing, us. That is the whole content of the double decree, the whole content of the 'Yes' and the 'No' that God pronounces as one word, the whole content the election of grace.

What of our election? We are elected 'in him', but not immediately. Our election in Christ is mediated by the elect community. There is here a high ecclesiology: the Church is not the *post factum* conglomeration – or even communion – of those who have been elected in Christ; rather, there is a historical community which forms the context for the particular environment of Jesus Christ, and as such is called to witness to him. Just as the single election of Jesus Christ has a twofold form, a 'Yes' and a 'No', so the single elect community presents a double aspect. Jesus Christ is both the Messiah of Israel

---

[36] *C.D.* II/2, p. 161.

[37] Ibid., p. 163. The comment concerning the creed is my own, but Barth will speak of hell in this connection on p. 164.

[38] Ibid., p. 164.

[39] 2 Corinthians 5:21.

and the Lord of the Church,[40] thus the elect community, the body of Christ, is both Israel, which handed over its Messiah to the Gentiles to be crucified, and the Church, which received its risen Lord from the dead. In the one aspect the single elect community thus witnesses to human rejection of God's election, and in its other aspect it witnesses to God's rejection of this human rejection, to God's election of humanity.[41] The one aspect is the community in its passing form, the other the community in its coming form. Israel and the Church are until the eschaton bound together in the one community which exists between these two poles, witnessing to the world both the state of human disobedience and the divine mercy which refuses to accept that state.

Finally, Barth will turn to the election of the individual, although when he does it is with two hundred pages of treatment, indicating that he is hardly neglecting the subject.[42] What place for reprobation here? The gospel pronounces that each human person is elect in that Christ has born his or her merited rejection. Those who do not receive this promised election, and so seek to live as if they were rejected by God, do so in spite of God's election, in spite of Jesus Christ, and cannot thereby annul it, or separate themselves from him.[43] Again, there is one decree, one Lord Jesus Christ, in a double aspect: on the one hand, those who hold to the promise that he has borne their deserved rejection, that they are elect in him; and on the other hand those who seek to live as if they were not elected but rather rejected, and so join themselves to him, because he has borne all rejection. Both elect and rejected individuals must be seen in Jesus Christ.[44]

The central scriptural example of the determination of the rejected, according to Barth, is Judas Iscariot.[45] He is found in the 'closest conceivable proximity' to Jesus Christ, not the representative of an evil world in which the Church is called to make its home, but as one of the apostles. As one who lives as if he were rejected, he cannot avoid his apostolic ministry, but fulfils it in spite of himself – he, too, 'hands over' Jesus to the Jews and Gentiles, just as the apostles are called to 'hand over' Jesus to all nations in word and sacrament. Jesus could not have fulfilled his ministry without being 'handed over' by Judas; his actions are an integral part of the gospel story. To the end, however, even in the gifts of bread and wine, Jesus is for Judas, although Judas is against Jesus. Although he decides to live as one rejected, he does not thereby nullify his own election. The Scripture will only speak of 'the place prepared for him',

---

[40] *C.D.* II/2, p. 198.

[41] Ibid., pp. 198–200.

[42] Ibid., pp. 306–506.

[43] Ibid., pp. 317–22.

[44] Ibid., pp. 351–4.

[45] Ibid., pp. 458–506.

indicating by the passive that even his fate is not his own to choose, but remains in the hands of the electing God.

This, in too-concise summary, is Barth's doctrine of reprobation. I can now, I think, assert two of the theses with which I began: Calvin, and the tradition that came after him, had almost nothing theological to say about the reprobate; Barth, by contrast offers a long and richly theological account of God's 'No' as it is pronounced in Jesus Christ. Is it not then fair to say that, in contrast to Calvin and the tradition, Barth had a doctrine of reprobation? Again, I have already described the asymmetry in Calvin's account, and shown the asymmetric picture drawn by Beza and Perkins; Barth's constant stress on the single decree of election, with its two sides, is much easier to describe as a 'symmetrical double decree' than what had gone before, as indeed Barth himself notes.[46]

My final thesis concerned the significance of this move. I have already indicated that central to Barth's concerns here is the desire for the doctrine of election to be truly gospel, of all words the best. I have also argued that Calvin's failure to have any significant doctrine of reprobation is the reason for the failure of his doctrine in this area to be gospel, as he, too, desired it to be. Here is the first consequence of Barth's doctrine of reprobation: it allows the doctrine of election to be truly gospel in a way it could not be without such a doctrine. In saying this I am, of course, agreeing with the majority line: Barth's great insight in his doctrine of election was to replace the *decretum absolutum* of the tradition with the name of Jesus Christ. However, I do not think it has been sufficiently recognised that this is only decisively innovative with regard to reprobation; in the case of election it merely sets on a sounder systematic base the things the tradition had always been trying to say. Thus I reassert my starting point: Barth's account of election is more theologically satisfying than the tradition in large measure because he knew how to theologise about the 'No' that God pronounces.

What are the consequences of this? Two in particular seem important. First, if truth is finally found only in Jesus Christ, then to speak of human being outside the Church – not just the particular issue of reprobation, but any attempt to describe human cultural endeavour, human political realities, human family life, even, in their sinful aspects at least – will be severely curtailed by a failure to link such being to the name of Jesus Christ in theologically powerful ways. Second, if we wish to speak of the possibility of the final destiny of some men and women being the experience of God's severity – if, that is, we still wish to speak of hell – then here too we can only do so in

---

[46] Ibid., p. 161. Pierre Maury's paper at the 1936 Calvinist conference in Geneva that was so formative for Barth's account of election had made this point. See McCormack, *Karl Barth's Critically Realistic Dialectical Theology*, pp. 456–8.

theologically interesting ways if we are able to speak of this reality also in connection with Jesus Christ.

The witness of the Christian tradition concerning the reality of hell (understood as the possibility, at least, that some people will endure God's severity for all eternity) is almost univocal;[47] in some contrast, recent theology often seems rather embarrassed by this unanimity. There are, it seems to me, two basic reasons for this: the sense that anything like the traditional doctrine of hell is so far out of step with modern sensibilities that it has become incredible;[48] and the sense that there is no good theological reason to hold to this doctrine. The latter problem, I suggest, might be removed by considering the theological discussions that I have just been outlining, which did indeed remove hell from any essential connection to the major themes of Christian theology. In this, however, I have suggested that it was mistaken, and that a more adequate account of the decree may offer a way of giving a theological account of perdition that is not strange and disconnected, but woven into the central themes and stories of Christian theology.

Should we want to do this? It seems to me that we should want at least to explore the possibilities. The warnings about hell in the Scriptures are frequent and explicit, and so it is not a theme that we should be willing to discard too readily, or without an adequate alternative reading of these texts. Further, the fact that modern sensibilities find this an uncomfortable doctrine is not, I think, a good reason to discard it, although it may be a good reason to re-examine it.

I suggested in the first three chapters of this book that one of the problems in listening to the tradition is the otherness of the historical contexts of the doctors of the Church – and, indeed, that one of the problems in listening to Scripture is the otherness of the historical contexts of the prophets and apostles. This problem is, however, also in a way a benefit. Encountering – listening to – people who do not think the way we do, who assume different things in different ways, offers us the opportunity to have our own prejudices challenged. Hearing the unanimity of the tradition on the doctrine of hell enables us to question the prevalent assumptions of our age, and ask if perhaps they are simply wrong.

---

[47] On which see my paper 'The Justice of Hell and the Display of God's Glory in the Thought of Jonathan Edwards', *Pro Ecclesia* IX/4 (2000), pp. 389–403, and the various references there.

[48] A good example of this tendency is Marilyn McCord Adams's paper 'Hell and the God of Justice', *Religious Studies* 11 (1975), pp. 433–47, which proceeds by offering a series of examples, and suggesting that we would surely consider such and such an action unjust in each case. The argument's fundamental source of authority is thus modern consensus.

They may not be, of course: it may be that our age is able to see certain things more clearly than anyone before could, and so to correct persistent defects in the tradition. To take only one example, the spectre of anti-Semitism that haunts Christian history so persistently is partly at least challenged by Barth in the course of the discussion I have sketched, and has been challenged much more powerfully since. There is no doubt, surely, that this is a theological advance, a necessary and long-overdue correction of an appalling error in the tradition. However, a clash between the tradition and the assumptions of our own age at least offers us the opportunity to ask the question. A respect for, and a disciplined listening to, the tradition can enable us to speak prophetically in our own day, calling our contemporaries to hear the challenge of the gospel.

Chapter 9

Of Neoplatonism and Politics: Samuel Taylor Coleridge 'On the Constitution of Church and State'

The interface between theology and politics is often considered a dangerous boundary to attempt to map, and not only because it involves two of the three subjects that one should traditionally avoid raising in polite conversation. A piece in *The Times* newspaper recently quoted a *Catholic Herald* columnist who identified the apparent danger rather well: 'to venture upon the interface between religious belief and political conviction may easily generate more heat than illumination. The difficulty is compounded by the radical differences between these two areas of human belief and practice. Organised religion depends on the acceptance of eternal and changeless verities; grown-up politics recognises that the ordering of society requires compromise and pragmatism.'[1]

Well, I will have something to say about Ms Segger's characterisation of religious belief as being about 'eternal and changeless verities' before this chapter is finished, but for now let me simply observe that this comment raises in an acute form one possible problem or criticism of the practice of doing theology by listening to the tradition. What are we to make of those moments when the tradition is discussing something that is not strange, or controversial, or difficult today, but is instead simply utterly irrelevant? That is the question I want to explore in this chapter, by looking at Samuel Taylor Coleridge's response to a major political question of his day, one that seemingly has no possible relevance to life in ours.

I choose Coleridge not just because I find his theology fascinating (and, incidentally, his poetry captivating), but because the particular characteristics of his thought might be regarded as making the problem particularly acute. If

---

[1] Jill Segger, quoted in William Oddie's 'Credo' column entitled 'Is the Catholic Church the Conservative Party at Prayer?', *The Times*, 12 May 2001.

the religious belief in question is of a broadly Neoplatonic cast, as Coleridge's was, then Ms Segger's observation applies a fortiori. An account that identifies God with the eternal and changeless, and sees the chief end of religious devotion in forging an escape from this mutable world of matter into the realms of spirit, which are enabled to share in these central perfections of God by his grace, is likely to be particularly impatient with politics, that most this-worldly of pursuits. Given this, I want to suggest that Samuel Taylor Coleridge's combination of theological theorising and political commentary might be regarded as unusual, and to explore the lineaments of his account.

J. R. de J. Jackson has collected together the major critical commentary on Coleridge,[2] which displays an interesting and radical divergence of opinion: particularly just after his death (when, naturally, there were a number of attempts to sum up his contribution), there is near unanimity that Coleridge was a great thinker, but total disagreement over whether what he left was a series of brilliant but disconnected fragments, or a unified system of thought. Few doubted that Coleridge's voice was worth listening to on the various subjects he treated in the fields of philosophy, literary criticism, university reform, theology and politics: what was in doubt was whether he spoke with one voice across that range (a doubt that could only have been compounded by rumours of plagiarism).

   Coleridge was, it seems, almost incapable of writing sustained prose: it is not just his essays that start out on one subject end up somewhere completely different; paragraphs and occasional sentences suffer the same fate.[3] This inability to produce systematic exposition might suggest a lack of systematic thought, and so to the charges (in his own words!) that his work was no more than 'a motley Patch-work, or Farrago of heterogeneous Effusions', and that he was just a '...wild eccentric Genius that has published nothing but fragments & splendid Tirades ...'[4] Further, even what he did publish delighted in circumlocution, allusive reference and obscurity, sometimes (as in _Aids to_

---

[2] J. R. de J. Jackson, _Coleridge: The Critical Heritage_, 2 vols (London: Routledge & Kegan Paul, 1970; and London: Routledge, 1991).

[3] In his _Coleridge, Philosophy and Religion_ (Cambridge: Cambridge University Press, 2000), Douglas Hedley has suggested that the literary form Coleridge was best in was marginalia, which might be considered to be a demonstration of this point: see p. 17.

[4] A note in one of his own copies of _The Statesman's Manual_. See _The Collected Works of Samuel Taylor Coleridge_, Kathleen Coburn (ed.) (Bollingen Series LXXV) (London: Routledge & Kegan Paul), p. 114 and n. 2. (I am quoting, as far as possible, the modern critical edition of Coleridge's works, _The Collected Works of Samuel Taylor Coleridge_, Kathleen Coburn [ed.], cited above. Other primary sources include: _The Collected Letters of Samuel Taylor Coleridge_, E. L. Griggs [ed.] [Oxford: Clarendon Press, 1957–71]; and the _Notebooks_, Kathleen Coburn [ed.] [London: Routledge & Kegan Paul, 1957–].)

Reflection) deliberately, as an attempt to encourage serious, meditative reading
– 'reflection';[5] at other times, one suspects, simply because Coleridge was by
the end of his life a delightfully other-worldly intellectual figure who thought
that his readers would instantly recognise a fragment of Greek from a Middle-
Platonist philosopher, recall its context in the original work, and so understand
the appositeness of the allusion! (Byron, ever impatient with anything with the
appearance of pretension, famously commented on Coleridge's prose works in
the 'Dedication' to *Don Juan*: 'And Coleridge, too, has lately taken wing / But,
like a hawk encumber'd with his hood / Explaining metaphysics to the nation
– / I wish he would explain his Explanation.')[6]

Almost throughout his adult life, Coleridge promised a work that would
explain his system of philosophy, usually called something like the *Opus
Maximum*, or the *Logosophia*. There are various plans of the contents of
this, almost always astonishingly ambitious, and more than once Coleridge
announced that a part at least of it was in press. I have every sympathy for
readers who lost patience with Coleridge, and find it entirely understandable
that many reached the conclusion that this fabled work, and the system it
promised, were alike smokescreens to hide the fact that there was no coherence to Coleridge's thought, no programme to his writing, and that a 'motley
patchwork' was a fair description.

It is becoming clear, however, that this judgement is flawed. Various
scholars have begun to notice the Christian Platonist philosophy that unified
Coleridge's various fragments, and to see that the patchwork was in fact a
mosaic, if only we look closely enough. Like so many other thinkers, Coleridge
is presently benefiting from the publication of a major scholarly edition of every
scrap of material, published and unpublished, that he left, and this process will, I
think, be greatly accelerated when the manuscript chapters of the *Opus
Maximum* that Coleridge did write are finally published in this edition. The first
part of this discussion, on Neoplatonism, is an attempt to pre-empt this process
slightly, being an exposition of a part of that manuscript.[7]

Coleridge begins with his standard account of God's own life as the eternal
self-actualisation of divine will.[8] 'The principle on which our whole system has
been built, that the Will is … that which God eternally *is* …'[9] Coleridge thinks

---

[5] On this, see again Hedley, *Coleridge, Philosophy and Religion*, pp. 88–152.

[6] Stanza 2.

[7] Manuscript chapter 'On the Divine Ideas' (Huntingdon Library, San Marino,
California: MS HM8195).

[8] On which see my essay on Coleridge in *The Nineteenth Century Theologians*, Colin
E. Gunton and Christoph Schwöbel (eds) (Oxford: Blackwell, forthcoming), and
references there.

[9] *On the Divine Ideas*, f. 109, emphasis original.

that it is a truth available to philosophy, that is, to anyone who is able to think clearly enough, that will is the most basic reality: nothing comes to be unless it is somehow willed into being, and so we can be sure that of all that is, will is most fundamental. As Coleridge puts it, '[will] is not the cause of all reality because it is the cause of its own but it is necessarily causative of its own reality because it is causative of all possible reality'.[10] In a sense, this is a variant on the form of argument that Aquinas uses in the five ways: something must lie behind each thing, whether that is constructed in terms of cause, motion, or purpose; one is then faced either with an infinite regress or with an unmoved mover, first cause, or final purpose. For Coleridge, movement, cause and purpose all have their basis in volition, and so the most basic reality is will, the cause and origin of all other reality.

This primordial will is the ground of the nature of all that eternally is, which is to say the ground of the divine nature. It is not, thinks Coleridge, appropriate to regard this abysmal depth, this *bubos abubos*, as God, still less as God the Father, or somehow the origin of God the Father, who alone is the unoriginate, the Unbegotten. Rather, the eternal life of God, the *actus purissimus,* which God eternally is, is to be identified with this willing. Father, Son and Holy Spirit *are*, dynamically and eternally, and they are what they will to be. As Coleridge puts it, 'The ground is not to be called God … It is the abysmal depth of the eternal act by which God as the alone causa sûi [*sic*] affirmeth himself eternally.'[11]

The problem faced by every attempted proof of the existence of God in the Christian tradition now comes into play: proving first causes, unmoved movers, grounds of being and the like seems easy enough, given the number of attempts so to do in the tradition; the harder work, as the more intelligent exponents of this way of thinking have tended to realise, is identifying what has been proved with the God revealed in the gospel history, who is most properly named as Father, Son and Holy Spirit. Aquinas, for instance, sees the problem and avoids it by using the five ways as proofs of attributes which are antecedently known to belong only to God by revelation – each supposed proof ends with the careful statement that there is a first mover, or whatever, and that 'all own this to be God'. Coleridge himself makes the point: 'no man can deny *God* in some sense or other, as *anima mundi, causa causarum, etc.*, but it is the *personal, living, self-conscious* God, which is so difficult to combine with an infinite being infinitely and irresistibly causative'.[12] It is easy to prove the existence of various supposed gods, the problem is in identifying the objects of these proofs with the true God.

---

[10] Ibid., f. 21.

[11] Ibid., f. 73.

[12] Quoted in J. R. Barth, *Coleridge and Christian Doctrine* (Cambridge, Massachusetts: Harvard University Press, 1969), p. 97.

Coleridge, however, thinks that this can be done. At various points in his writings he hints that Plato had thought his way to an adequate doctrine of the Trinity, although he is clear that the later Platonist tradition, and particularly Plotinus,[13] fell away from this insight decisively. The argument goes like this: the eternal willing of primordial will has three moments, corresponding to the three persons of the Trinity. First, Will wills to be and so comes to know itself to be. Hence, the first moment is the existence of that which can know, absolute Mind, the Father; the absolute Mind again cannot be inactive any more than absolute Will could be, and so thinks of its own being, as it is the only worthy object of its own thought. So, the second moment is the existence of that which can be known, as absolute mind forms the perfect idea of itself, the Logos, or Son. Finally the absolute act by which the Father knows the Son and the Son is known by the Father is the 'Spirit of Love and Holy Life', the unity which preserves the oneness of God in the eternal act of self-realisation, or the closing of the circle.[14] These relationships of origin are not primordial in the sense that they happened and are over; rather they are eternal, the full content of God's dynamic life. Coleridge's own summary of the account is worthy of quotation:

> ... in & together with the act of self-realisation the supreme mind begetteth his substantial idea, the primal self, the adorable *I am*, its other self, & becometh God the Father, self-originant (or lest this word should lead to the conception of a Beginning, self-existant, self-caused) & self subsistent even as the Logos or Supreme idea is the co-eternal Son self-subsistent but begotten by the Father while in the mutual act of self-attribution the effusion and refundence,[15] the inspiration and respiration of divine Love, the Son is, (or may I innocently say of the Eternal that he becometh?) Deus alter et idem, and these words express the Tri-unity:- the Deus, the paternal, the Filius, the Deus alter, and the Spirit, the Deus idem in patre et filio per quem pater et filius unum sunt, qui et ipse cum patre et filio est unus Deus.[16]

As an aside, it is perhaps worth asking whether Coleridge is here suggesting that the Trinity is a truth available to unaided human reason? It might seem so, but within Coleridge's epistemological scheme the question is a meaningless one:[17] all true philosophy is a participation in the divine logos, as far as

---

[13] On whom see variously *On the Divine Ideas*, ff. 87, 151–63; or Coburn (ed.), *The Collected Works of Samuel Taylor Coleridge*, 11.I, pp. 413–16.

[14] *On the Divine Ideas*, ff. 67–71.

[15] This word is unclear in the manuscript.

[16] *On the Divine Ideas*, ff. 73–5: the final Latin reads 'God that [is] in the Father and the Son, through whom the Father and the Son are one, who also himself with the Father and Son is one God.'

[17] On which see again my contribution in Gunton and Schwöbel (eds), *The Nineteenth-Century Theologians*.

Coleridge is concerned, and so 'unaided human reason' is simply not a meaningful category. Certainly Coleridge has a strong doctrine of general revelation, of God in Christ making himself available to be known beyond the boundaries of the Church, although he equally thinks that all that may be gained this way is difficult, partial and shadowy compared to the luminous simplicity of the Scriptures. Plato, the greatest philosopher the world has known, did begin to glimpse this in the utmost depths of his profoundest meditation, but the boy pushing the plough knows far more of it, if only he has read his Bible.

Returning to the main exposition, Coleridge now has in place his account of God's eternal life, an account that he seems to regard as relatively simple and uncontroversial.[18] The problem is the reality of history, change and particularity: philosophy can only deal with eternal and necessary concepts, which are reached by 'abstracting from time',[19] and so to understand the relationship of the eternal and necessary to the particular and contingent is the chief intellectual problem facing humanity. Coleridge stresses the sharpness of the difficulty: '[t]he passage from the absolute to the separated finite, this is the difficulty which who shall overcome? This is the chasm which ages have tried in vain to overbridge.'[20] Coleridge, of course, has an answer, but he wants to make quite sure that we realise the seriousness of the problem so that we will be certain to spot the brilliance and significance of the answer.

Coleridge's answer follows the lines of traditional Christian Platonism: all possibilities are present in the divine mind as eternally existent ideas, gathered up in the Logos, the *idea idearum*.[21] The same argument, however, that proved the real existence of the Logos, the argument that to be known perfectly by the divine mind is enough to ensure existence (something I suspect Coleridge developed from his reading of Berkeley), demands the actual existence of all these ideas within the Godhead. The argument 'that led us to admit the self-subsistence of the adequate idea of the supreme mind must hold equally good of whatever ideas are distinctly contained in that adequate idea'.[22] In the eternal willing to be, the *actus purus sine ulla potentia* which is God's own life, whatever is willed is necessarily actual, ontologically real, and whatever is not willed is necessarily not even potential, and so has no existence. Thus the eternal ideas are eternally actual; they have a real ontological existence of their own.

---

[18] The force of Byron's complaint becomes luminously clear at this point!

[19] *On the Divine Ideas*, ff. 9–11.

[20] Ibid., f. 11.

[21] Coleridge uses this phrase in this context in various places, for example Coburn (ed.), *Notebooks* IV, p. 5294.

[22] *On the Divine Ideas*, f. 19.

'[R]eason', says Coleridge, meaning the divine Logos, '... has compelled us to the conclusion that whatever is distinct in the Deity must be real[,] substantially distinct & distinctly substantial ... and that these distinctions [between the ideas] are both real and actual as in whom and through whom the eternal act of the Father and the Son, the uniting, receiving & communicating Spirit lives & moves.'[23]

Coleridge insists on the absolute oneness of God's life, and so of these various ideas. How this is to be done, how both the reality of the distinction and the absolute unity are to be simultaneously defended, seems to him to be the proper statement of a basic problem of philosophy, 'the problem of steering a course between atheism & pantheism, and between fatalism and polytheism',[24] the age-old problem, that is, of the One and the Many.

To find a solution we must first define the terms. What is an 'idea'? Says Coleridge, 'I know of no other answer than that a divine Idea is the Omnipresence or Omnipotence represented intelligentially [*sic*] in some one of the possible forms, which are the plenitude of the divine Intelligence, the Logos ... as such the Ideas are necessarily immutable in as much as they are one with the Eternal Act by which the Absolute Will self-realised begets its idea as the other Self.'[25] Just so, 'to suppose God without Ideas, or the realizing knowledge of all the particular forms potentially involved in the absolute causativeness, would destroy the very conception of God'.[26]

There is still a tension in this logic, however, of which Coleridge is well aware. These forms are described as having real and distinct existence within God's own life, but no particular (other than the three Persons) can exist inside the Godhead, as God is, *ex hypothesi*, simple. Coleridge's solution is to notice that the existence of these particulars is volitional, inasmuch as it is in the eternal self-actualisation of will that is God's own life that gives them any existence. Given this, Coleridge thinks, so long as they will not to have particular existence, but only to exist within the being of God, there will be no problem.[27] He thus feels confident in asserting 'the reality of the existence of distinct beings in the plenitude of the Supreme Mind, whose essence is will and whose actuality consists in their Will being one with the Will of God'.[28] Otherness-without-separation, or alterity as Coleridge calls it, is after all a necessary feature of the description of God's life that he has given, in that the Son, *Deus alter*, exists in this relationship to the Father by the Spirit. The ideas,

[23] Ibid., ff. 19–21.
[24] Ibid., f. 23.
[25] Ibid., f. 31.
[26] Ibid., f. 33.
[27] Ibid., ff. 35–9.
[28] Ibid., f. 89.

who are contained within the Son, the *idea idearum*, can similarly will to exist only in this way, only within the fundamental relationship of alterity, of distinction in unity, that is the Son's particular way of relating and so being within the Godhead.

This move, however, introduces a hitherto unsuspected possibility: each idea now presumably has the potential to will to be differently: it is not inconceivable that one or another might assert its particularity, might seek to set itself up over and against God as an independently existent being. To so will, thinks Coleridge, is to become 'the father of self, alien from God, a liar from the beginning & the father of lies'.[29] To so will is demonic, but the possibility of this independent and particular existence, however demonic, is nonetheless now present. This is as far as Coleridge thinks philosophy, the science of the eternal and necessary, will take us. The possibility of evil, of particulars willing to be apart from God, is now established. The outcome of this possibility can only be established by looking at contingent facts. Coleridge thinks it is demonstrable that evil does, in fact, exist in the world, and so is prepared to assert that this possibility came to pass, that there was a heavenly fall.

And there the manuscript ends, after a brief digression comparing this system to that of Plotinus. I suspect that the development would have followed Origen to some extent: there are hints elsewhere in Coleridge's writings that he took with utmost seriousness the idea of a heavenly fall.[30] Certainly the forms or ideas are central to Coleridge's account of the being of creation, as to know the reality of what is, rather than merely its appearance and effects, is to know its form, or the idea of which it is an instantiation.

Notice here the connection between the forms, which are the mediators of causation and so of creation, the ideas and the Logos, in whom all the ideas have their existence: it seems that Coleridge here has an answer to a criticism of the Christian Platonist tradition that has been developed particularly by Colin Gunton.[31] In this version of Christian Platonism, at least, it is not that the forms displace the Son as the mediator of creation, as the criticism has it, but that the forms are the way in which the Son is the mediator of the Father's creating action. Coleridge is very clear on this point when he insists that 'whatever actually is … is possible only by a communion with that life which is the light

---

[29] Ibid., f. 45.

[30] See, for example, the summary of the key points of Reformed Christianity in the 'Confessions of an Inquiring Spirit' (Coburn [ed.], *The Collected Works of Samuel Taylor Coleridge*, 11.II, pp. 1111–71), where he includes as the second point 'The Eternal Possibilities; the Actuality of which hath not its origin in God. – Αποστασις. Chaos Spirituale.'

[31] See, for instance, Colin E. Gunton, *The Triune Creator: A Historical and Systematic Study* (Edinburgh: Edinburgh University Press, 1998), p. 102.

of man…', an idea which he describes as 'the great master key, not only of all speculative science, physical as well as metaphysical'.[32]

Again, the linked criticisms often made of Platonic philosophies and theologies, that they somehow denigrate both the material and the particular, cannot, I think, be sustained against Coleridge. Taking particularity first, Coleridge's answer to the problem of the one and the many is to locate particularity in the ideas, which exist in Christ. It might be doubted whether this is adequate defence: the will to be particular, after all, has here been identified as the source of all evil. This only raises the question, however, of the nature of created particularity: what Coleridge denies is the ability of any creature to be an isolated individual, a self that does not need God or other creatures. The particularity that remains possible within Coleridge's account is to have distinct being within the loving embrace of God, to find self only in self-surrender to him.[33] It does not seem to me a failure of theology to deny that any creature can be *a se*, and so to insist that proper creaturely being remains constantly contingent on God's upholding.

What of materiality? Here, Coleridge's account of the imagination comes to the fore. Douglas Hedley makes the point by a comparison of Coleridge (and, incidentally, Schelling) with Plato and Plotinus.[34] Plato, famously, would have banished all artists from the Republic: a material object is itself an imperfect instantiation of an eternal form, and a painting or sculpture of that object is thus merely an imperfect representation of an imperfect instantiation, and so has no value or interest. Porphyry by contrast, saw a more positive role for the material world in representing symbolically the intelligible world of the forms so that those who were unable to philosophise could nonetheless grasp intuitively, or better imaginatively, the true nature of reality. Plotinus, finally, took this a step further in arguing that there could be a positive role for art as well, that of making clearer the symbolic nature of material reality and so enabling us to see the eternal ideas there symbolised.[35]

The role of the artist, particularly the poet, was a burning question for Coleridge,[36] and his most sustained investigation into the subject, the

---

[32] *On the Divine Ideas*, f. 63. A similar point is made in marginalia to Henry More; see Coburn (ed.), *The Collected Works of Samuel Taylor Coleridge*, 10, p. 113 and n. 3.

[33] Coleridge makes almost this argument in defining true individuality in ibid., 9, p. 292.

[34] I.e. Hedley, *Coleridge, Philosophy and Religion*, pp. 128–35.

[35] Plotinus, *Ennead* iv.3 11, 1–8.

[36] On which see again my contribution to Gunton and Schwöbel (eds), *The Nineteenth Century Theologians*, although when I wrote that I had not seen how this could be used to establish the materiality of the world in the later Christian Platonist philosophy.

Biographia Literaria, follows this Plotinan line in its famous theory of the imagination.[37] As Coleridge was later to write, the imagination is:

> that reconciling and mediatory power, which incorporating the Reason in Images of the Sense, and organizing (as it were) the flux of the senses by the permanence and self-circling energies of the Reason, gives birth to a system of symbols, harmonious in themselves, and consubstantial with the truths, of which they are the *conductors*.[38]

We may describe the material world, then, as the means by which eternal truths are communicated to those unable or unwilling to reach them through the work of philosophy. God graciously incarnates the ideas in a vast symbolic system to enable all his (intelligent) creatures to intuitively know and grasp the truth. To pre-empt the political part of this paper slightly, a fine example of this occurs in *On the Constitution of Church and State*, where Coleridge acknowledges that the philosophical idea of the state he derives will never cross the minds of a vast proportion of the populus, but nonetheless is known by all, the evidence adduced being that 'no man who has ever listened to laborers ... in any alehouse ... discussing the injustice of the present rate of wages ... will doubt for a moment that they are fully possessed by the idea'.[39]

I have questions about this account of materiality, mainly to do with the implication that all that is is created for utilitarian purposes, and not simply as a gratuitous expression of God's bounty, but I do not think that Coleridge can be accused of failing to take with due seriousness the goodness of the created order.

Thus far, I have argued that Coleridge's system is not susceptible to the standard criticisms of Platonist-influenced theology, and can succeed in taking with due seriousness the particularity and materiality of the created order. I have one further criticism, which I think will stick, and which I will return to at the end, but for now let me just observe that if the things I have said so far are correct then Coleridge's Christian Platonism might well have more to say in the political realm than my initial observations suggested would be likely. It seems to me that this is indeed the case, as I wish to demonstrate by a reading of one of Coleridge's other late works.

Coleridge was involved in politics all his life, as a dreamer and radical in his early years (of sufficient interest to the government during the paranoia following the French Revolution to acquire his very own secret agent, who

---

[37] Coburn (ed.), *The Collected Works of Samuel Taylor Coleridge*, 7.I, p. 304.
[38] Ibid., 6, p. 29.
[39] Ibid., 10, p. 16.

tracked Coleridge for most of the summer he spent with Wordsworth in Nether Stowey, and probably never realised what a privilege he had, being paid to eavesdrop on the conversations that resulted in the *Lyrical Ballads!*), as a reactionary defender of the establishment by the end. It is the latter period that interests me now, not because of the content of his later politics, particularly, but because of his attempted theological defence of them.

The key text here rejoices in the title *On the Constitution of the Church and State, According to the Idea of Each; with Aids towards a Right Judgment of the Late Catholic Bill*. Two points of exegesis of the title demonstrate its relevance: first, the aim of the work is to promote 'right judgment' of the 'late Catholic Bill', that being the Catholic Emancipation Act of 1829, a key constitutional change designed in part to prevent tensions between Protestant and Catholic communities in the British possessions in Ireland. This is straightforward politics: important and far-reaching politics, perhaps, as questions around British membership of the single European currency are now, but nonetheless politics. Second, Coleridge proposes to discuss Church and State 'according to the idea of each', and the text makes it clear that the word 'idea' is philosophically charged. This is a Neoplatonist, or at least Christian Platonist, account of what the Church and State properly are, in the mind of God, applied to a pressing and ephemeral political question; this book is about the surprising overlap of Neoplatonism and politics.

The Catholic Emancipation Bill was in many ways a natural progression from the repeal of the Test Acts and Corporation Acts, which had taken place in 1828. These contained the various laws that restricted civil participation to members of the Anglican Church, by forbidding those who refused to sign the Articles of Religion university education, or any political or civic employment. Originally targeted at Dissenters, these acts had also restricted the advancement of Deists and other free thinkers, or at least of those who were keen to avoid hypocrisy. Once Dissent was allowed its place in the civic realm, it seemed natural to many that Roman Catholicism should alike be accepted; others argued, not unfairly given the then prevailing circumstances, that the Pope was not just an alternative religious leader but the head of a foreign territorial power in Europe, and that admitting people into government who had taken an unconditional oath of allegiance to the head of a foreign territorial power could perhaps be regarded as imprudent. Such objections resulted in prohibitions being placed on religious orders, with the Jesuits being specifically mentioned, but were not considered sufficient to prevent a lay Roman Catholic who had taken an oath of loyalty to the Crown being given the same rights and privileges as any other citizen.

Coleridge's discussion of this question is an extensive analysis of the proper place of a national church within the nation, which is then applied to the issue at hand. At the heart of the analysis is Coleridge's belief that the instantiation of an eternal idea in the temporal and material realm will inevitably be bipolar, appearing in two apparently contradictory modes which are nonetheless held together and essentially united by the underlying idea: like God, ideas are *idem et alter* existing in dynamic unity. The ideal nation, then, will only be understood by holding together the State, the political pole, and the national church, the cultural pole. The national church is a misleading title, perhaps, since it is not necessarily Christian (although it is a great boon to the nation if it should happen to be); rather, the national church is the semi-organised movement that preserves, develops and passes on the civilisation and culture of the nation. Its members, whom Coleridge calls the 'clerisy', include those who work in universities, those who produce and preserve the nation's artistic heritage, those who practise medicine, and also school teachers and the parish clerks, whose role is to pass on the most useful and accessible parts of the nation's culture to all its people. The crown of this culture is necessarily theology, the mistress-science, which deals directly with morality and reality (in the ideas), but much else is comprehended alongside it.[40]

The opposite pole to the national church, the State, is itself polar, being composed of 'two antagonist powers or opposite interests … PERMANENCE and … PROGRESSION'.[41] Permanence is vested in the land-owning classes; progression is achieved by merchants, manufacturers and the professions. Alongside these two, the national church is the 'third estate', 'the necessary antecedent condition' of both.

All this constitutional theory is an analysis of the eternal ideas of nation, Church and State, and so philosophical. For the great mass of people, such theory will be merely opaque, and so there is a necessity for living symbols that represent and make apparent these underlying realities. The monarch is the symbol of the nation, head of both Church and State. In the Church the Crown is chief patron of the nation's culture, the person in whom all that is best in the nation is to be visible and concentrated. In the State, the monarch is the head who provides the higher unity that prevents the opposition of permanence and progression descending into class warfare. As the symbol of the nation, the monarch is not merely a private individual but the instantiation, the incarnation if you like, of the nation: the royal 'we' is no affectation but simple truth. The bipolar state, composed of the permanence and progression, has its

---

[40] There are various significant speeches and lectures dating from the foundation of my own institution, King's College, London, which speak of its students – then largely destined for medicine, law or the Anglican church, with a few remaining in the universities – as a 'national clerisy', indicating that Coleridge's conceptions had some influence on educational policy, at least.

[41] Coburn (ed.), *The Collected Works of Samuel Taylor Coleridge*, 10, p. 24.

own symbol in a parliament of two houses, one representing the permanence by giving its seats to hereditary land owners, and the other representing the progression by allowing members of the commons to be elected to its ranks. Crucially, it is nonetheless one parliament.

The philosophy here is important: Coleridge is able to cut through many of the more difficult problems of political philosophy by postulating the reality of the nation, in this case the United Kingdom, and the making visible of that reality in the Crown. That a political thought may never have crossed my mind is besides the point; I am still a member of the nation because I am a subject of Her Majesty the Queen, and so belong to my fellow countrymen without any need for a postulation of a social contract or similar mythology.

Coleridge's argument on Catholic Emancipation is now fairly easy to trace: whilst Christianity, and the Christian Church, transcend all political and social boundaries, every particular nation necessarily contains a national church, and any Christian nation will want to ensure that that church is Christian. Thus the support and maintenance of an established church is simply the proper ordering of national life. Dissent disrupts this, but is at least contained within the body politic, and so an acceptable disruption.[42] The introduction into the nation of members of the clerisy whose loyalties lie beyond the boundaries of the nation is, however, too great an evil to be permitted. Coleridge also seems to accept that the Roman pontiff is indeed the Antichrist,[43] which must have been something of a deterrent when Catholic emancipation was in view!

I have skated rather quickly over the main lines of Coleridge's argument, but I hope there is enough there to show how his Christian Platonism directly affects his political opinions, and to demonstrate that those opinions are extremely conservative. Coleridge appears to believe that the British constitutional arrangements and ecclesiastical establishment as they existed *c.* 1825 imaged forth the eternal model of perfect statehood, which should only be preserved, and if necessary replicated elsewhere. Now, I have nothing against conservatism as such, and I happen to think that the constitutional settlement achieved in 1688 and largely in place until very recently in this country has a fair amount to recommend it (although three centuries is probably too short a time to really test such an arrangement). However, I think Coleridge is driven to this conservatism by a flaw in his theology.

I mentioned earlier that I had one more criticism of Coleridge's Christian Platonism. It is this: whilst I think it is unfair to suggest that, for Coleridge, the forms replace God the Son in mediating creation, I think it is fair to say that

---

[42] It appears that Coleridge was in favour of the repeal of the Test and Corporation Acts even before this happened. See ibid., 10, p. 88, and n. there.

[43] Ibid., 10, pp. 131–45.

the account that is given of God the Son is driven by a vision of the Logos as the sum of the forms, and not by the gospel history of the man from Nazareth. Even if Coleridge had completed his great work, it is difficult to believe that there would have been much Christology amongst the *Logosophia*; the historical particularity of the Incarnation finds little or no place within Coleridge's systematic thought. This becomes particularly clear in a discussion in the *Statesman's Manual*, where Coleridge claims that Christianity is especially differenced from all other religions by being *grounded* on *facts* which all men alike have the means of ascertaining ...'[44] He is making a point about the felt need of redemption, and so the assertion is not as bizarre as it may first appear, but, even so, it is clear that the particular human history of Jesus Christ is not foundational to Christianity, in Coleridge's opinion.

This judgement, thus stated, is probably a little too sharp: there are places in Coleridge's writings where he does attempt to take the gospel history seriously, seeing it as the particular point where the eternal and historical meet,[45] or perhaps the ultimate symbol, where the *idea idearum* is instantiated – here we must say incarnated – in the phenomenal realm. This, however, is just doing the same as all the modern proponents of divine passibility,[46] denying that the events of manger, river and tree are redemptive, but instead making them merely revelatory of some eternal realm where any truly significant event must take place. Coleridge does this in a rather more nuanced way than this modern tradition, to be sure – he is some distance from being so dull as to believe that impassibility can be safely discarded – but the fundamental failure is the same.

And, finally, this failure of Neoplatonism results in a failure of politics. The point about the gospel history – the scandalous point, to Lessing, and all those who have learnt from him, which here would seem to include Coleridge – is that religion is not, *pace* the journalist with whom I started, only about 'eternal and changeless verities', but has at its very centre the historical and contingent. 'In the fifteenth year of the reign of Emperor Tiberius, when Pontius Pilate was governor of Judea, and Herod was ruler of Galilee, and his brother Philip ruler of the region of Ituraea and Trachonitis, and Lysanias ruler of Abilene, during the high-priesthood of Annas and Caiaphas, the Word of God came to John son of Zechariah in the Wilderness' (Luke 3), and the Word of God came to him again for baptism at Jordan river, and it is in these contingent places and times and ways that we encounter the eternal. The New Testament, after all, begins with a genealogy, a list of begettings which could at every turn have been different, and arguably should have been at several. At the end of it, the

---

[44] Ibid., 6, p. 55 (emphases original).

[45] So, for instance, ibid., 9, p. 205, or 11.II, pp. 1155–6.

[46] I owe this point to Weinandy, *Does God Suffer?*, pp. 223–4.

Virgin Mary is called blessed by this and every generation only because the eternal verities depended precisely on whether she was prepared to respond to the angel's perplexing proclamation of grace with faith and submission.

Coleridge's theological system does not, I think, denigrate the material or the particular; but it does denigrate the contingent, and so when he turns from Neoplatonism to politics the picture we get is of an eternal blueprint for the perfect republic, a politics that has no space for the contingencies of history and so will claim to work equally as well in fabled Atlantis, Socrates' Athens or Regency Britain. Thus, I think that the reason for the utterly reactionary nature of Coleridge's account of the proper ordering of the nation in *On the Constitution of Church and State* is not temperament or political taste, but a failure of theology.

Is it, then, the case that mixing religion with politics is both difficult and dangerous, that theology should restrict itself to the 'eternal and changeless verities', and accept that politics is about 'pragmatism and compromise', as Ms Segger suggested? I think not: it is a theological failure which makes the difference here, which means that Coleridge's account of politics has too much of the eternal and changeless in it. Further, I have already suggested that Coleridge is in the intellectual mainstream of Enlightenment thought in his distrust of the importance of the contingent: it is difficult to think of a genuinely influential nineteenth-century thinker, in Europe at least, who did not regard Lessing's ditch as a near-unbridgeable chasm. Just so, most of the significant economic and political theories – whether Marxist, Keynsian, or monetarist – of the modern age are just as focused on that which is universally true in all times and at all places as Coleridge's Neoplatonism. In his political thought, the error Coleridge makes is not a result of his theology, but a result of the failure of his theology: it is not down to a lack of appreciation of modern political theory, but instead too much agreement with it. A 'one size fits all' prescription that assumes that politics is about going beyond the exigencies of a particular situation and applying a universal panacea is endemic in all serious political thought in the modern era.

What is the alternative? Ms Segger suggested politics was about 'compromise and pragmatism'; it is usually assumed in political discourse and argument that the alternative to universal theorising is mere pragmatism and expediency, valueless, convictionless, cynical politics that is to be decried and despised. If my criticism of Coleridge is right, then good theology might point the way to a different account, an account which acknowledges the importance of eternal values but stresses that values only make sense in relation to present particulars, which sees the contingent not as a problem to be circumvented and compromised with in order to apply the grand narratives, but as something to be valued and taken seriously in its own right.

The problem, I suggest, with Coleridge's politics is that it is not theological enough and so, like all other political theories of the modern era, remains focused on only universal truths. The gospel should teach us to be suspicious of such exclusive grand narratives, and to focus more on the needs and possibilities of the particular situation. Modern politics, I submit, is too much about 'eternal and changeless verities'; it needs to get its hands dirty, to discover the messiness of human life as it is actually lived. It may be that only a healthy dose of theology will bring it back down to earth.

Chapter 10

Listening to the Past:
On the Place of Tradition in Theology Again

In most introductory accounts of the work of theology, somewhere the question of authority is discussed. Usually, this takes the form of a list of possible sources of authority for theological work, with more or less explanation or exploration of how these sources might function as authorities. Generally, four items appear on the list: Scripture, tradition, reason and experience. These, it is asserted, are places to which appeal may be made to establish a theological point.

Such discussions often appear to me to be flawed, not least in not recognising that these different possible sources of authority function in different ways. Reason, for instance, narrowly understood, is merely the exercise of logic – surely no theological system will deny that logical arguments, insofar as they are valid, and based upon accepted premises, are an appropriate part of theological method? This might suggest a method in which Scripture supplies premises, and reason tools with which to work on those premises. This is totally inadequate as an account of how theology is done, of course, but at least begins to recognise the different roles of these differing alleged sources of authority.[1]

I sketched in the first chapter of this book some ways of relating to the Christian tradition that accorded it, or at least some part of it, normative status alongside Scripture. I further indicated there that such discussions were not at the forefront of my thinking in this book. My aim in this chapter is to sketch an

---

[1] Even the suggestion that reason is authoritative inasmuch as theological positions that are demonstrable from 'self-evident' propositions should be accepted seems to me uncontroversial, the controversy rather concerning the existence of propositions that are self-evident. That is, my objection to natural theology is not founded on any refusal to accept a valid argument built on observations about the world that reaches conclusions about God; rather, it is built on the suspicion that there happen to be no valid arguments of this sort.

account of the role of appeal to tradition in theology that accepts the basic *sola scriptura* principle. If final authority in theology rests only with Scripture, is there any role for appeals of the form 'Calvin says x, so x must be true'? Such a role was not established by the arguments in the first two chapters. There, I suggested that we could not hear the teaching of Scripture aright without listening to the tradition, but this does not of itself ascribe any authority to the voices of the tradition, it just insists that they are necessary guides to enable us to hear the words that are authoritative in the Scriptures. I now want to suggest that we can go further than this, however.

An obvious text to reflect on when considering the possibility of ascribing authority to the Christian tradition is Jesus' account of the revelatory work of the Spirit: 'When he comes, the Spirit of truth, he will guide you into all truth. For he will not speak from himself; but he will speak only what he hears, and he will announce to you all that is coming. He will glorify me by taking from what is mine and announcing it to you' (John 16:13–14). It seems clear that this promise does not primarily refer to further revelation, as Jesus has claimed to have revealed all things to the disciples (15:15), and even here the Spirit will only announce what he has received from Jesus. In any case, John's Gospel offers a powerful picture of Jesus as the full and final revelation of God's truth (most obviously in the prologue, but the theme is pervasive in John).[2] Instead, this is a filling out of a theme that has been regular in the earlier part of the Gospel: the acknowledgement that, whilst Jesus reveals all during his lifetime, it is only after death, resurrection and ascension that his disciples will understand what he has revealed, said and done.[3] The work of the Spirit, then, is to bring remembrance and understanding of, and insight into, the words and works of Jesus. As Beasley-Murray puts it, 'the task of the Paraclete will be to lead them that they may comprehend the depths and heights of the revelation as yet unperceived by them'.[4]

The statement at the end of verse 13 might seem to deny this, asserting as it does that the Spirit will announce what is to come. This has caused much discussion, but most recent commentators agree that a straightforward reading

---

[2] See, for instance, C. H. Dodd, *The Interpretation of the Fourth Gospel* (Cambridge: Cambridge University Press, 1953), pp. 170–86, 263–85, where this theme in the prologue is discussed at some length.

[3] See, for instance, John 2:22, 12:16, 13:7. This reading of the passage is supported by (e.g.): G. R. Beasley-Murray, *John* (Word Biblical Commentary 36) (Waco, Texas: Word Books, 1987); T. L. Brodie, *The Gospel according to John: A Literary and Theological Commentary* (Oxford: Oxford University Press, 1993); R. E. Brown, *The Gospel according to John* (Anchor Bible, 2 vols) (Garden City, New York: Doubleday, 1966–70).

[4] Beasley-Murray, in the commentary on that text.

referring to predictive prophecy is out of tenor with the thought of the Gospel, whilst acknowledging that John would have been well aware of the existence of Spirit-inspired prophecy within the churches.[5] Two alternative accounts are proposed: first, in keeping with the eschatological flavour of the passage, the things which are to come might well be read as end-time events, beginning perhaps with the happenings of Easter and ascension, but also looking forward to the return of Christ. This accords well with the assertion in verse 14 that this work is a part of the Spirit's glorification of Jesus, since glory is itself an eschatological category. Second, an account which parallels the challenge of Isaiah 41:21–9 is suggested,[6] whereby the work of the Spirit is the continued interpretation and application of the once-for-all gospel into new places and situations.

There are various ways of giving theological content to the process of spiritual illumination which Jesus points to here. Theologians from more 'catholic' traditions often claim this promise for the institutional church, identifying a magisterium or some other structure that, it is claimed, is able to make authoritative pronouncements which either determine the interpretation of the Scriptures or actually add to the content of the faith.[7] Writers from more Protestant traditions, by contrast, have sometimes interpreted this text polemically to be no more than a reference to the inspiration given to the apostles for the purposes of writing Scripture, which came to an end with the death of the apostolic generation and the closure of the canon. It seems to me, on the basis of the exegesis sketched above, that neither of these views are wholly adequate, and that it is better to see this as a promise both to the whole Church, and to each particular believer within the Church. If this is the case, then it seems clear that the promise is not of infallibility or completeness, or at least until the eschaton, when we shall 'know fully, even as now we are fully known'.[8]

This position seems appropriate for another reason: theologically, the work of the Spirit is always eschatological, in that it is the particular place of the Spirit

---

[5] See, for instance, the three commentators referenced above.

[6] I owe the parallel to Beasley-Murray.

[7] Classically in the first decree of the Council of Trent, which asserted that, alongside Scripture, 'traditions concerning both faith and conduct' were to be venerated, whether 'directly spoken by Christ or dictated by the Holy Spirit' ('... *vel oretenus a Christo, vel a Spiritu sancto dictatas* ...'). Vatican I makes the same point, referring to Trent: 'revelation ... is contained in written books and unwritten traditions, which were received by the apostles from the lips of Christ himself, or came to the apostles by the dictation of the Holy Spirit ...' ('... *quae ipsius Christi ore ab apostolis acceptae, aut ipsis apostolis Spiritu sancto dictante* ...'). Texts are from N. P. Tanner (ed.), *Decrees of the Ecumenical Councils: Volume II (Trent – Vatican II)* (London: Sheed & Ward, 1990).

[8] 1 Corinthians 13:12.

in the economy of God's workings to draw the creation on towards the consummation that awaits it. Gifts and experiences of the Spirit's work now are real and marvellous, but they are only the 'first fruits' which are the promise of the full harvest to come, a down payment on the future that, God has pledged, lies in wait. Just so, to suggest certainty or completeness in our theological knowledge now on the basis of this pneumatological promise seems to me to be mistaken.

What, then, does this, admittedly provisional and partial, pneumatological leading actually look like and amount to? It seems to me that the action of the Spirit here does not so much invite us to make confident assertions, so much as to be hopeful and cheerful in the face of the problems and difficulties of theological knowing. Faced with a problem that seems insuperable, we can trust in the promise of the Spirit that it will be overcome, and that it will not prove fatal to the faith of the Church – or to our faith – in the meantime. We can proceed, patient of our own infirmities and dullness, and confident in both our own work and in the coming future knowing that in all the confusion and messiness of our life and our thoughts we are not abandoned to our own slender resources but upheld by the Spirit. One day we shall know fully; the theological task shall be accomplished. Until then, we can be sure that it at least will not fail. God will not abandon his Church to error. That is the fundamental content of the promise;[9] the question is how it can be applied to establish an account of the authority of tradition.

In Chapter 2 I hinted at an argument that may be used to ascribe a form of authority to the tradition.[10] There I suggested that there are certain writers in the history of the Church who have been generally recognised as being particularly successful in exploring the internal logic of the gospel, and its ramifications for the particular situation in which they found themselves. I referred to these writers as the 'doctors' of the Church. What lay behind that discussion was the sense that theology, the exploration of the logic and implications of the gospel of Christ, is difficult: it is not always easy to explore successfully, or even to discern the measure of success of a particular exploration. Given this, if we are able to accept that we have good reason to believe certain writings to be generally successful in this work, not only does a patient examination of those writings become an important part of our own theological work (the argument of Chapter 2), but it should also be possible to

---

[9] I am happy to regard the gifts of prophecy, knowledge and discernment that are exercised in the churches as a part of the fulfilment of this promise as well, although I do not think that such direct revelatory experiences are central to what is meant here. Jesus had in mind, I think, something less spectacular, and more important, than such occasional insights, life changing as they can be for particular individuals.

[10] See pp. 30–2 above.

construct an argument to suggest that such writings, where they agree widely on certain points, establish a presumption in favour of those points.

What reasons might there be, then, for according this 'classic' status to certain writings, or for denominating certain writers as 'doctors'? Earlier, I bracketed the question of how this identification might be made, but certain facets of that question become important now. The basic condition, of course, is that a piece of work conforms to, and explores the relevance of, the gospel. The problem, however, is that this condition is difficult to apply: as I argued in the first two chapters of this book, it is a difficult task to appropriate and apply the witness of Scripture to a different context. All that we have to measure the success or failure of an interpretation by, then, is other attempts to explore the same themes, themselves as, or more, partial and prone to error as the work we are seeking to judge. (If this seems a harsh claim, consider again the limiting case of heresy: however obvious it is now that Arius's denial of the full divinity of Christ was a failure of the gospel, and that Alexander's and Athanasius's responses were more adequate, the point was in dispute for several decades in the fourth century, with faithful and learned pastors who sought only to follow the teaching of Scripture found on both sides of it. In any case, given the recurrence of Arian-like heresies amongst groups who claim to found their doctrine only on Scripture [the Jehovah's Witnesses of today, for example], it is clear that this error is not easy to dismiss, but requires discernment and thought.)

All of which is to say that the problems of discerning the truth which lead to the need for guides within the tradition, the doctors, also make it difficult to identify such guides. Nonetheless, it seems to me that the attempt can, and must, be made. A first point might be the general esteem in which a book or teacher is held: if most of those who have had opportunity to pass judgement regard it as generally successful, then that is a presumption in its favour. Many people, attempting to discern what it means to be faithful to Scripture in a particular context, and all agreeing that a particular exposition provides a helpful and convincing account, are more likely to be right than wrong, in the absence of any other considerations. This point is strengthened if the consensus extends to those who themselves may be regarded as having some expertise in the work of theology, as the agreement of experts on a topic within their sphere of expertise always carries a certain weight.

This agreement is again more weighty if it extends to widely differing contexts, or across time. A particular context will have its own presumptions or blind spots, which may lead to a great deal of agreement on points which actually have nothing to do with the gospel, or are in fact a denial of it. If, however, an argument is judged to be successful by Christians from different cultures, places and times, it is more likely that the agreement is a result of a shared commitment to the gospel, rather than something else that they share, simply because less else is shared. I suggest then that where there is general agreement on a particular point amongst Christian believers from a wide variety of intellectual and historical contexts, then that agreement itself is evidence for the correctness of the point. This is particularly the case with texts that are widely acknowledged to be theological classics; that have been generally judged to represent the gospel successfully. In these cases, whilst it is possible that such texts may be wrong on particular points, there must be a presumption that any position that is found in several such texts is correct, at least until a stronger counter-argument is offered. (I am certainly not suggesting that such a counter-argument may never be found: the example of anti-Semitism, discussed briefly in Chapter 8, is surely sufficient to establish that point. I will return to this later.)

This is a broadly historical and sociological account of the authority of tradition, but that is not a major problem here, I think. If whatever authority the tradition has comes through pneumatological action, something like this is to be expected. The work of the Spirit, as well as being fundamentally eschatological, is also essentially immanent: the Spirit works within creation, establishing the creation's ability to be itself to the praise of its Creator.[11] The work of the Spirit in the Church, again, is in giving life and gifts to the Church (and the churches) from within. Just so, the work of the Spirit in this case ought to be, if not wholly explicable in human terms, at least congruent with created causes and so hidden to some extent. That the Spirit is at work in the processes sketched above is in some sense a guarantee of their efficacy. This is, in a sense, a work of providence; the role of the Spirit here is in ensuring that in and even through the confused, messy and ambiguous actions of creaturely agents the will of the Father still comes to pass. Through such processes the Spirit is at work, quietly, in the hearts of believers and the mind of the Church, leading us into all truth.

The effect of this work of the Spirit, as I discussed above, is not to create certainty or infallibility, but rather hope and patient confidence. In the promise of the Spirit's help in the work of declaring the gospel, we do not presume that every prayer will be answered, every problem overcome, every hearer converted, but rather trust that in the face of difficulties and setbacks and seeming lack of success our work will not be in vain. Just so, in theological work, the promise that the Spirit will guide us into all truth does not announce an overcoming of all problems or a final solution to every question, but instead an assurance where the truth or relevance of the gospel is at stake that God will not abandon us but will work providentially through the

---

[11] On this point, see Colin E. Gunton, *The Triune Creator: A Historical and Systematic Study* (Edinburgh: Edinburgh University Press, 1998), pp. 169–71, 177–8, 188–9, 222–4.

messiness of very human arguments and decisions to ensure that the decisions taken are not disastrous.[12]

All of which establishes a form of authority that resides in the tradition. It is a relative, dependent and partial authority, but authority nonetheless. Faced with a question of faith or morals, and a consistent witness in the tradition in favour of a particular answer, it is theologically appropriate for a Christian believer or theologian to accept that answer as correct unless and until a stronger argument to the contrary appears. The usefulness of this assertion depends, of course, on the relative strength ascribed to this form of 'argument from tradition'. How strong an alternative argument is necessary to success-fully oppose it?

The strongest form of an argument from tradition, and so the limiting case, will be an appeal to the ecumenical creeds, particularly, perhaps to the Nicene Creed.[13] This formula, more or less universally accepted by Christian churches as a basic statement of faith over the past fifteen hundred years and more, to be recited particularly during the celebration of the Eucharist, is perhaps as close to a consensus position as can be found within Christian history. Could evidence of another form be found that would be strong enough to cause us to reject one of the clauses of the Creed?

There are, it seems to me, four possible forms of argument that might be offered to oppose a particular position derived from the tradition: exegetical, logical, experiential and authoritative. In the first case an appeal would be made to (a reading of) the text of Scripture; in the second to a (perceived) logical impli-cation or contradiction within Christian theology; in the third to (claimed) human experience; and in the fourth to a (supposed) theological authority.[14] Each of these offers a possible valid argument that might give us reason to believe that a theological proposition is adequate, were there no other compel-ling reasons.[15] Can any of them provide a weighty enough reason to reject a credal position?

---

[12] Thus there are good biblical and theological reasons to side with Calvin against the Anabaptists, in the debate I outlined in the first chapter (pp. 14–17), or so it seems to me. To assume that God had abandoned his Church to such an extent that it needed refounding, rather than reforming or renewing, is to fail to trust in this promise of Jesus.

[13] For the sake of the illustration I am ignoring the *filioque* debate in what follows.

[14] The parenthetical phrases are not attempts to undermine these forms of argument, but acknowledgements that none of them is trivial either.

[15] I am not sure that an appeal to experience can ever establish a theological proposi-tion, even if there is no counter-evidence. For the sake of argument, however, I include it.

Starting from the end, it seems clear to me that no authoritative pronounce-
ment could cause us to reject anything in the Creed. However authority is
identified within the Church, and particularly given the arguments I advanced
in the second chapter concerning the continuing life of the Saints and doctors,
any appeal to authority may be met by a list of authorities in favour of the Creed
so compelling that there will be no question of their defeat. The same would
seem to be true of human experience. Whatever experience causes me to doubt
the truth of a credal proposition, the sheer number and variety of human lives
that have been lived without contradiction of these truths is overwhelming.
This may not be the case if I embrace some form of relativism or solipsism that
enables me to disregard the experiences of others, but such a position would
seem to be wholly incompatible with any Christian theology, and so the point is
not relevant.

Logic and exegesis are more interesting. It seems clear to me that a demonstrated logical contradiction between two credal propositions, or proof that
the Creed in fact denies something plainly taught in Scripture, would alike be
sufficiently strong to cause us to reject the Creed on one point, at least.
However, I think it is so unlikely as to be virtually impossible that such an
argument will ever be discovered, in either case. The Nicene Creed has
been regularly recited and embraced by many billions of people, on every
continent, and over nearly seventeen hundred years. Any obvious logical
contradiction would have been spotted thousands of times over by now, as
would any serious inconsistency with the teaching of Scripture. The fact that
the Creed is still traditioned, handed on, is itself compelling evidence that
there are no straightforward problems of these kinds with it.

It is possible, of course, that I might come to believe that I have spotted a
problem like this, not straightforward, but convincing to my mind at least. A
rigorous exploration of the original texts leads me to doubt the resurrection,
perhaps. Or I construct an argument, long, complex and abstruse in parts, but
which appears valid to me, which does call into question the coherence of the
credal assertions. It would still seem to me to be the case that this is not a strong
enough argument to call into doubt the adequacy of the Creed, in that
the probability that I might be wrong in some way seems greater than the likelihood that there is a flaw in such a basic document that has never been noticed
before. I have no more evidence than all the great minds in all their various
situations who have reflected on this text long and lovingly; it seems improb-
able in the extreme that I will see something they have missed.[16]

There is, that is to say, a proper humility about doing theological work that
is a part of the establishment of the authority of the tradition. The knowledge

---

[16] There are two exceptions here: textual and archaeological discoveries. It is conceivable that textual criticism might establish a scriptural point that is wholly new, and that

that the Spirit has been active in guiding the Church, in particular, should not encourage any of us to believe that we have seen something that has been missed by so many others, unless we can give a convincing explanation of why they were wrong, and of why we can see more clearly than they could. This is not an invitation to obscurantism or fideism, not a suggestion that we should pretend we cannot see questions where we can. It is rather to acknowledge that there is a logical distinction between the fact that I cannot see a way through a problem and the assertion that there is no way through it. It is both intellectually honest and appropriately humble to respond to a theological question with an awareness that it currently appears to me to be insoluble, but also an acceptance that others have believed they could solve it, and that there is no way of demonstrating conclusively that they were wrong in their belief and that I am right in mine.

For these reasons, which rely finally on the promise of Jesus and the providential action of the Spirit, I find it difficult to envisage a situation in which there could be sufficient evidence to doubt the Nicene Creed.[17] Such a central part of the tradition, then, becomes in effect an authoritative document. Its authority comes only from the recognition that it is a remarkably successful repetition of central truths found already in the Bible, but because of that it has genuine authority as a privileged interpretation of Scripture, against which other claimed interpretations may be measured and tested. In this limiting case, there are central parts of the tradition that are in fact authoritative. That the Creed says x is sufficient reason to assert that x is true, theologically.

Perhaps the next step down from the ecumenical creeds are the central confessional points of particular strands of Christianity. Here the *filioque* debate[18] comes into view, as do Roman Catholic insistences on the visible

---

[16] (*continued*) does require doctrinal adjustment; suffice to say that I can think of no case where this has been so of any doctrine, however minor, and the confidence I expressed above in the providential workings of the Spirit lead me to suppose that it will never come to pass, at least with regard to central doctrines, such as those of the Creed. Archaeology equally might throw up evidence that must be taken into account (an indication that Pilate died before the trial and crucifixion of Jesus, perhaps), but there seems little reason to suppose it will, and little point in answering such a hypothetical problem before it arises.

[17] As Robert Jenson points out in his *Systematic Theology* (Oxford: Oxford University Press, 1997–9), pp. 23–41, certain decisions taken by the Church are irreversible: if they are wrong, faith has passed from the earth. It seems to me that the Nicene Creed is the clear example of this.

[18] The *filioque* debate was the presenting cause, at least, for the formal split between Eastern and Western churches. The Pope claimed the right to alter the creed to read '... the Holy Spirit, who proceeds from the Father *and the Son* ...' ('*filioque*' in Latin); the Eastern churches disputed both that right and the appropriateness of the addition.

unity and right ordering of the Church, the Lutheran emphasis on justification, the Reformed codification of the 'doctrines of grace' in the Canons of
Dort, Wesleyan accounts of 'Scriptural holiness' and so on. In each case there
is a long and rich process of tradition, but also a fundamental disagreement. For
a thousand years, the Western churches have been exploring what the gospel
means and looks like on the assumption that the *filioque* is an adequate representation of what Scripture has to say about who God is, and the Eastern
churches have for the same time been exploring the same matter on the
assumption that the *filioque* is a failure to listen to Scripture. Each of the other
debates are of the same form, if more local and more recent.

One way of responding to all this that has been distressingly popular is to
simply identify one's own party with the Church and deny that members of
other traditions are in any interesting sense Christian. This seems to me to be
clearly mistaken; if everyone who disagrees with me on any point of theology
is to be excluded from the Church, then not only will the Church be very
small, but I will be elevating my own opinions to be the measure of Christian
orthodoxy. The whole argument about tradition in this book has been predicated on the sober recognition that it is actually quite easy to go wrong in
theology, and that we need the insights of precisely those within the Church
with whom we disagree if we are to learn and progress. Just so, I cannot
presume to judge others on the basis of my own understanding.

As I pointed out in Chapter 5, the Synod of Dort offers an interesting
insight here. Contained within the synod's determinations was the sense that
there were ways of being wrong that were not betrayals of the gospel, and so
not to be anathematised (supralapsarianism was the example to the fore), as
well as ways of being wrong which were betrayals and must be rejected
(Arminianism). Whether that synod was right in its examples might be
doubted, but the principle is an interesting one: recognising the partial nature
of all theology, and particularly our own, can we find ways of identifying those
to whom we must extend an appropriate generosity as fellow Christians, even
whilst sharply disagreeing with them? Within the modern ecumenical movement, assent to the historic creeds has been the standard chosen, which seems
to me to display some wisdom.

The creeds essentially codify the patristic synthesis concerning the doctrine
of God. The occasions for the promulgation of creeds were generally
Christological or Trinitarian heresies, which made claims about who God is
that were judged unacceptable. Now, in seeking to discern who, however
wrong we may think them, still should be regarded as a Christian brother or
sister, and who has left the faith some way behind, it seems to me that the
doctrine of God is crucial. Two people who both alike confess one God in
three Persons, and the hypostatic union of divine and human in Jesus Christ,
are seeking to serve the same God as each other; someone who denies one of

these crucial points is, from a Christian point of view, running after idols of their own construction. Given this, however wrong I may think someone who confesses these points is on other matters of faith and morals, they are on the same path as I am on, also imperfectly; the difference between us can only ever be in degree. Someone who confesses a different God, by contrast, is doing something different to what I am seeking to do.[19]

The question then is whether commitment to the ecumenical creeds is a sufficient and necessary condition: is there anything that must be confessed to ensure that we are worshipping the same God that is not in the creeds, or is there anything in the creeds that is not relevant to this question? Arguments could be had (particularly today, perhaps, about the virgin birth), but it seems to me that the form of argument from tradition which I have described above should be enough to settle the issue: all major Christian traditions have insisted on belief in the creeds without addition[20] or diminution as the touchstone of Christian faith; just so, we today should accept this, unless a very strong counter-argument can be adduced.

(The *filioque* is a particular problem here, in that it is clearly a debate concerning theology proper [i.e. the nature of God], and thus appears, at least, to suggest belief in a different God. There are, however, at least two good reasons for supposing that this is not in fact the case. First, it has never, or rarely, been taken this way in official pronouncements and theological discussion between West and East; Catholicism and Orthodoxy have both always recognised that they are in a closer relationship than either is in with Judaism or Islam, for instance. Second, the clause is an addition to the common creed, rather than a denial of any point of it, and an addition which can be interpreted in ways which are not inimical to shared beliefs.)[21]

The disputed tradition, then, insofar as the ecumenical creeds are accepted as codifying the essential teachings of Scripture concerning who God is, remains, I think, a single tradition, encompassing various debates and questions within the

---

[19] Thus, incidentally, the complaints sometimes heard about the ancient decisions that they were all about faith, and not about morals, miss the point slightly (as well as being historically inaccurate: any reader of the canons of the ecumenical councils will be struck by the amount of moral legislation that went on alongside the writings of creeds; and even Augustine, the example often to the fore, regarded the sin of schism as fundamentally a failure of love, as I indicated in Chapter 7).

[20] Other points to be believed are adduced, of course, but in baptismal and eucharistic liturgies it is usually clear that belief in the creed alone is sufficient.

[21] Most notably in the suggestion that the *filioque* be read as enshrining the Greek fathers' teaching that the Spirit proceeds from the Father through the Son. On this, and other attempts at ecumenical rapprochment, see Tom Smail, *The Giving Gift* (London: Darton, Longman & Todd, 1994), pp. 116–43.

totality of what is handed on from generation to generation. Such debates matter: they concern the sufficiency of Christ's atoning work, the demand for ethical living made upon Christian believers and so on, none of which subjects should ever be regarded as anything other than serious and important. There are, however, as the generosity of the Canons of Dort would teach us, serious and important disputes which nonetheless do not threaten our Christian unity, or divide the Christian tradition in any irreparable way.

There is even, I think, an authority that can be ascribed to the confessions of these disputed strands of the tradition. Insofar as they have survived and commended themselves to successive generations of believers in widely differing circumstances, they can be assumed to be not too far from the truth (a judgement based on the providential work of the Spirit) and convincing and coherent within themselves. Thus, where there are a series of disputed points, an argument of a similar form to those above might be constructed to suggest that acceptance of a particular strand's account of any one of those points is itself good reason to accept the others, in the absence of any more convincing argument.

I am conscious that the account of doing theology explored here is conservative, in the sense that it argues for a respect for the past, rather than a freedom to plough our own furrows. I make no apology for that. For any serious Christian theology, the test of truth will always be in the past, in the person of Christ, and the writings of prophets and apostles who interpreted his coming. All who come after are seeking only to interpret and explore and spread the news of his coming. There is, of course, also an appropriate looking forward, trusting in the continuing providential work of the Spirit, and waiting with eager expectation for the day when he shall return and make all things new. Even on that day, however, there is, as far as I can discern in Scripture, no new revelation, only a making clear of what has already been told. We will see nothing different; we will just(!) see the same Christ face to face, where now we look through a glass darkly. We can and must pray and trust that, guided by the Spirit, and in the light of the promise of Christ, we will see certain things more clearly than those who came before – or else why be about the work of theology? When we do so it will, however, be only as those who, in the popular medieval image, are like pygmies standing on the shoulders of giants, and seeing some little thing better than the giants. Of course, in the goodness of God we must trust that there are giants in our own day also; but we have no privileged access to knowing who they are, and we certainly can never claim that status for ourselves. Whilst humility is remembered as a theological virtue, conservatism will remain an appropriate theological stance, and historical theology, which is to say the patient, careful and respectful study of the writings of the doctors of the Church, will continue to be a central part of theological work.

Index